The Department Store

THE DEPARTMENT STORE

A SOCIAL HISTORY

Bill Lancaster

LEICESTER UNIVERSITY PRESS
LONDON AND NEW YORK

LEICESTER UNIVERSITY PRESS
A Continuum imprint
Wellington House, 125 Strand, London WC2R 0BB
370 Lexington Avenue, New York, NY 10017-6503

First published in 1995. Re-issued in paperback 2000.

British Library Cataloguing in Publication Data

A CIP catalogue record for this book is available from the British Library

ISBN   0 7185 1374 6   (hardback)
         0 7185 1985 X   (paperback)

Library of Congress Cataloging-in-Publication Data

Lancaster, William, 1948–
   The department store : a social history / Bill Lancaster.
      p. cm.
   Includes bibliographical references and index.
      ISBN 0-7185-1374-6 (HBK). — ISBN 0-7185-1985-X (PBK)
      1. Department stores—Great Britain—History. 2. Industrial
relations—Great Britain—History. 3. Department stores—Social
aspects—Great Britain—History. I. Title
HF5465.G73L36 1995
381'.141'0941—DC20   95–18851
                                                                              CIP

Set in Monotype Bembo by Ewan Smith, London

Printed and bound in Great Britain by
Biddles Ltd, Guildford and King's Lynn

CONTENTS

For my mother, a former Fenwick girl.

ACKNOWLEDGEMENTS

During the five years that it has taken to research and write this book, many scholars, institutions and individuals in the department store trade have provided support and encouragement. Tony Mason's advice that my idea to write a book on this subject was worth pursuing gave me the confidence to move beyond my previous work on labour history.

Staff and students at numerous postgraduate research seminars have listened with patience and creatively criticised various papers based upon my department store obsession, as have audiences at many conferences and workshops. To all of them I record my grateful thanks. Michael Dintenfass, Jeremy Gregory and Joan Hugman read parts or all of the manuscript and their comments have proved invaluable. My postgraduate student, Philip Woodward, has provided me with many insights into the mysteries of retailing. Paddy Maguire's wit, gentle criticism and friendly support never failed to rekindle my enthusiasm. Rob Colls' friendship, support and advice, always delivered with Geordie warmth, are deeply appreciated. Anita and John Bain-Tyrrell and Michael Tichelar provided comfortable sanctuary on my numerous research visits to London.

Erik Kelderens of the International Association of Department Stores in Paris kindly guided me through the Association's archives and made my stay in Paris extremely comfortable. Chris Fenwick allowed me access to his company's archives, was generous with his time and shared his considerable knowledge on the workings of a department store.

Many former employees from a wide range of stores have allowed me to interview them, providing a source of material to this study which has proved invaluable. Numerous libraries and their staff have delivered excellent, friendly service, but the staff of the British Library Newspaper Collection at Colindale deserve special thanks for providing an unbroken flow of the trade press. The University of Northumbria helped this work along by providing me with both study leave and enthusiastic students for my course on retail history. Suzi Beach has had the pleasure and occasional tribulation of accompanying me on countless tours of department stores, her sharp eye for detail often proving invaluable. Marion Wilson typed the manuscript and as always offered cheerful comments on the text. Needless to say, any faults that remain in this work are those of the author.

INTRODUCTION

This book is the first historical survey of the British department store. The fact that this should have to be stated in 1994 highlights a curious omission in our historiography. Every school child learns of Britain's pre-eminence in manufacturing, motive power and trade during the nineteenth century, yet the equally important developments in retailing are largely ignored. Mr Smith's railway station newspaper stalls and Mr Boots's chemist shops, along with a few late nineteenth-century grocery chains, occasionally make an appearance in an A level lesson or an undergraduate lecture. But the department store, arguably a British invention and the primary engine in the retail revolution, is generally ignored. This omission is even more curious when we consider the strength and vitality displayed by British economic historians during the post-war period.

Perhaps economic historians have been motivated largely by questions concerned with Britain's industrial decline. Production has held centre stage at the expense of scholarly activity in the area of consumption. The recent plethora of texts that focus upon consumption have largely been the work of sociological and cultural studies practitioners. These works in the main reflect the decline of Marxism as a scholarly discourse and the trek by a generation of intellectuals to the supposedly greener pastures of post-modernism. Needless to say, most of this work lacks an historical perspective. Moreover, the barrage of neologisms and the cerebral dancing to the tune of the 'fractured discourse' leave most historians at best bemused and often reaching for the analgesics.

British social history in recent years has moved away from its post-1960s focus upon work and working-class life. Interest in sport, leisure and gender has accelerated and many social historians are paying increasing attention to the world of goods. The major contribution of this process, however, has been mainly concerned with the later early modern period. Responding to McKendrick's seminal thesis on the consumer revolution of the late eighteenth century, these scholars have challenged his argument for a discontinuity in consumer behaviour during the late eighteenth century and his theoretical analysis.[1] The richness of this debate is testimony to the contribution that social history can make to the study of consumption and at the same time brings into sharp relief the lack of similar work during the modern period. McKendrick's thesis sits upon that convenient, if somewhat artificial, divide between the early modern and the modern and his work is as important to nineteenth and twentieth-century studies as it is to the earlier period.

There are a number of scholarly texts that deal with retailing in the modern period. J.B. Jefferys's *Retail Trading in Britain 1850–1950*, published in 1954, is an analysis of retailing trends that relies heavily upon official statistical data. Dorothy Davis's *A History of Shopping*, published in 1967, surveys with much insight six centuries of retailing, but given the scale of her chronology the modern period is covered only briefly. W.H. Fraser's *The Coming of the Mass Market 1850–1914*, published in 1981, is a useful study which analyses the relationship between the emergence of mass production and retailing and marketing. Michael Winstanley's *The Shopkeeper's World*, 1983, is a highly useful judicious account of the milieu of small retailing. John Benson and Gareth Shaw produced a collection of essays in 1991, *The Evolution of Retail Systems, 1800–1914*, which comprise a useful comparative volume surveying retail methods in Europe and North America. Finally, Peter Mathias's, *The Retail Revolution*, 1967, is a survey that is mainly concerned with the rise of multiple grocery chains during the late nineteenth century.

Histories of individual department stores have been produced but the quality of these works ranges from the scholarly to the compilation of celebratory anecdotes. Asa Briggs's pioneering 1956 study of Lewis's is rich in analysis and foreshadows many of the themes addressed in this volume; it is also a work that cannot be ignored by students of retailing.[2] Michael Moss and Alison Turton, two business archivists, published their *A Legend of Retailing, House of Fraser*, in 1989. This work is a detailed encyclopaedic history of Fraser's and its constituent stores which will be a key source for students of retailing for many years. The quality of many other store histories is extremely mixed but many can be of great utility. Rowen Bentall's *My Store of Memories*, 1974, is an endearing account of his family's business; it is also richly evocative and detailed.

Britain may be a nation of shopkeepers but foreign scholars have given the subject more attention. American historians, thanks to the marked Veblen tradition in humanities and the social sciences in the United States, are particularly strong in the field of retailing. The two monuments of American interwar business studies, R.M. Hower's study of Macy's and R.W. Twyman's work on Marshall Field, have no British equivalent.[3] During the 1980s American scholars pioneered new perspectives on department store history. Michael B. Miller's *The Bon Marché, the Department Store 1869–1920*, 1981, in a subtle mix of cultural, social and economic history, has had an impact beyond the confines of historical scholarship. Susan Porter-Benson's history of women workers in American department stores has enriched both the study of retailing history and the wider world of feminist studies.[4] The work of William Leach during the 1980s, culminating in his 1993 *Land of Desire*, has placed the department store at the centre of American cultural history. Leach's scholarship ranges from art, feminism and display to the economics of corporate capitalism. Despite reservations expressed in a later chapter, *Land of Desire* is a triumph of cultural and social history. Finally H. Pasdermadjian's 1954 study, *The Department Store*, written for the International Association of Department Stores, remains the classic international work on the subject.

This book makes no claim for a consumer revolution centred around the development of the department store. The contributors to *Consumption and the World of Goods* clearly demonstrate that the desire to shop and own goods pre-dates the modern period. The argument of this book is that consumption and retailing is a process that is in a constant state of evolution and that for much of the nineteenth and part of the twentieth centuries the department store was a key institution in this development. Nevertheless, a series of important changes is identified which served to shape the emergence and subsequent history of the British department store.

The first was the process of industrialisation and urbanisation that took place in north British cities during the first half of the nineteenth century. It is argued that these forces, together with their impact on class structure and the politics of free-trade Liberalism, provided the climate for a new type of drapery establishment. These shops which featured fixed, marked prices and cash payment emerged in northern cities during the 1830s and 1840s and their then novel trading methods were adapted to other non-drapery items. The term 'proto-department store' has been applied in this work to these shops. Possessing four or more distinct trading areas, they accord to Jefferys's classic definition of a department store.[5] But the structural model presented by Jefferys, whilst useful to historical analysis, lacks the qualitative dimension that has distinguished the department store from other forms of retailing.

This dimension, which includes factors such as atmosphere, display, fashion and novelty, has often been imitated by other retailers, particularly variety stores. It is nevertheless a vital ingredient, indeed the very flux to the department store formula.

The second area of change identified in this work is the discovery of the qualitative factors. This study is mainly concerned with the British department store, but by the late nineteenth century the large store was becoming an international phenomenon and entrepreneurs in retailing were even more adept than their counterparts in industry at incorporating new methods into their businesses. It is no surprise that Paris was the city that developed the qualitative dimension during the 1860s and 1870s. The Boucicauts, their store the Bon Marché, and the notion of 'democratic luxury', together with 'odd-pricing' and exhibition-style displays, fundamentally changed the nature of retailing and brought the department store to maturity.

By the early 1900s the techniques of the Boucicauts were being applied in a somewhat *ad hoc* manner by many British stores. But as these methods were slowly, almost reluctantly, absorbed in Britain, another key series of changes was taking place in the USA. The scale and rate of growth of American cities, new building technology and, importantly, the lack of clear distinctions between high and low culture were factors that shaped the development of American department stores. This process was witnessed in many cities, particularly New York and Philadelphia, but above all in Chicago.

When Chicago hosted the Colombian Exposition in 1893 the city was at the peak of its vitality. Architectural innovation, a thriving economy, partly based upon Chicago's role as the distribution capital of America, and a refusal to recognise traditional cultural boundaries, underpinned State Street's claim to be the world's premier shopping location. By 1900 Marshall Field's was the largest store in the world. From the bargain basement to the Tiffany dome, the store exuded features that were to become the norm during the new century. Customer services, staff policy and highly innovative window displays, together with new forms of merchandising, set the large American stores in general, and Marshall Field's in particular, apart from their European equivalents. These methods were dramatically imported to Britain by Gordon H. Selfridge, Field's dynamic manager, when he opened his large Oxford Street store in 1909.

The war years apart, the period 1909 up until 1939 witnessed the incorporation of American techniques by British department stores. Although never completely Americanised, British stores continued to reflect the nation's distinctive class structure; these years were the 'Golden Age' of the department store. Their share of the market was increased as they followed Selfridge's formula of making stores 'community centres'. Palm Court orchestras, the demonstration of new electrical products and theatrical events, ranging from gymnastics to menageries in the toy department, all served to increase the flow of customers and broaden the class base of department store shoppers. The fact that they survived and prospered during this period, against a backcloth of falling prices and aggressive competition from the new variety stores, is testimony to the success of Selfridge's methods.

The second part of this book examines key themes that play a central role in the study of the department store. Industrial relations are examined in order to highlight the complexity of department store work and also to offer explanations on the apparent docility of the workforce. For much of the period under review women have been the major economic decision-makers in the world of department stores, certainly as customers and increasingly in key employee positions such as buyers. The economic, sexual and political ambiguities of women's involvement in department stores form the main focus of this section. In recent years a range of theoretical perspectives has been developed to help facilitate a deeper understanding of consumption. These include concepts and models derived from sociology, anthropology and cultural studies. That the present author rejects much of this literature is not a reflection of a general hostility to theory, indeed Weberian concepts are occasionally applied in this work; rather it is a confirmation endorsed by many historians, that the complexity of the historical process rarely fits the neat formulas produced by social science. The volume concludes with a thematic survey of post-war trends and their impact upon department stores. The shopping precincts of the 1950s and 1960s and the malls of the 1970s and 1980s, together with legislative changes, such as the ending of Resale Price Maintenance, through to Sunday trading have wrought considerable change upon department stores. The fact that so many continue to thrive and prosper is testimony to the endurance of this 'great Victorian invention'.

Notes

1. N. McKendrick, J. Brewer, and J.H. Plumb, *The Birth of Consumer Society*, Europa, London, 1982. J. Brewer and R. Porter (eds), *Consumption and the World of Goods*, Routledge, London, 1993.

2. A. Briggs, *Friends of the People. The Centenary History of Lewis's*, Batsford, London, 1956.

3. R.M. Hower, *History of Macy's of New York 1858–1919. Chapters in the Evolution of a Department Store*, Harvard University Press, Cambridge, Mass, 1943. R.W. Twyman, *History of Marshall Field and Co., 1852–1906*, University of Pennsylvania Press, Philadelphia, 1954.

4. S. Porter-Benson, *Counter Cultures, Saleswomen, Managers and Customers in American Department Stores 1890–1940*, University of Illinois Press, Urbana and Chicago, 1988.

5. J.B. Jefferys, *Retail Trading in Britain 1850–1950*, Cambridge, 1954, pp. 325–6.

CHAPTER ONE

THE NORTH BRITISH PROTO-DEPARTMENT STORE: ORIGINS AND DEVELOPMENTS

The origins of the British department store are firmly rooted in the twin processes of industrialisation and urbanisation. It is tempting to locate the Victorian department store as yet another institution spawned by Britain's revolutionising industrial system. New shops for new products based in the centre of growing urban areas is a neat formula. Like most handy historical equations, however, it hides more than it reveals. Shops, shopkeepers, customers, goods and city centres all existed before Britain's economy stumbled down the road to revolution. What could be sold nearly always determined what was produced. The picture is further complicated when we keep in mind the fact that the majority of consumer goods continued to be produced for much of the nineteenth century by the expansion of the old industrial system of sweatshop and small workshop rather than the factory.[1] Similarly, customer taste could prove to be stubbornly pre-modern and the ability to purchase could rise and fall as dramatically as the new economic cycle, especially lower down the social order. Even geography could be as much a hindrance as a help. Urbanisation could maroon traditional centres of trade and the unfolding pattern of city expansion confused more traders than it enlightened. In short, the department store's background was as complex as the national economy. Its emergence and success was as much slow and hesitant as it was spectacular. Its ultimate triumph by the end of Victoria's reign was the summation of a retail revolution that was as profound as that experienced by industry.

The department store first appeared cheek by jowl with the industrial revolution in the cities of northern Britain. Which store was first is probably an insoluble and, ultimately, not a very important question. The two major claimants to the title, Bainbridge's of Newcastle upon Tyne, and Kendal, Milne and Faulkner of Manchester, both developed expanded drapery businesses in the late 1830s.[2] Within two decades most major northern cities boasted a draper who was expanding beyond

7

the traditional trade stock of textile pieces. An expanding draper's may hardly ring of revolution but we need to place this process in context.

Shops in city centres up until the 1830s tended to be highly specialised. Their turnover was relatively slow, margins were high and overheads heavy. Not surprisingly prices were high in such establishments, with a clientele to match.[3] Contemporary directories confirm that drapery businesses were the most numerous. Central Newcastle, for example, boasted 50, divided into woollen, linen and cotton, in 1838 when Emerson Muschamp Bainbridge set up shop.[4] The majority of people could not afford to patronise such places, relying instead on pedlars, 'Scotch travellers', visiting fairs and other itinerants for the majority of non-food purchases. This somewhat simplistic depiction of city centre retailing omits one major new development. Late Georgian and early Victorian Britain witnessed the rapid growth of purpose-built indoor markets and arcades.

We lack a comprehensive history of indoor markets, although some work has been done by architectural historians on arcades.[5] The striking feature to the modern observer of these developments in the early Victorian city centre is the emergence of the high street, together with Galleria arcades and proto shopping malls. Indeed the term 'Mall' is not too far-flung when we apply it to Newcastle's Grainger Market. This vast structure, completed in 1835, was enclosed by four streets and housed 243 units organised into alleys. The majority of covered markets were built as part of the rationalisation of city centres; untidy and potentially unruly street markets were enclosed in these new structures. The Grainger Market, designed by John Dobson, was built specifically to house the numerous butchers displaced by Richard Grainger's comprehensive redevelopment of central Newcastle; Europe's first planned city centre which pre-dates Haussmann's Paris by two decades. The 143 butchers and 60 greengrocers along with sundry fancy goods traders in the Grainger Market acted as a magnet to this city redevelopment. Moreover, with marked prices, a corporation weigh house and surveyor, the Grainger Market provided a new risk-free shopping experience.[6]

The opportunity provided by this new attraction was soon seized by Bainbridge. Well experienced in the local drapery trade, Bainbridge recognised that the rationality of the new market could be applied to other retailing areas. Traditionally drapery relied on better-off customers, credit transactions and high mark-ups. The ethos of such shops was, to say the least, daunting to the less well-off, nor did it take a great knowledge of retailing to make the equation between credit, slow turnover and high prices. Bainbridge, an active Methodist lay preacher, also recognised the important changes in social structure wrought by Newcastle's growing economy. The city's pre-eminence as the centre of the world's coal trade produced armies of clerks, officials and junior managers as well as miners. The period was also witnessing major working-class recruitment to Methodism. Moreover, working-class wages on Tyneside were often high by national standards and the sober, God-fearing Methodists enjoyed increasing levels of disposable income.[7] Bainbridge extended the rationalisation of shopping in the Grainger Market across the street to his new shop in 1838. What he offered was clearly marked prices, good quality products considerably cheaper than his rivals and an insistence on cash payment. This cash nexus at once liberated and democratised his shop. New customers from new social strata and those in search of drapery in order to express their respect-ability flocked to the lay preacher's establishment. Bainbridge had discovered the retailers' philosopher's stone that was to prove to be as profound as steam power to industry.

Low profit margins and cash sales resulted in an acceleration of stock turnover and it also allowed the pioneer to purchase with cash from his suppliers at a considerable discount to that paid by his traditional rivals. Liberalism had now entered the hidebound world of retailing. Its early pioneers were soon to advertise aggressively its benefits and moral superiority over the 'old corruption' of the traditional shopocracy as vociferously as Manchester industrialists campaigned against the Corn Laws.[8]

In the midst of the Anti-Corn Law campaign, Manchester ex-perienced similar retail developments to those under way in Newcastle. The centre of Manchester, unlike Newcastle, mirrored local industry in its organic growth. An important element in the piecemeal growth of central Manchester was the opening of a bazaar in Deansgate in 1832.[9] The bazaar format was inspired by similar ventures in London which in turn took their lead from Paris. The Parisian arcades and bazaars reflected the ideas of the Utopian socialist, Fourier, who envisaged phalansteries – new community structures of producers and merchants.[10] By the time this model reached pragmatic Manchester it was somewhat diluted. John Watts, a Cheshire farmer turned draper, opened up bazaar-style premises in 1832 in Deansgate, letting out counters to individual traders. In order to control this undertaking, Watts formulated a constitution which all traders had to abide by. Clearly marked prices, 'with no abatement', was a key house rule.[11] This, however, was a product of necessity rather than a retailing insight. Watts, similar to bazaar operators in London, emphasised novelty: 'The Bazaar and the Exhibition of Works of Arts, Including DIORAMA and PHYSIORAMA, ETC.' prefaced his first prospectus. Counters could be hired for a period of as little as a week, an obvious strategy for a proprietor whose quest was for difference and spectacle. The problem with such short lets was that traders were unable to enter credit arrangements with customers. Watts, on the other hand, was anxious that price haggling should not lower the demeanour of his 'palais des arts'.[12]

Watts, the bazaar impresario, had reached the marked price stage by a different route from that followed by Bainbridge. His concern was order. It was three young stall-holders, Kendal, Faulkner and Milne, who realised the retailing implications of their proprietor's house rules. Watts appears to have had diverse business interests in expanding Manchester and was increasingly devoting his attention to wholesale drapery. He therefore proved willing to accept an offer from the three young drapers to buy the Deansgate premises, and they took over the bazaar and converted it into a marked price drapery establishment.[13]

Both Bainbridge, and Kendal, Milne and Faulkner, were responding to new social and economic forces and seized the opportunity offered by the growth of city centres. There were undoubtedly others who embarked on the path of marked prices in this period but only the above were to emerge as department stores. More were to follow: in the late 1840s, Anderson of Glasgow, with his 'Polytechnic', continued where Watts left off in Manchester and combined showmanship with retail innovation.[14] Others we will encounter later, but first it is necessary to follow the pioneers on their next, and arguably most important, phase of growth.

Both firms, independently but responding to the same forces of demand, crossed the threshold of product diversity in the late 1830s and early 1840s. Product barriers within retailing were jealously guarded. Breaches of this tradition were seen at best as ungentlemanly and at worst as war. The customers of the new drapers, however, presented a huge potential for growth. A visit to Bainbridge to buy material to be worked up at home or by a seamstress into clothes or house furnishing, created other demands. A dress, for example, gave rise to a demand for gloves, stockings, ribbons, bags etc. – a range of items which the

Table 1 Geographical distribution of white-collar workers, 1901.

Place	Percentage of workers
Edinburgh	10.9
London	10.1
Aberdeen	8.6
Bristol	8.3
Liverpool and Birkenhead	8.1
Newcastle	8.0
Cardiff	7.9
Glasgow	7.8
Manchester and Salford	7.5
Hull	7.3
Birmingham	5.6
Nottingham	5.3
Sheffield	4.9
Northampton	4.9
Oldham	3.8
Wiltshire	3.1
Lincolnshire	3.1
Buckinghamshire	2.5

Source: G. Crossick, 'The emergence of the lower middle class in Britain: a discussion', pp. 19–20, in G. Crossick (ed.), *The Lower Middle Class in Britain*, Croom Helm, 1977.

emerging Paris fashion industry called 'nouveautés'. The northern draper preferred the term 'novelties' and both Bainbridge and Kendal, Milne and Faulkner were quick to move into this market. Similarly, household fabric needed curtain fixtures, tassels, cords and other items. A matching rug or tapestry soon opened the door to an avalanche of needs required by these new shoppers. Moreover, the quality name that the pioneers established in fabric rubbed off onto other product areas. What retail and marketing theorists now call 'brand linkage' was first practised in these proto-department stores.[15] The growth of the new stores was enhanced by the demographic expansion of their lower middle-class clientele. Table 1 clearly demonstrates this process.

The stores were also fortunate in that their emergence was partly a response to a new form of demand. Urban historians have noted the demise of the 'Walking City' and its replacement by the 'Streetcar City' as the nineteenth century progressed. This process was responding to two developments: a transport revolution, which will be discussed below, and a tendency for cities to divide into spatial segments that were largely defined by class and status.[16]

It is, of course, tempting to package the above developments into the overburdened concepts of 'respectability', 'class formation' and even the 'labour aristocracy'. Social historians are now well aware of the dangers of simplistically applying these terms to the historical process, especially in the political arena. It is now acknowledged that working-class respectability was not the product of the 1840s and 1850s, rather it had deep roots in artisan communities that stretch back to the eighteenth century.[17] Even more difficult problems surround the idea of the 'labour aristocracy'. Traditionally used as a political concept it has, in recent years, increasingly been linked to changes in the life-style of some sections of the working class.[18] Aspidistras, pianos and better housing form a new focus of interest replacing an older obsession with collaboration and class treachery. What is certain is that status distinctions became more important as the nineteenth century unfolded and accelerated with the stabilisation of the economy in the 1840s. People saw themselves in terms of their occupation and how that connected to the immediate community; the strongest social imperative was to live amongst people of the same or a similar station who shared your manners, values, interests and life-style.[19]

The expanding city was, however, full of uncertainties. The 'Walking City' of the early nineteenth century was much firmer social terrain. A quick glance at city directories from this period will confirm this point. A variety of social groups, with major differences in income, lived in close proximity to each other and enjoyed face-to-face relations. The growth in population and the physical size of communities demanded a more complex social code. Residence and life-style was the most accessible solution to the problem of social anomie caused by the swamping of older, smaller communities. Housing and goods offered new solidarities to replace the old order of deference and community. This generalisation, of course, is largely confined to the larger cities and conurbations. As Waller has reminded us, the expansion of smaller towns was of equal importance in Britain's process of urbanisation.[20] But in qualitative terms, the city was in the van. New habits, fashion and styles were city-born and with the growth of transport, old boundaries were broken.

Improvements in transport, particularly within cities, were incremental rather than revolutionary. Unlike American cities, better transport was usually a response to urban growth, not its cause. The number and quality of horse-drawn buses increased to facilitate access between city centre and expanding suburb.[21] We need to keep in mind that the period under review was witnessing only the first 'ring' of the centrifugal development that was typical of so much urban expansion. Newcastle again serves as a good example. Here the fabric of the old city was torn asunder by Grainger's redevelopment. The old heterogeneous community was dispersed into new socially-distinct suburbs. The middle class moved to Elswick, half a mile from the city centre, and were soon followed by the lower middle class and skilled artisans into this purpose-built suburb. The better-off, those with a carriage or who could afford the higher transport costs, soon escaped to the more exclusive environs of Jesmond and, later, Gosforth. The working class underwent a similar process, with Byker and Scotswood forming the first staging post, while Heaton, built later in the century, attracted the higher-paid skilled workers.[22] It is pointless to dwell too long on these aspects of urban history which have been adequately addressed by Daunton, Dyos, and Reeder.[23] What we need to keep in mind is that the early department store, although centrally located, was still in relatively close proximity to its customers in the new suburbs. As the century progressed, cities both expanded in size and became more centre-orientated thanks to new transport innovations. Nothing illustrates this more graphically than Bainbridge's boast in 1912 that 2,500 trams daily passed their door.[24]

Based in the new suburb, the housewife faced the task of creating the new solidarity of goods. The expansion of the early department store is almost a mirror image of the emerging middle-class household. Kendal, Milne and Faulkner in 1847 offered a wide range of drapery products, haberdashery and rugs and floor coverings. Vacant premises next door allowed the firm to expand into funeral undertaking, up-holstery and furniture. Bainbridge's followed a similar path; these expanding drapery establishments still had a long journey before becoming full-blown department stores but their policy of seeking out new lines and products was proving successful. The key to this success was that they took the fear out of shopping for the new lower middle class and better-off working-class housewife.[25] Clearly marked prices facilitated budgeting and also took away the dread of showing your moderate circumstances and unrefined taste that was ever present in the specialist shop. Yet these new stores were neither palaces of temptation nor arbiters of taste. Many of the items on offer still required the labour of the housewife or a seamstress for conversion into finished products, while the furniture and household goods on offer were sturdy but plain. Similarly, display methods were primitive and selling techniques unsophisticated. The truth of the matter was that up until the mid-century, and indeed for some years after, demand reflected the plain and simple needs of the lower middle class.[26] Households were established and identities created which mirrored the sobriety and thrift of this new social group. The next stage in the progress of the department store required improved levels of disposable income, new attitudes and perceptions of products by consumers and a conscious effort by the entrepreneur to create a new shopping environment where demand could simultaneously be satisfied and reborn. It is, perhaps, no surprise that such a formula was invented by a Parisian couple rather than by a north British Non-conformist!

Notes

1. N.R. Craft, *British Economic Growth During the Industrial Revolution*, Clarendon Press, Oxford, 1985; R. Samuel, 'The workshop of the world: steam power and hand technology in mid-Victorian Britain', *History Workshop*, 3, 1977.

2. For Bainbridge's, see A. and J. Airey, *The Bainbridges of Newcastle*, A. and J. Airey, Newcastle upon Tyne, 1979, pp. 40–50. The best account of the early history of Kendal, Milne and Faulkner is to be found in M. Moss and A. Turton, *A Legend of Retailing, House of Fraser*, Weidenfeld and Nicolson, London, 1989, pp. 343–5.

3. H. Pasdermadjian, *The Department Store, Its Origins, Evolution and Economics*, Newman, London, 1954, p. 9.

4. *Richardson's Directory of Newcastle, 1838*.

5. M. MacKeith, *Shopping Arcades, a Gazetteer of Extant British Arcades, 1817–1939*, Mansell, London, 1985. J.F. Geist, *Passagen Arcades, The History of a Building Type*, MIT Press, Cambridge, MA, 1983.

6. For the redevelopment of Central Newcastle, see B. Allsop, *Historic Architecture of Newcastle upon Tyne*, Oriel Press, Stocksfield, 1977.

7. North-east Methodism is surveyed in R. Colls, *The Pitmen of the Northern Coalfield*, Manchester University Press, Manchester, 1987, Chapters 7–12, *passim*.

8. Moss and Turton, op. cit., p. 344.

9. Ibid., p. 343.

10. Geist, op. cit.

11. A. Adburgham, *Shops and Shopping, 1800–1914*, George Allen and Unwin, London, 1981, p. 20. This work dates the opening of the bazaar as 1831.

12. Ibid.

13. Ibid., p. 21.

14. A. Briggs, *Friends of the People. The Centenary History of Lewis's*, Batsford, London, 1956, p. 155.

15. For example, by 1847, Bainbridge's had '23 separate sets of takings'. A. and J. Airey, op. cit., p. 47.

16. S.B. Warner, *Streetcar Suburbs. The Process of Growth in Boston, 1870–90*, Harvard University Press, Cambridge, MA, 1978, is the classic statement on this model.

17. J.K. Walton, *Lancashire: A Social History, 1558–1939*, Manchester University Press, Manchester, 1987, especially Chapter 13.

18. R.Q. Gray, *The Labour Aristocracy in Victorian Edinburgh*, Clarendon Press, Oxford, 1976, especially Chapter 5.

19. Ibid.

20. P.J. Waller, *Town City and Nation, England 1850–1914*, Oxford University Press, Oxford, 1983, especially Chapter I.

21. See for example T.C. Barker, 'Urban transport', in M.J. Freeman and D.H. Aldcroft (eds), *Transport in Victorian Britain*, Manchester University Press, Manchester, 1988.

22. B. Lancaster, 'Newcastle capital of what?', in R. Colls and B. Lancaster (eds), *Geordies, Roots of Regionalism*, Edinburgh University Press, Edinburgh, 1982.

23. M.J. Daunton, 'Urban Britain', in T.R. Gourvish and A. O'Day (eds), *Later Victorian Britain, 1867–1900*, Macmillan, London, 1988, pp. 37–69. H.J. Dyos (ed.), *The Study of Urban History*, Edward Arnold, London, 1968, especially D.A. Reeder, 'A theatre of suburbs', pp. 253–72. See also D. Fraser and A. Sutcliffe (eds), *The Pursuit of Urban History*, Edward Arnold, London, 1983.

24. Bainbridge's *Souvenir Store Guide*, 1912.

25. Pasdermadjian, op. cit., Chapter I, *passim*. Bainbridge's had always attracted the more prosperous working class; for example, in 1892 they still had a 'pit clothing' department. A. and J. Airey, op. cit., p. 115.

26. Pasdermadjian, op. cit.

CHAPTER TWO

LUXURY DEMOCRATISED

Historians of aesthetics and design have long drawn attention to the revolution in the popular perception of manufactured goods created by the Great Exhibition of 1851 and afterwards. Toshio Kusamitsu has argued that some of the precedents and inspiration for the 1851 event came from earlier artisan exhibitions where craftsmen displayed their wares: inventive genius alongside artefacts of a scientific and artistic nature.[1] While undoubtedly important, these venues, similar to the early department stores, were relatively small beer when compared with the Great Expositions of 1851 and later exhibitions. Historians, generally, are suspicious of placing too much emphasis on one event; discontinuities in the historical process have to be qualified and set in a broader context. The phenomena of the expositions are no exception to this rule.

The London Exhibition of 1851 did draw a mass audience and did heighten the popular awareness of the achievements of British power and the industrial revolution. But it did not bring about an immediate consumer revolution.[2] It is more useful to see the Crystal Palace Exhibition as the beginning of a process that was to take two decades to bring about noticeable change to retailing. Nevertheless, the next development in the evolution of the department store is inexplicable without reference to expositions. The spectacular rise of the Bon Marché in Paris and the genius of the Boucicauts in this establishment's development has been the subject of a pioneering scholarly monograph.[3] It would be pointless to spend too long on this well-ploughed furrow, but we do need to dwell on some of the key points that emerge from Miller's study and other recent works on Parisian consumer society in the second half of the nineteenth century.

Paris in the 1850s was becoming the show-case of Louis Bonaparte's Second Empire. Inspired by the grandiose vision of the Utopian socialist, Saint-Simon, Bonaparte embarked on the redevelopment of Paris and a revolution in French business life. Fired by the success of the 1851 London Exhibition, the French were anxious to establish Paris as the centre of European civilisation and culture, and the first instalment in wrenching the crown from London was the Grand Exposition in Paris of 1855.[4] A legend of retailing is that of the Paris draper, Aristide Boucicaut, having lost his way in the middle of the 1855 Exposition. Instead of being confused Boucicaut found himself enraptured by the spectacle of the goods on view and delighted in the surprises that met his every turn. It is difficult to confirm this story but the connection between the Paris exhibitions and the development of the *grand magasin* is undeniable. The Bon Marché's first rival, the 'Louvre', was built as a hotel for the 1855 show. When Boucicaut rebuilt his Left Bank store in the 1860s he chose Eiffel and Boileau as architects; Eiffel in particular was highly skilled in the new technology of iron and glass which had been pioneered by exhibition buildings.[5] The historian of the Bon Marché has described the new store as 'Dazzling and sensuous ... a permanent fair ...'[6] The Bon Marché acknowledged its debt to the expositions by becoming a regular exhibitor, even participating in the international fairs of Chicago and St Louis. This process of imitation reached full circle when the journalist, Maurice Talmeyr, described the 1900 Paris exposition as a 'sort of Louvre or Bon Marché'.[7]

The major innovation of the Bon Marché and its Parisian competitors was the creation of a new shopping experience in a new environment, a development as profound as the twentieth-century shopping mall. A diversity of elements went into the making of this new environment. The use of price tickets on objects displayed at the 1855 exposition is often cited as being relevant to the development of the Parisian store. Fixed prices, clearly displayed, however, had been in use in Paris by a number of drapery houses, following a similar path to that of Bainbridge and Kendal, Milne and Faulkner since the 1840s.[8] These Paris stores, like their British, and indeed as we shall see below, their American, counterparts, were developing into other markets, particularly 'nouveautés' or fancy goods. What was significant about 1855 was the combination of price tags, sumptuous display and the ability to browse, explore and dream of potential ownership. The sociability of the exhibition with attendances measured by the million heightened this experience. In a sense just admiring the goods on display indicated appreciation of modern society; ownership offered full membership of the club. Boucicaut realised that spectacle and browsing were integral to the success of the exposition and these elements had tremendous potential for retailing. His various innovations at his Left Bank premises went some way towards these aims but he realised that the piecemeal development of department store premises mitigated against achieving the full theatrical effect of the expositions.

Boileau and Eiffel's building which came to occupy the entire square bordered by the rues Babylone, Sèvres, Bac and Volpean eventually covered 52,800 square metres. It was also the first building specifically constructed as a large department store. The historian of the Bon Marché has described the Boileau Eiffel design in the following passage:

> Together they devised a plan that would employ a framework of thin iron columns and a roofing of glass skylights to work to the best advantage of a giant retail operation. The role of the iron was to provide for open spacious bays in which large quantities of goods could be displayed and through which vast crowds could move with ease. The skylights capping what, in effect, was a series of interior courts, were to permit a maximum influx of natural light, which was deemed necessary for display purpose.[9]

The sheer size of the new emporium was a key to success. Its numerous departments and floors facilitated a vast traffic of customers and potential customers. The Bon Marché offered a new type of liberty. Anyone could enter, browse in departments, wander from floor to floor, without spending a centime. The earliest proto-department stores were too small and formal to offer such anonymity. Customers in the Bon Marché were encouraged to wander by means of stunning visual displays. Goods draped across gallery rails sucked crowds up to the upper floors. Boucicaut was anxious to recreate the experience of the exhibition. He knew only too well that a customer who entered the Bon Marché to buy an umbrella would soon be back for something else. Even the browsers would leave the store with new desires in their minds. Boucicaut and the Bon Marché were in the right place at the right time. As Miller has argued, if he had not been born he would have been invented. The north British stores, the American dry goods emporiums and the Paris 'nouveautés' shops of the 1840s met the needs of the emerging lower middle class. Boucicaut, by contrast, sold to a more mature bourgeoisie with growing levels of disposable income. This confident class were the inheritors of the modern world; lacking title and land they turned to an unfolding realm of finery and consumer goods to signify their presence.[10]

The growth of the French economy in the second half of the nineteenth century has been well documented by economic historians.

Both Miller and Williams have explored the fascinatingly complex relationship between the new value system based on consumer goods, fashion and bourgeois culture. The issues generated by this theme will be discussed later but let us conclude this section by mentioning some aspects of Boucicaut's achievements. The Bon Marché defined, through its goods, the mould of upper middle-class life. But it also served as a model for the growing middle class generally. Its cultural message was skilfully propagated by displays at exhibitions, a vast array of printed advertising material and, perhaps most importantly, by its mail order catalogue.[11] Every item from table linen to children's clothing offered the security of bourgeois membership. Zola went as far as arguing that the department store went beyond providing a new solidarity by taking on the role of cathedral to the new culture of consumerism:

> the department store tends to replace the church. It marches to the religion of the cash desk, of beauty, of coquetry, and fashion. [Women] go there to pass the hours as they used to go to church: an occupation, a place of enthusiasm where they struggle between their passion for clothes and the thrift of their husbands; in the end all the strain of life with the hereafter of beauty.[12]

The triumph of the *grand magasin*

The successful formula of Boucicaut was soon imitated in his home city. The redevelopment of Paris readily lent itself to the building of large stores on island sites astride the new boulevards.[13] His earliest competitor, the Louvre, expanded to occupy the complete building that was originally planned as an exposition hotel. Printemps, which originated in 1865, built perhaps Paris's most beautiful store on the boulevard Haussmann and was joined in 1895 by Galeries Lafayette; a move that was eventually to secure the boulevard's primacy in the world of Parisian shopping. In 1870 Samaritaine was founded on the rue du Pont-Neuf and it needs to be underlined that both Printemps and Samaritaine were started by ex-employees of Boucicaut's.[14] These developments secured the pre-eminence of Paris in international shopping; this was further secured by the triumph of Worth and others in the world of *haute couture*. Paris was also fortunate in possessing a flexible industrial base ideally structured for the mass production of luxury goods.[15]

Boucicaut's revolution was broadcast to an international audience in the first instance by the flocks of visitors drawn to Paris by the lure of the expositions.[16] In 1878 the fair attracted 16,000,000 visitors; in 1889, 32,000,000, and in 1900 it culminated in an attendance of 48,000,000. International interest in Paris fashion generated further exposure of the *grands magasins* in an avalanche of newspaper, weekly and magazine articles. Parisian taste and style became the standard of the international bourgeoisie.[17]

In many ways the *grands magasins* of the last years of Second Empire Paris were light years removed from the proto-department stores of northern Britain. Yet we need to bear in mind that when Boucicaut founded the Bon Marché in 1852 it was smaller than either Bainbridge's or Kendal, Milne and Faulkner. Moreover, similar to his British counterparts, Boucicaut financed his store's expansion internally, by ploughing back profits and later by investing his workers' savings in the fabric of the company.[18] But Paris was a rapidly expanding capital city whose nineteenth-century growth, from just over half a million to 2½ million dwarfed that of the cities of northern Britain. To find comparable stores to that of Paris in the last quarter of the nineteenth century we need to look across the Atlantic to the booming cities of Chicago, New York and Philadelphia, a phenomenon which will be examined later. What is surprising, however, is the relative backwardness of Paris's great rival, London.

William Whiteley's emporium in Westbourne Grove began to break the log-jam of conservatism in London retailing in the late 1860s. Whiteley, an apprentice draper from Wakefield, took his first holiday in 1851 when he visited the Great Exhibition. Overawed by the event and the retailing potential offered by London, the young draper left Wakefield for London in 1855, the day after completing his apprenticeship. Whiteley worked for several city drapers and saved intensely in order to start his own business.[19] Whiteley's first act of genius was to recognise the potential of Westbourne Grove as the shopping centre of the expanding suburbs on the edge of Hyde Park.[20] The area's potential was rapidly being enhanced by major improvements to London's public transport system. Whiteley's hunch on the Grove's potential was confirmed with the opening of the Metropolitan Underground Railway which included a new station near his target area. His store opened in 1864, a few months after the completion of the railway. Whiteley was also well aware of the area's rich customer base. The suburb's historian has commented on social developments in the 1850s and 1860s, 'The middle-aged and respectable heads of the Victorian households who moved into Bayswater paid £2000 or more for some of these houses and also maintained a retinue of some six to ten servants per family'. David Reeder further notes that, '[B]y the 1860's the social cachet of Bayswater had caught on to the extent of attracting families of colonial administrators ... Bayswater had become a symbol of Imperial London.'[21]

Whiteley followed a similar path to the northern proto-department store entrepreneurs. Concentrating initially on traditional drapery stock, by the late 1860s he added gloves, jewellery, furs, umbrellas and artificial flowers. In the early 1870s, by purchasing adjoining premises, Whiteley began to show his flair and ambition by converting them into an estate agency, hairdressing, tea-rooms and a furniture shop.[22] Whiteley, like Boucicaut, also possessed the showman's instinct. But while Parisian stores pioneered new forms of advertising, Whiteley specialised in self-publicity, dubbing himself the Universal Provider, and the vast range of goods on offer became a source of journalistic interest. Spoof letters flooded the correspondence columns of newspapers extolling the virtues of the Universal Provider's emporium. Whiteley also became an un-official master of ceremonies to the pantomimes of imperial London. In 1887 he decorated his entire Bayswater frontage with material and royal and imperial insignias. By 1897 he was draping buildings in St James's Street.[23]

Whiteley created Westbourne Grove as a major London shopping venue. Others rushed to cash in on the traffic which Whiteley generated. His more traditional business neighbours frequently protested at the multiplication of the Universal Provider's departments, but even the most conservative small trader began to realise the benefits of basking in the sunshine of Whiteley's Westbourne Grove.[24] The newer traders were more ambitious, seeking to emulate rather than bask. In 1873 Tom Ponting from Gloucester opened a store in the Grove and in 1894 a Mr Bourne and his brother-in-law, Mr Hollingsworth, set up shop. It is worth noting that both these traders had the prescience to understand the rapidly shifting geography of London's retailing, wrought by popula-tion growth and a rapidly improving transport system. The Ponting brothers concentrated the family capital in Kensington High Street, while Bourne and Hollingsworth boosted Oxford Street when they moved there from Bayswater in 1902.[25]

Geography was the making of Whiteley in the nineteenth century; it was to prove his undoing in the twentieth century. Bayswater's position as the centre of the empire was short-lived. Reeder had described how the success of Westbourne Grove bore in parts the seeds of its own destruction:

> [S]ome residential streets were taken over for shops, more boarding houses and private hotels. The district also contained a working population of milliners, shop assistants and others for whom new commercial and social institutions were provided, mainly by the Westbourne Park Baptist Chapel, founded in 1877. Bayswater also became more cosmopolitan as Jewish and Greek families moved into the district.[26]

Nevertheless his flair and style revolutionised British shopping. His business at its peak in the nineteenth century resembled a music hall farce but his customers appeared to have found it endearing. Frequently surrounded by sexual innuendo of both his own and his customers' making, and following a series of fires reputedly started by disgruntled employees, the store gained a *risqué* reputation. Yet the customers came in droves; from the royal family and aristocracy, to the Paddington proletarians who flocked to the January sale, while London society was conveniently in 'the country'. Whiteley's was very different from the bourgeois spectacle of the Paris *grands magasins* but it also served the similar function of making shopping more than just shopping.

Whiteley, for example, attracted, 'Proletarian bargain hunters from Notting Hill [who] claimed the sale as their own, and resented, in rough language, the intrusion of plutocrats from Prince's Square or Lancaster Gate, who operated under the pretence of buying to stock charity bazaars or aiding the district visitor'. 'If only they would stay at their Gammages' must have been a popular sentiment amongst those wishing to avoid such examples of class *frisson*.[27] Perhaps in the London suburbs local entrepreneurs could cater for a wide clientele in an environment well away from the imperial elite.

While Whiteley was a genius of location, others just landed on their feet. Harrods is unusual in starting life as a grocer's rather than a draper's store. Henry Charles Harrod from Clacton began the business as a grocer and tea dealer in Cable Street, Stepney, in 1835. When business improved he moved to Eastcheap in 1849. His involvement with his close friend, Philip Burden's, ailing business resulted in Harrod taking over Burden's grocery shop in the then notorious district of Knightsbridge. This area at the mid-century was dominated by the barracks and had a reputation to suit. The Great Exhibition across the road in

Hyde Park in 1851 rapidly transformed the area from raunchy to ultra-respectable. Harrod's son, Charles Digby Harrod, had the insight to develop business within their increasingly up-market neighbourhood. Concentrating initially on foodstuffs, young Charles gradually developed a trade in perfume, flowers, stationery and medicine. By 1880 Harrod employed over 150 workers and was actively expanding his premises into adjoining property. New departments selling china and ironmongery were added and the store was enjoying steady success when the disastrous fire of 1883 virtually destroyed the premises.[28]

An earlier, now legendary chance encounter on a bus, between Harrod and the sponge merchant, Edgar Cohen, resulted in Cohen being invited to assist the heartbroken grocer in rebuilding his fire-damaged business. With Cohen's help, the store was rebuilt but the fire appears to have diminished Harrod's business appetite. By 1889 the firm, now largely in Cohen's hands, was floated as a public company. Newspaper accounts of the rebuilt store clearly indicate that the three-storey premises was rapidly moving away from its recent past as an expanded grocer's. The upper sales floors were entirely devoted to a wide variety of household items ranging from brass fenders to billiard tables. Cohen's major contribution to the salvage and rescue of Harrods, however, was the appointment of Richard Burbidge, a former manager of Whiteley's, as general manager.[29]

Burbidge was quick to realise that while Westbourne Grove thrived on Whiteley's music hall farce, Knightsbridge required an ethos of pomp and circumstance. Whiteley was an innovator, the first in the field, and this novelty was the secret of much of his success. But by the 1890s the market was expanding and maturing, whilst the newer shopping centres of Knightsbridge, Oxford Street and the mushrooming new suburban high streets offered shoppers an alternative to the Universal Provider. This competition was heightened by the growing labyrinth of London's underground railway system, and a rapidly improving surface transport network. The London middle-class housewife could now easily visit Westbourne Grove, Kensington High Street, Knightsbridge, and Oxford Street.[30] Moreover, the suburban high street mounted a spirited campaign to retain its local customers. Finchley Road, Hampstead, boasted the new John Barnes department store; Holloway, Jones Brothers; Streatham, Pratts; Clapham, Arding and Hobbs; Brixton, The Bon Marché; Lewisham, Chiesmans; whilst as early as December 1888 the enterprising Roberts store in Stratford, London, was tempting customers with a Christmas Grotto complete with Santa Claus and Cinderella. The *Draper's Record* enthused at Roberts's Christmas innovation, which appears to have been the first of what is now a department store institution, and reported that 17,000 children visited Santa at Stratford during the Christmas period (see Figures 1 and 2).[31]

The suburban stores in London certainly faced stiff competition from the central emporiums. The last two decades of the nineteenth century witnessed the emergence of many of London's premier department stores. Prompted by Whiteley's success and the growing fame of the Parisian stores, particularly the Bon Marché which was regularly featured in the trade journals, a new generation of entrepreneurs, many of them ex-employees of Whiteley, established their own businesses. These new men were joined by a few traditional but ambitious established businesses.[32] Dickens and Jones, which had been in Oxford Street since 1790, moved to Regent Street in 1835 and grew rapidly during the 1890s into a full-blown department store. Marshall and Snelgrove, originated in Vere Street in 1837, experienced a spectacular expansion in the 1880s. Swan and Edgar had been in Piccadilly since 1812 and started extending its premises in 1866. Debenham and Freebody originated from 1813 when William Debenham took over an old drapery concern and enjoyed a similar process of expansion to that of its rivals.[33]

One final set of players emerged on the central metropolitan department store scene during this period: the middle-class pseudo cooperative stores. The first of these institutions was the Post Office Supply Association, which was founded in 1864 by clerks in the General Post Office as a tea club. By 1866 its name had changed to the Civil Service Supply Association and in 1868 retail premises were acquired on The Strand.[34] The Army and Navy Stores began life in 1871 as a wine club founded by a small group of officers. In 1872 they established retail premises in a part of Vickers Distillery in Victoria Street. The cheap prices that these institutions offered on a vast selection of goods, both having quickly expanded into non-foodstuffs, gave them immense appeal. Harrods, who competed with the Army and Navy for clientele, were forced to advertise goods at 'Co-operative Prices'. The Army and Navy was an extremely large establishment by 1887, employing 5,000 workers and enjoying a membership of over 50,000. It must, however, be remembered that many of these workers were employed either servicing their vast mail order trade, 4,000 letters being received every day for items in their 1,000-page catalogue, or worked in their considerable manufacturing establishment. Despite the vast number of members visiting the stores and its refreshment rooms, the Army and Navy continued to resemble a warehouse, albeit a middle-class one, during this period.[35]

It was not until the 1920s that the Army and Navy succumbed to the idea of providing display windows. What is certain is that these middle-class co-operatives could not match the working class in the spirit of co-operation. Trouble between the ranks, for example, resulted in the formation of the breakaway Junior Army and Navy Stores in 1879. Both societies were riven with disputes over prices, profits and shareholding and in the twentieth century both became private companies.[36]

Provincial Britain enjoyed a similar burgeoning of department store activity. Bainbridge of Newcastle upon Tyne had the advantage of a ready-made island site in the block of buildings arranged by Grainger's redevelopment in the Market Street/Grainger Street area. This firm, however, only succeeded in burrowing through the block to the Bigg Market and only ever occupied part of the site. Nevertheless they still experienced considerable growth. When E.M. Bainbridge, the firm's founder, died in 1892 the store had 11,705 square yards of floor space and employed over 600 workers in the Market Street store. Bainbridge's range of goods and services was as wide-ranging as any of the London stores. The firm offered funeral, house-removal and carpet-beating services.[37]

Kendal, Milne and Co., as the firm was known after Adam Faulkner's death in 1862, enjoyed major growth in the 1870s and 1880s. In the early 1870s the old Bazaar was extensively rebuilt as part of the Deansgate improvement scheme and the store became a central feature of this redevelopment. Kendal, Milne's sales area now covered four floors and like Bainbridge's departments multiplied. Moorish-style tea-rooms were opened in 1890 and in that year the store, with 900 employees, claimed to be the largest outside London.[38]

In the closing years of the nineteenth century the influence of Paris could be detected throughout urban Britain. The premier trade journal, the *Draper's Record*, ran a weekly column on products and innovations in the Paris stores. Numerous British stores followed the Paris model of store building which emphasised gallery floors, sweeping staircases and dramatic glass roofs. Jenners of Edinburgh, Fraser's of Glasgow and Liberty's of London are very fine extant examples of this period. Some

Figure 1 Going to see Santa Claus – Mr J.R. Roberts's Christmas Bazaar
(*source*: British Library).

Figure 2 The home of Santa Claus – Mr J.R. Roberts's Christmas Bazaar
(*source*: British Library).

even paid Boucicaut the ultimate compliment: Lewis's of Liverpool abandoned their effort to promote a middle-class clientele in their rather down-market Ranelagh Street store by opening the city's own Bon Marché in Basnett Street.[39] Similarly, Mr Smith, the south London printer, enriched by an enormous accumulator win on the horses, invested his fortune in Brixton's emporium of the same name.[40] Even humble wool and draper's shops in northern coalfield pit villages boasted the name of the illustrious Left Bank establishment. Illustrations of store interiors and reports in the trade press, however, indicate that most British stores developed into hybrid versions of the *grands magasins*. Displays were generally mundane rather than spectacular and many stores continued to expose their origins in the unostentatious world of lower middle-class respectability. Figure 3, an illustration of Bainbridge's interior in 1898, clearly shows the persistence of the formal world of service, replete with the fussy floor-walker and the chair at the counter, a format which had been present since the 1840s. This was far removed from the thronging crowds that wandered freely through the stores of Zola's Paris.

This difference in retailing style, which emphasised the less 'democratic' nature of British stores, was highlighted by the activities of the Fenwick brothers in the 1890s. Arthur and Trevor Fenwick were the sons of J.J. Fenwick, Newcastle's premier draper and dress designer, who was often dubbed the Worth of the North. Fenwick senior had been highly successful in developing an up-market image by locating his shop, in 1882, in the then exclusive residential Northumberland Street. Fenwick was not averse to diversification, establishing fur, silk and a Liberty's franchise, but these activities were carried out in separate individual shops on Northumberland Street. Fenwick appeared to prefer a number of separate boutiques rather than a single multi-department outlet. J.J. Fenwick had a strong affinity with most things French. Perhaps this was a product of his family background of small traders in Huguenot Richmond, North Yorkshire, or more likely a wish to emulate the success of Worth in the unlikely terrain of Newcastle. Nevertheless, he could count the Duchess of Northumberland and over fifty titled ladies amongst his customers. He adopted the word 'Modiste' for his telegraphic address and broadened his customer base amongst theatrical and artistic circles. The costumes for the musical *Trilby* were Fenwick creations and he became Ellen Terry's favourite dressmaker. After only nine years' trading on his own account he was able to

Figure 3 Bainbridge's, Newcastle, interior 1898 (*source*: Newcastle upon Tyne City Libraries).

purchase extensive premises in Bond Street, London, and frequently took his team of mainly continental models to the south of France to show his collection. His famous 'walking skirt' which exposed the ankles was a sensation of the 1890s and much prized by the 'new woman'; Fenwick himself, perhaps because of its *risqué* implications, dubbed the garment the 'Anti Microbe Skirt'.[41] Local artists were equally lured by Fenwick's talent. The notable artists' colony at Cullercoats sent their fishwife model to Northumberland Street to be garbed by Fenwick himself in 'traditional' peasant fisherwoman clothes.[42]

Fenwick's two sons, Fred and Arthur, were sent to Paris in the early 1890s to study the fashion industry. Fred became far more interested in retailing than *haute couture* and spent most of his time observing the *grands magasins*, particularly the Bon Marché. Fred returned to Newcastle with a vision of transforming the Northumberland Street premises into a *grand magasin*. He did have a major advantage in the business's strong French image, but his father was initially hostile to opening up his exclusive 'showrooms' to all and sundry. Fenwick's seriously failing health diminished his resistance, and by the time of his death in 1905 the revolution was well under way. In 1901 the store attracted 295 customers per day; the following year this had risen to 3,000. The main factor in this remarkable expansion was the introduction of the 'silent sales assistant'. Announced in the local press on 27 November Fenwick promised:

> A welcome to customers to walk around the store. Assistants are not allowed to speak to visitors. Walk around today, don't buy. There is time for that another day.[43]

This offer was revolutionary in the city that 65 years earlier had, perhaps, been the birthplace of the department store. A pitman's wife could now enter the same premises used by the Percys. Whether she bought anything was another matter. But the Fenwick message was extremely subtle and loaded with economic and social implications. What the young Fenwicks wanted was what they termed a Paris-style 'walk round' store. Careful marketing ensured that some items were affordable to the less well-off, but of equal importance was the creation of an ambience which gave full vent to the complexities of the British class system. The better-off could be seen being better off by the things they purchased. Poorer folk could enter a new world of material fantasy, they could see it and even touch it and expect its glamour to rub off on their own small purchases. It is, no doubt, easy to mock such a marketing strategy, since after all it fits neatly into many somewhat conspiratorial theories on the quiescence of the British working class. Yet the immediate and continued success of Fenwick's is undeniable. Moreover, in the longer term this success clearly reflects the fact that the items purchased by poorer folk were of good value. People do not return to retail institutions week after week purely for novelty.

Fenwick's silent sales assistant created a fuss amongst their Newcastle rivals and some countered with mocking advertisments in the Newcastle press, but the Northumberland Street store created a social centrifuge; an apparently random, yet deliberately created juxtaposition of goods and customers which contained all the atmosphere and excitement of the Parisian *grand magasin* on the banks of the coaly Tyne. The result was that Fenwick's outpaced their rivals and began a process of rebuilding and expansion that has continued throughout the twentieth century.

Brown's of Chester shared Fenwick's classy origins but pioneered a different route to success. This firm has its origins in the marriage of Susannah Towsey, a local draper, to John Brown, who ran a nearby druggist shop, in 1788. The drapery business enjoyed a boom during the revolutionary period supplying muslin for the growing market in the 'Naked Fashion' style. Susannah died in 1812 and her business was taken over by her son William, joined in 1819 by his brother Henry. Their fashionable business enjoyed a prime site on Eastgate Street Row and they were reaping the benefits of Chester's growing popularity with the local gentry. This popularity, moreover, was accompanied by a redefinition of public space in the Rows area. In 1813 a Society for the Suppression of Vice was formed in order to secure the Rows for the promenading gentry. Heads of households were urged to keep their servants away from the area as traders and the local authority battled with 'rowdies and dissolute women'. Traders in the Rows, including William Brown, formed a rote system for policing the area in 1828. This measure, together with a more effective police force, eventually secured the district for the enjoyment of the upper classes.[44]

Brown's was also in the forefront of the Rows architectural improvements. Its neoclassic façade, built in 1828, was at first out of place with its more humble neighbours, but they quickly followed suit, producing Chester's pleasant blend of medieval and neoclassic buildings. The development of Chester as a middle-class resort continued throughout the nineteenth century and the Brown family played an

increasingly important role in this process. The Browns dominated local
Liberal politics in the last quarter of the nineteenth century; both
William and Charles Brown were town councillors, Charles being
elected mayor six times.[45] The 1820s were dominated by the campaign
to rid the Rows of 'rowdies and dissolute women', but by the 1870s
the edification of Chester had reached a more grandiose level. The
district of Flookersbrook, which dominated the entrance to the town,
presented a sorry picture of stagnant quarries and was transformed by
the Brown brothers into one of Chester's prettiest suburbs. They also
bought, for preservation, key town centre buildings, carefully constructed
new roads and under their guidance the Council improved the Dee
and created riverside promenades. The current image of 'Ancient
Chester' as a quintessential English shire town is very much a product
of these Victorian developments, which were largely prompted and
superintended by the Browns. Despite the Browns' considerable energy
and interest in improving the town, the business continued to grow
considerably. The firm certainly benefited greatly from Chester's popularity amongst the upper classes. Drapery continued to be important
and Brown's up-market style paralleled Chester's image. French sales
assistants were recruited from Paris and an extensive furniture business
was established. The family firm also diversified into textile manufacturing and gold mining in North Wales, as well as being major local
property developers.[46]

The decline of male family members in the early years of the present
century, especially ones with an interest in the business, presented the
firm with serious management problems. Brown's solution to this
difficulty was to restructure the company into a limited liability firm
headed by Mr J.M. Harris of Liverpool. This proved to be an in-
spirational development. Harris possessed first-rate business acumen, with
flair, vision and a strong sense of Brown's role in the twentieth century.[47]

Harris, who took over the reins of Brown's in 1908, had an acute
sense of the changes in retail patterns offered by the motor car. Moreover, he saw the car not as a threat to Chester but as a potential source
of new business. Chester retailers had prospered in the nineteenth
century by the town's cultivation of upper-class visitors; Harris realised
that the car offered a beneficial new twist to this theme. An old
customer of the period recounted:

> If my memory serve aright, the inspiration was to some extent prompted by
> the coming of the motor car. To this far-seeing business man it was clear that

the ladies of the household of what were known as the Merchant Princes of Liverpool would prefer a shopping day involving a run in the car through the Wirral to the always ancient and interesting city of Chester, rather than to the ferry crossing of the River Mersey ...[48]

This Saturday retreat to the shire town by middle-class suburbanites has been an important feature of twentieth-century retail development. But this was more than a chance discovery by middle-class motorists. They did not just stumble upon Chester, with its quaint tea-rooms and fine stores, beautiful architecture and genteel ambience that accorded so well with the growing middle-class cult of 'Englishness'. Harris brilliantly promoted his store as an alternative to the large establishments in Liverpool and Manchester. The muck and grime of these industrial cities were in many ways an affront to the new middle-class image of England. Black-and-white timbered Chester offered the newly mobile middle class a continuity of 'Englishness' that stretched between the leafy suburb and the ancient county town. Harris lured these customers by newspaper advertisements (see Figure 4), leaflets through letterboxes and by promoting motoring products in the store.

Harris's formula paid immediate dividends: adjoining property was acquired and the number of departments expanded. In a short period Brown's had been transformed from an up-market drapers with a furniture section into a fully-fledged department store, replete with restaurants and home delivery service by smart liveried, motor vans. 'Brown's of Chester', as it first termed itself in 1913, could justly claim on the eve of the Great War to be the 'Harrods of the North', and embarked on a battle with its regional rival, Lewis's Bon Marché in Liverpool, which it was ultimately to win. Harris did not totally revolutionise Brown's, rather he skilfully blended the old with the new. For example, the store continued to specialise in French fashion and Paris goods. Regular fashion shows featuring French models and gowns were started in 1913 and the firm's advertisements often priced fashion items in francs.[49] Brown's was certainly not an establishment frequented by the wives of clerks and artisans, indeed its classy reputation was to prove a hindrance later in the century. The customer mix that Harris's clamoured for were the well-heeled suburbanites of the Wirral and the stores' traditional gentry and aristocratic clients. Harris achieved this mix by astutely appealing to the snobbish sensibilities of such customers. Consider the following promotional ploy:

From eleven in the morning till late afternoon one side of Eastgate Street was lined with the motor cars of county people, and many thousands must have passed through the showrooms that day to the strains of music from Miss Giles's orchestra. The proceedings were described (in part) as follows: 'County ladies as shop assistants! This was the novelty to see when on Tuesday afternoon everybody's lady friends flocked to Eastgate Row. The goal of every pilgrimage was Browns! ...

It was a red-letter day in the calendar of Chester shopping. Never has any Chester shop contained at the same time so many members of the aristocracy. In the mingling of well-dressed ladies who thronged the splendid showrooms a large proportion were members of notable county families, and the ordinary customer becoming the purchaser of a bewitching gown or a dream of a hat could easily have had the great honour of being assisted in her choice by the unimpeachable taste of a lady as high up in the world of rank and fashion as a Duchess or a Marchioness ...

Decorated with flowers and plants, glittering with mirrors, radiant with soft tones of colour, and graced by an animated company of stylish and handsome women, the beautiful showrooms, new and old, made a picture of shopping splendour rarely seen in the provinces, and, as for the latest creations in gowns and the new spring styles in hats, they presented such glowing visions of the adornments that captivate the heart of lovely woman that no fair creature of mortal mould (and a well-filled purse!) could possibly have held aloof from the irresistible appeal to add to her wardrobe new articles of grace and beauty ...[50]

'County ladies as shop assistants!' at this charity event were obviously the lure of those with a 'well-filled purse'. Brown's achievement was to develop a style that allied the better-off bourgeois with the gentry and aristocrat, an amalgamation made possible by the motor car. Brown's remained more like Harrods than Fenwick of Newcastle, yet all three clearly were responding to social and economic change in their own locality. Indeed in the case of Fenwick and Brown's both were succeeding thanks to their managements' finely-tuned awareness of their existing and potential customers' social sensitivities.

So far we have examined the development of the department store in large cities and the shire town; there is, however, another important example that warrants discussion. The department store by the sea is an important British institution and its emergence throws light on both business and social history. Beale's of Bournemouth encompasses many such themes. This store originated as a fancy goods shop in 1881 when James G. Beale, 1848–1928, moved to Bournemouth from Weymouth.[51] Bournemouth during this period, like so many other South Coast

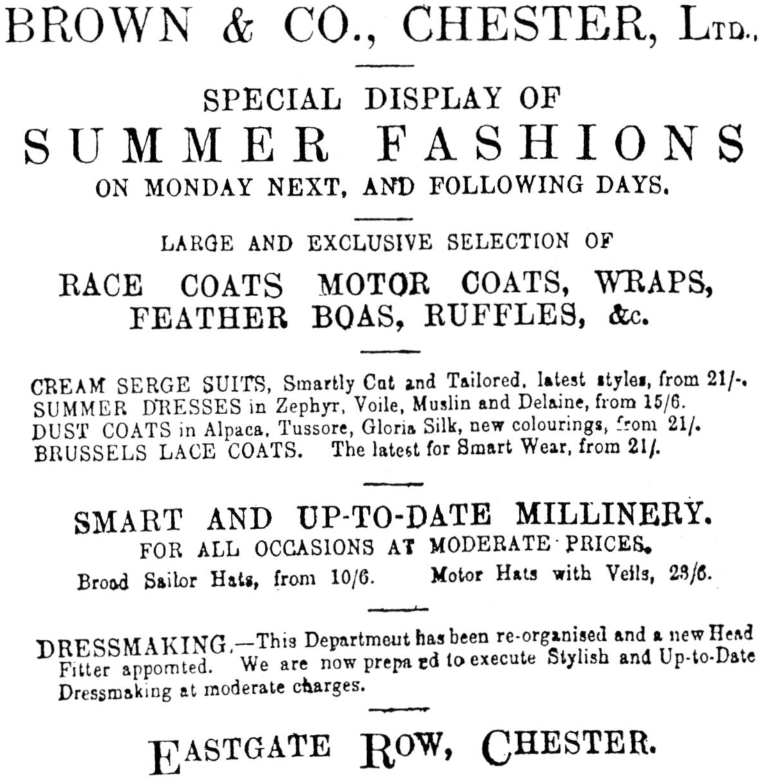

BROWN & CO., CHESTER, Ltd.,

SPECIAL DISPLAY OF

SUMMER FASHIONS

ON MONDAY NEXT, AND FOLLOWING DAYS.

LARGE AND EXCLUSIVE SELECTION OF

RACE COATS MOTOR COATS, WRAPS, FEATHER BOAS, RUFFLES, &c.

CREAM SERGE SUITS, Smartly Cut and Tailored, latest styles, from 21/-.
SUMMER DRESSES in Zephyr, Voile, Muslin and Delaine, from 15/6.
DUST COATS in Alpaca, Tussore, Gloria Silk, new colourings, from 21/.
BRUSSELS LACE COATS. The latest for Smart Wear, from 21/.

SMART AND UP-TO-DATE MILLINERY.
FOR ALL OCCASIONS AT MODERATE PRICES.
Broad Sailor Hats, from 10/6.   Motor Hats with Veils, 23/6.

DRESSMAKING.—This Department has been re-organised and a new Head
Fitter appomted.   We are now prepa ed to execute Stylish and Up-to-Date
Dressmaking at moderate charges.

EASTGATE ROW, CHESTER.

Figure 4 An advertisement of 1908 in which motor cars and motor hats for
women highlight the growing popularity of motoring.

watering holes, was engaged in the tourist-excursionist conflict. To
paraphrase John Walton's seminal study on this topic the conflict was
essentially over the strategy of many resorts to attract the better-off
long-stay holiday-maker.[52] The realisation of such a goal was perceived
by many interested parties as necessitating the exclusion of poorer day-
trippers. Beale's reaction to this problem was to abandon his bucket-
and-spade shop and his largely excursionist clientele, and move
up-market into drapery, which included his acquisition of the Liberty
agency. Beale was clearly falling in line with Bournemouth's emerging
self-image as an up-market resort. The move quickly paid off. The shop
rapidly developed into a department store, Beale astutely perceiving
that tourists on holiday do not stop shopping and their needs presented
many opportunities. His sons were sent to work at Harrods and

Whiteley's to gain experience and by the late 1890s they assumed control
of the store. The founder continued to be active and, besides being
highly involved in local Nonconformity, he was elected a progressive
councillor in 1900 and returned as mayor in 1902.[53]

The subsequent political career of the founder of Beale's has many
parallels with that of the Brown brothers in Chester. He became the
leading campaigner for municipal improvements, including major rebuilding of the seafronts and the development of an efficient tram
service, and according to his entry in the Dictionary of Business
Biography, he was in the forefront of the process of creating Bournemouth as a high-class shopping centre. He also diversified his interests
when he founded the Carlton Hotel, Europe's only independent five-
star establishment. Beale obviously backed the right horse when he
gave up buckets and spades to pursue the tourist's purse.[54]

Jolly's of Bath is another striking example of the shire/seaside town
store. This store's origins were in the holiday town of Margate. Its
owner, James Jolly, was assisted by his son who wearied of Margate's
excursionist trade. Young Thomas Jolly was determined to find a 'higher
class of holiday trade' and took seasonal premises at Bath. By the 1850s
Jolly's was referring to itself as the 'Parisian Depot' and employed 58
workers.[55] Jolly's experienced a strikingly similar trajectory to Brown's
of Chester. Michael Jolly became an active local politician; he reformed
the local police force and landholding systems and saved the neglected
baths and pump rooms from decay. Jolly was twice elected mayor, and
like the Browns of Chester, he had a clear vision of Bath as a refurbished
historic town which would act as a magnet to visiting shoppers. And
again like Brown's, it was during the Edwardian period that the store
developed a multiplicity of departments.[56]

The South Coast developed a necklace of department stores during
this period which stretched from Bobby's in Margate via Volkes of
Brighton, Hubbards of Worthing, Knight and Lee in Southsea, Bobby's
again in Torquay and Spooners of Plymouth. No doubt some of these
have histories as heroic as Beale's, but the major point that needs to be
underlined is the integral role played by the department store in the
development of the seaside resort. Indeed the quality of the store
reflected the image of the resort and, as Beale's illustrates, the department
store was both a product of the emerging resort and a major force in
its development.[57]

By 1900 Britain possessed a range of department stores catering for a wide variety of communities. Indeed the wide spectrum of stores reflected the growing complexity of British society. The large central London stores served the well-heeled clientele of imperial London, richly peppered with the better-off suburbanites and the odd brave adventurer from lower down the social order. In the same period we see the rise of the suburban stores catering for less wealthy customers, but often matching the guile of their West End rivals. In the provinces the same process was at work. We have already examined some of the major developments carried out by retailers in Newcastle, Manchester, Chester and Bournemouth and it is worth noting that other cities and towns shared these experiences.

The emergence of large stores in Glasgow paralleled the city's growing fortunes and claim to be the second city of the empire. Glasgow is interesting because here we witness the stark division between 'posh' and popular. Buchanan Street in the last quarter of the nineteenth century became dominated by grand establishments such as McDonald's and Wylie and Lockhead, the latter in 1885 boasting an iron-framed glass-roofed building, whose four galleried floors echoed the Parisian style. At the bottom of Buchanan Street, Fraser and McLaren's six-storey edifice dominated the corner with Argyle Street, Glasgow's more 'popular' shopping area, and close by, Arnott's was enjoying considerable success. Thus, within a few minutes' walk, the stores of Glasgow reflected the growth of both the city's wealthy merchant and industrial magnates and its considerable lower middle class.[58]

Birmingham, Glasgow's great rival to 'second city' status, was, by the admission of its leading citizen, 'undershopped'. Birmingham's leading historian has suggested that this backwardness was produced by the proliferation of small businesses and an historically small city centre.[59] Briggs's famous thesis on social class in Birmingham, a city of small businessmen and workers enjoying daily contact on first-name terms, may also illuminate the apparent backwardness of retailing in the city. Distinctions between bosses and workers were often blurred and of little consequence, and the pressure to create social hierarchies through patterns of consumption may have been less felt in Birmingham than elsewhere. Table 1 also highlights Birmingham's relatively small white-collar population in comparison to Glasgow, Manchester and Newcastle. It is useful to dwell on Birmingham's backwardness, as the city's experience in retailing highlights the socio-economic background that was an essential condition for department store growth. This city of small units of production also proved, in Cole's words, 'to be a desert of co-operation'.[60] Indeed Brummies seem to have preferred arcades to large stores. The Great Western Arcade (1875) and the City Arcade (1898) may well have reflected the small business culture of Birmingham.[61] The city did, of course, eventually possess a few department stores, but we need to keep in mind the rather puny growth of Rackham's prior to the 1920s and the experience of the Lewis's store in late Victorian Birmingham. The historian of Lewis's has noted the 'failure to secure spectacular increases' in Birmingham and the store's increasing emphasis on cheapness with a repertoire of Penny Readings, sales of bankrupt stock and low-price tea.[62]

Leeds, like Birmingham, appears to have preferred arcades to department stores.[63] Edinburgh and Cardiff are also high on the list of white-collar populations shown in Table 1. Both capitals obviously possessed a high proportion of administrative workers. Edinburgh also enjoyed the fruits of being the centre of Scotland's separate education and legal institutions. The prosperity of Edinburgh's growing bureaucracy is reflected in Jenner's magnificent Princes Street premises and its rival on Princes Street, Robert Maule's whose Rendezvous restaurant was a fashionable social centre in the late Victorian period.[64] Cardiff never managed to equal Edinburgh in capital city distinctiveness but it certainly outpaced the 'Athens of the North' in economic growth. Daunton has expertly analysed Cardiff's prodigious development during the second half of the nineteenth century, based largely on the expansion of the port, which overtook the Tyne as the major exporter of coal in the 1890s. The growth of the port gave rise to a highly mobile population at the lower levels of the social hierarchy but the city, like Newcastle, also needed a large white-collar presence to service its commercial activity[65] (see Table 1). The rapid growth of James Howell and Co. of St Mary Street in the 1890s, and David Morgan's nearby, symbolised Cardiff's economic pre-eminence in the principality, with half the population of Wales living within 25 miles of the city centre. The local newspapers' boast in 1905 that Cardiff was 'the Chicago of Wales' was a fairly accurate one.[66]

Leeds also enjoyed enormous growth during the nineteenth century, rising from 53,000 in 1801, to 445,000 in 1911.[67] Yet Leeds lagged behind other major cities in department store development. Leeds was, of course, famous for its markets, but the centre-piece of these retailing amenities, Kirkgate Market, with its 44 shops inside the new iron and glass structure of 1857, was a minnow in comparison to Newcastle's earlier Grainger Market with over 220 outlets in Dobson's late Georgian building. Kirkgate was, however, the birthplace of Leeds's greatest contribution to retailing, Marks and Spencer, which began life as a cheap and cheerful Penny Bazaar in the 1880s.[68] The most stunning aspect of Leeds's retail growth was the development of the arcade system in the city centre. Charles Thornton's arcade of 1877–78 was the first of five which formed a virtual redevelopment of the central area. The historian of retail facilities in Leeds has argued that the arcade system was a response to the peculiarities of Leeds's ancient urban geography which left the city with a shortage of vacant land fronting the main streets. Thus development in central Leeds was forced literally backwards into the courts and alleys behind the main thoroughfare.[69] It is no surprise that the major indigenous department store in Leeds, Schofield's, began life as a corner draper's at the entrance to the Victoria Arcade in 1901.[70] But note the lateness of Schofield's arrival which was perhaps hampered by the enormous choice provided by individual traders inside the arcades. We lack the demographic data available for other places in Table 1 and it would be churlish to construct comparisons with Birmingham, but Leeds did enjoy prosperity during the Victorian era based on an increasingly diversified economy. By the end of the period under review, Leeds did possess some department stores, especially branches of Marshall's of London and Robinson's of Darlington, but with the exception of Schofield's rather small store, for a city of its size, Leeds failed to produce a major department store entrepreneur.

The same could not be said of Liverpool. William Henderson, David Lewis and Owen Owen founded Liverpool's three major stores and the latter two were to have an import beyond Merseyside. Lewis began trading in Ranelagh Street in 1856 as a men's and youths' tailors. Ever cautious, Lewis slowly developed other lines; by the 1870s he had branched out into women's clothing and tobacco, soon followed by cheap books, tea and other items. His core business in the early years remained boys' clothing, and he claimed fifty thousand such customers a year in his advertisements. Lewis, like most department store owners, combined retailing with manufacturing, employing 'a brigade of cutters' in his own workshop. Lewis and his family successors were highly skilful at developing a popular store for a mainly working-class clientele, and their formula was exported to other northern and midland towns which was to add a new dimension to retailing in provincial England.[71] Owen

Owen, in contrast, opened his modest store in London Road in 1868, but his target customer base was Liverpool's large, mainly Nonconformist Welsh population. His store quickly expanded and was soon attracting customers from the North Wales hinterland.[72] It is easy to forget the 'Welshness' of Liverpool during this period when so many historical works on the city focus upon its Anglo-Irish dimensions. Yet Liverpool was the host of the Eisteddfod in 1884 of which Owen Owen was a prominent donor. Owen Owen's main distinction, however, was as a speculator in retail real estate. Having trained at the family business in Bath and successfully put together a large portfolio of property in Liverpool, the young draper from Machynlleth helped finance his brother's store in Westbourne Grove.[73] This was followed by a major stake in the Bon Marché, Brixton, and a foray into the development of Kensington High Street, where he developed the Derry and Toms building in 1896, Oxford Street and Regent Street.[74] Owen was also a major shareholder in John Barnes of Finchley and a central figure in the London–Welsh business/political circle.[75] Despite its prodigious growth and huge size – over 700,000 people in 1901 – Liverpool was not an easy city for department stores. It could be concluded, for example, that the growth of the Owen Owen group in the present century was largely financed by the founder's property speculations outside the city. Liverpool possessed a great port but it was by no means a prosperous city. The commerce of the port could be highly seasonal and it lacked the steady coal trade that underwrote the success of Cardiff and Newcastle. The docks had a large population of surplus labour and workers were often lucky to gain three days' work per week. Similarly, Liverpool's large army of clerks were often 'insecure and ill paid' and were increasingly under pressure as women moved into clerical professions.[76] The domination of transport and the city's small skilled manufacturing base appear to have resulted in Liverpool's fragmented department store structure. This is best illustrated by Lewis having to develop their up-market trade separately from the main Ranelagh Street store. This took the form of establishing Lewis's Bon Marché store in the more salubrious setting of Basnett Street. Lacking the solid skilled working- and lower middle-class base of Cardiff, Glasgow, Manchester and Newcastle, Liverpool failed to develop the 'democratic' stores that featured prominently in many other provincial cities.

By the Edwardian period, Britain possessed a large number of department stores. Yet this development was highly uneven, reflecting the complexities of the nation's social and economic structure. Stores in London were increasingly concentrated in the Kensington High Street, Knightsbridge and Oxford Street areas, whilst the pioneering Whiteley's and its Westbourne Grove neighbours began to decline in importance. The rise of the London suburban stores was symptomatic of the growing prosperity of these districts and the innovation of local entrepreneurs. The large provincial cities with sizeable lower middle and skilled working classes such as Glasgow, Manchester, Newcastle and Cardiff all experienced the growth of their central retail areas driven by the success of their large stores. Smaller provincial towns also shared in this process, particularly the South Coast resorts and the emerging shire towns, especially Bath and Chester; while many lesser industrial towns in the north saw the arrival of a branch of Binns, the Sunderland store which pioneered an early chain of department stores, or Robinson's of Darlington who pursued a similar programme of expansion. There also existed a large number of smaller, independent stores catering for the needs of their individual communities. Unfortunately, little exists for the historian in the way of records on such *petits grands magasins* like the Beehive of Whitehaven, Roomes of Upminster and Lilley's of Cambridge. There is much work here for local historians.

Notes

1. T. Kusamitsu, 'Great Exhibitions before 1851', *History Workshop*, 9, Spring, 1980.

2. P. Greenhalgh, *Ephemeral Vistas, The Expositions Universelles, Great Exhibitions and World Fairs, 1851-1939*, Manchester University Press, Manchester, 1988, is the most complete survey on this subject.

3. M.B. Miller, *The Bon Marché, Bourgeois Culture and the Department Store, 1869-1920*, George Allen and Unwin, London, 1981.

4. Greenhalgh, op. cit., p. 35.

5. Miller, op. cit., p. 42.

6. Ibid., p. 167.

7. R.H. Williams, *Dream Worlds. Mass Consumption in Late Nineteenth Century France*, University of California Press, Berkeley, CA, 1982, p. 62.

8. Miller, op. cit., p. 25.

9. Ibid., p. 42.

10. Williams, op. cit., pp. 107–10.

11. Miller, op. cit., pp. 61–5.

12. Ibid., p. 177.

13. On the redevelopment of Paris, see A. Sutcliffe, *The Autumn of Central Paris*, Edward Arnold, London, 1970; also P.G. Nord, *Paris Shopkeepers and the Politics of Resentment*, Princeton University Press, Princeton, NJ, 1986, Chapter 3.

14. Miller, op. cit., p. 41, n. 38.

15. L. Berlanstein, *The Working People of Paris*, Johns Hopkins University Press, Baltimore, MD, 1984, is a useful survey of the Parisian economy in the late nineteenth century.

16. Miller, op. cit., p. 61.

17. Greenhalgh, op. cit., p. 37.

18. Miller, op. cit., p. 54.

19. R.S. Lambert, *The Universal Provider: A Study of William Whiteley*, George C. Harrap, London, 1938. Chapter 1 presents a useful account of Whiteley's early career.

20. Ibid., p. 61.

21. D.A. Reeder, 'A theatre of suburbs', in H.J. Dyos (ed.), *The Study of Urban History*, 1968, p. 263.

22. Lambert, op. cit., Chapter 2, *passim*.

23. Ibid, pp. 87–91; 194–5; 235–6.

24. Ibid., p. 217.

25. Ibid., p. 99.

26. Reeder, op. cit., p. 264.

27. Lambert, op. cit., p. 168.

28. The best account of Harrods' early history is to be found in Moss and Turton, *A Legend of Retailing*, 1989, pp. 321–32. Tim Dale's *Harrods', the Store and the Legend*, Pan, London, 1981, is also useful.

29. Moss and Turton, op. cit., pp. 321–3; Dale, op. cit., pp. 9–21.

30. T.C. Barker's essay, 'Urban transport', in M.J. Freeman and D.H. Aldcroft (eds), *Transport in Victorian Britain*, pp 134–71 offers a useful account of the growth of London's railway system.

31. *Draper's Record*, 15 December 1888.

32. Apart from Burbidge at Harrods, John Barker, founder of the Kensington store, was a former employee of Whiteley. The Army and Navy stores were also managed by ex-Whiteley workers. *The Bayswater Chronicle* also noted 'Mr Whiteley's is the chief training ground for heads of department who are afterwards nobbled by the stores all over London.' Lambert, op. cit., p. 135.

33. For Dickens and Jones see Moss and Turton, op. cit., pp. 305–9; accounts of Marshall and Snelgrove, Swan and Edgar and Debenham and Freebody can be found in M. Corina, *Fine Silks and Oak Counters, Debenhams 1778–1978*, Hutchinson, London, 1978.

34. Details on this and other middle-class co-operative ventures are discussed in J. Hoard and B.S. Yamey, *The Middle Class Co-operative Retailing Societies in London, 1864–1900*, Oxford Economic Papers, 3, 1957.

35. Ibid. See also Moss and Turton, op. cit., pp. 272–8.

36. Hoard and Yamey, op. cit.

37. A. and J. Airey, *The Bainbridges of Newcastle*, 1979, pp. 62–6.

38. Moss and Turton, op. cit., pp. 343–5. See also the article by Graham Turner, *Daily Mail*, 4 August 1990.

39. Briggs, *Friends of the People*, 1956, pp. 35–8. Briggs notes that 'down to 1914, the Liverpool Bon Marché delivery vans were painted in the same striped colours as those of the store in Paris'.

40. Adburgham, *Shops and Shopping*, p. 169.

41. This account of Fenwick largely follows R. Pound, *The Fenwick Story*, Fenwick, Newcastle upon Tyne, 1972.

42. *The Fenwick Album, 1882–1982*.

43. Pound, op. cit., p. 56.

44. This discussion is largely based upon *Brown's of Chester, Portrait of a Shop* by Mass Observation, (ed.) H.D. Willcock, Lindsay Drummond, London, 1947.

45. Ibid., pp. 153–71.

46. Ibid., pp. 99–112.

47. Ibid., p. 180.

48. Ibid., p. 181.

49. Mass Observation Archive, *Brown's of Chester*, Box 5, File A.

50. Quoted in Willcock, op. cit., p,186.

51. J.F. Parsons, 'J.G. Beale', essay in the *Dictionary of Business Biography*, (ed.) D.J. Jeremy, 1984, pp. 226–9.

52. J.K. Walton, *The English Seaside Resort. A Social History, 1750–1914*, Leicester University Press, Leicester, 1983, Chapter 8.

53. Parsons, op. cit.

54. Ibid.

55. Moss and Turton, op. cit., pp. 337–42.

56. Ibid.

57. Details on Bobby's and Spooners can be found in Corina, op. cit., J.H. Porter's, 'The development of a provincial department store', *Business History*, 13, 1971, is a useful account of Broadbent's of Southport which enjoyed a clientele similar to the South Coast resorts.

58. Moss and Turton, op. cit., Chapter 3, has useful material on Glaswegian stores during this period.

59. Briggs, op. cit., pp. 79–83.

60. G.D.H. Cole, *A Century of Co-operation*, Co-operative Union, Manchester, 1944, p. 155.

61. MacKeith, *Shopping Arcades 1817–1939*, 1985, pp 12–16.

62. Briggs, op. cit., pp. 88–9.

63. MacKeith, op. cit., pp. 70–5. K. Grady, 'Commercial, marketing and retailing amenities, 1700–1914', in D. Fraser (ed.) *A History of Modern Leeds*, Manchester University Press, Manchester, pp. 194–5.

64. Moss and Turton, op. cit., pp. 351–3.

65. M.J. Daunton, *Coal Metropolis. Cardiff 1870–1914*, Leicester University Press, Leicester, 1977, Part I.

66. Moss and Turton, op. cit., pp. 332–6.

67. Fraser, op. cit., p. 48.

68. Grady, op. cit., p. 192.

69. Ibid., pp. 194–5.

70. Moss and Turton, op. cit., pp. 356–60.

71. Briggs, op. cit., Chapters 2 and 3.

72. D.W. Davies, *Owen Owen, Victorian Draper*, Gwasg Cambria, Aberystwyth, nd (1984?), pp. 40–1.

73. Ibid., p. 26.

74. Ibid., pp. 56–7; 62–3; 81–2.

75. Ibid., pp. 59–61.

76. Walton, 1987, *Lancashire*, p. 211.

CHAPTER THREE

BUILDINGS, FIXTURES AND FITTINGS

The physical structure of the stores also presented a wide variety of architectural styles and internal arrangements. Bainbridge's of Newcastle was fortunate in being located in a part of a central block in the heart of Newcastle's late Georgian Grainger town. It took the store, however, many years to burrow its way through the block and gain entrances in both Market Street and the Bigg Market. The store, which is now part of the House of Fraser Binns division, still contains a changing variety of space and levels, the testimony to its higgledy-piggledy growth in the nineteenth century. Nearby, Fenwick's of Northumberland Street contains a similar internal geography but on a much grander scale. Fenwick's has, however, made a virtue out of this possible drawback; this vast store is the easiest in Britain in which to get lost and offers the nearest experience to Boucicaut's Parisian ideal. Others, restrained by surrounding property, were forced to expand by opening separate premises nearby. Hannington's of Brighton, Roomes of Upminster, Knight and Lee of Southsea and Farnon's of Newcastle are amongst extant examples of this development. If the French built cathedrals of commerce in the late nineteenth century, the British stores, in contrast, resembled rambling Nonconformist chapels. Moreover, many stores expanded their manufacturing and wholesale activities on the same premises. Bainbridge's, for example, called their business a 'warehouse' well into the present century.

Very few, especially prior to 1900, could begin business in a large purpose-built store. The *grands magasins* of the boulevard Haussmann in late nineteenth-century Paris were in part the product of the city's increasing function as the centre of fashion and international con-sumerism. Generally, purpose-built stores in late Victorian Britain were the, perhaps unintended, consequence of the department store's major enemy – fire. Whiteley's in Westbourne Grove suffered four major infernos between 1882 and 1887. Prior to the first fire, Whiteley's early historian described the premises in the following terms, 'No galleries,

45

vaults and pinnacles of glass – only a long row of windows stretching down the dusty pavement'.[1] Whiteley's first fire of November 1882 devastated this property, but insured fully by the Royal Fire Office, the 'Universal Provider' was quickly back in business. The subsequent two fires were confined to nearby warehouse and workshop premises and, with rumours and press speculation that Whiteley was the victim of a mysterious arsonist, insurance companies greatly curtailed their risk with Whiteley. Nevertheless, out of the ashes in the Grove, Whiteley was able to construct a five-storey block crowned with a central mansard tower 'so characteristic of Parisian architecture'. Whiteley's fine new structure was hardly completed when fire struck again in 1887.[2]

Store fires were to bedevil the major cities of Britain throughout the second half of the nineteenth century. A major factor in the vulnerability of department stores was their growing dependence on artificial lighting. Stores became deeper, with less natural light whilst, at the same time, display systems were becoming more sophisticated and demanded greater illumination.[3] Oil lamps were replaced by the more efficient gas mantle served by growing labyrinths of small lead pipes. The *ad hoc* development of stores, in both depth and height, often utilised cheap and highly inflammable matchboard partitions and wooden floors were used extensively as extra storeys were added. Typically, a small fire would melt lead piping, causing gas to escape and quickly turn into a destructive inferno. Glasgow was particularly hard-hit, paradoxically, because of the innovative modern building techniques employed in the city's major stores. Glasgow was a pioneer of iron-framed building at the mid-century, but the local method of fixing wooden floors to iron girders made the premises highly vulnerable. Fraser and McLaren's premises on the corner of Buchanan and Argyle Street suffered severe damage in 1872 and again in 1888.[4] The replacement building of 1889 has been described by the store's historians as 'Built on six floors with a fine stone façade it boasted the most modern fittings, including electric lighting and heating equipment'. Nearby, Wylie and Lockhead's revolutionary building which was 'iron framed, had a façade of Corinthian pillars and plate glass and an arched glass roof', erected in 1854, was destroyed in 1867. Its replacement on similar lines suffered the same fate in 1883. The new store completed in 1885 had its iron frame encased with fire-proof material and was internally lit largely by natural light. This building, still trading as Fraser's, is arguably Britain's most beautiful store.[5] A number of Glasgow's famous architects were involved

Figure 5 Pettigrew and Stephen's Sauchiehall Street store, 1901. This magnificent example of a purpose-built Glaswegian store featured a gilt dome designed by Charles Rennie Mackintosh. The architect of the building was John Keppie, the senior partner of the firm that employed Mackintosh (*source*: British Library).

in the design and construction of department stores in the city (see Figure 5).

Brown, Muffs of Bradford gained purpose-built premises in 1871, thanks to the municipal redevelopment of the central area. These premises had to be rebuilt in 1878 after a fire, while the Harrods fire of 1883 subsequently led to a change of management and ownership which was to produce the store's greatest period of expansion, culminating in the building of the present-day store in the early years of this century.[6] A Whiggish interpretation of store infernos must, however, be avoided. Even in the 'electric age', stores have been highly vulnerable and difficult to insure. The loss of trade and drain on the balance sheet often set back business many years. Moreover, as we shall see in a future chapter, the risk of fire seriously soured industrial relations up until 1914.

Technological developments within the stores proceeded in a similar piecemeal manner. As stores expanded in size, the handling of cash became an increasing problem. The typical method was for a sales assistant, on completing the sale, to write out an order form and send a young member of staff to the counting house with the cash and form and return with the change and a receipt of sale. This system was labour-intensive, inefficient and presented security problems. This problem was solved by the Lamson pneumatic tube system in the 1880s or by similar means such as Bainbridge's 'Ariel Messengers' of the late 1880s which were powered by a six-horse power Otto engine which also drove the firm's carpet-beating machine and worked a cable tramway used for the conveyance of goods.[7] The pneumatic tube system proved remarkably enduring (see Figures 6 and 7) and survived in many stores up until the 1950s, long after the arrival of cheap cash registers.

As stores rose in height, access to upper floors became a problem. The Parisian stores favoured graceful curving staircases, such as those designed by Eiffel for the Bon Marché. Most British stores followed this solution and the use of mechanical lifts was also slowly introduced. The first known lift in Britain was installed in the nation's most innovative retail building, Wylie and Lockhead's, in 1855.[8] This piece of Glaswegian engineering inventiveness, according to the *Glasgow Herald*, consisted of a

> very ingenious hoisting apparatus, worked by a neat steam engine, which is intended not only to lift up bales from the Wagon entrance to the upper parts of the building, but to elevate those ladies and gentlemen to the galleries to whom the climbing of successive stairs might be attended with fatigue and annoyance. Parties who are old, fat, feeble, short winded, or simply lazy, or who desire a bit of fun, have only to place themselves on an enclosed platform

Figure 6 Tubes for taking carriers back to sales departments. Note the numbers of the 'terminal stations' (*source*: collection of the author).

Figure 7 The 'terminal station' of the tube system in a selling department (*source*: collection of the author).

or flooring when they are elevated by a gentle and pleasing process to a height exceeding that of a country steeple, and from the railing of the upper gallery they may look down on a scene of industrial and artistic magnificence which has yet not a parallel amongst us.

A more efficient device had been developed by Eliza Otis in the USA in 1852. Complete with brakes and powered by hydraulics this system was gradually installed in British stores in the 1880s.[9] The slow adoption of lifts in Britain was probably due to the lower traffic flows of British stores, building constraints caused by piecemeal expansion and, as the newspaper quotation above indicates, the fact that they were initially perceived as a novelty.

Novelty certainly accompanied Britain's first escalator installed in Harrods in 1898 (escalators had first been used in retailing earlier in the year at the Louvre in Paris and Bloomingdales in New York).[10] Customers unnerved by the experience were revived by shopmen dispensing free smelling salts and cognac. Richard Burbidge, Harrods' managing director, engaged the French firm, Piat, to install the escalator and also negotiated a licence agreement with them which gave Harrods patent rights in Britain.[11] Harrods did grant Owen Owen permission to install a similar escalator in his Liverpool store in the same year, but generally British stores remained aloof from this technology well into the interwar period.

Lighting, as noted above, was a growing problem during the last decades of the nineteenth century. The dangers inherent in gas lighting were becoming well known and in September 1887 the trade journal, the *Draper's Record*, condemned gas as a light source as it was the major cause of fires.[12] The problem, however, for many stores, was the availability of an alternative source of illumination. Electricity was the obvious answer; displays of electric lighting were a popular novelty at grand expositions of the period and store owners were quick to realise the display potential of the new bulbs. The major drawback was the highly variegated nature of electrical supply. Lewis of Liverpool was an early pioneer, taking his lead from the much publicised electric lighting of Macy's and Wanamaker's stores in the USA; in 1878 he decided to illuminate the whole of his new Manchester premises with electricity. Unfortunately the steam engine and generators employed at the new store could only manage to illuminate a powerful lamp on top of the store's flagstaff.[13] Bainbridge of Newcastle, a city that pioneered the generation of electricity and the light bulb, illuminated his store with the new source in 1890.[14] Glasgow was another centre of innovation; one store 'installed sixty lamps in the toy salon to create a dazzling hall of light' in 1882. Fraser's new showroom of 1889 employed the new system and its reliability was improved with the municipal supply of electricity in 1893.[15] Electric lighting also served to transform department stores into city centre evening magnets. *La Lumière électrique* reported that the lighting of Printemps in 1883 'enlivens the whole area'.[16]

If electricity was slow to assist the store in displaying its goods, new types of fixtures and fittings, particularly cabinets, were developed more quickly. The early method of placing large mirrors in dark corners to assist brightness and security, was replaced by the emergence of the glass cabinet.[17] Similarly, the trestle tables, like those in Kendal Milne's early bazaar premises, gave way to oak and mahogany counters, considered the most effective surface for displaying unrolled material, which remained the largest area of sales for stores during the period. Counters soon developed glass fronts. Wood and glass cabinets of great ingenuity were developed for the display of gloves and novelties. In this area Britain kept pace with the USA and France largely due to the activities of Frederick Sage, London's premier shop-fitter. Sage came to London from Ipswich in the early 1850s to work as a carpenter. In that same decade, he developed a range of new show-cases with light frames and plate glass, which revolutionised British display methods. When he died in 1898, his firm employed 600 workers and his products were the equal of those produced in the USA by the Phillips Silent Salesman Showcase Company.[18] Placing goods behind glass obviously added to their attractiveness and many stores installed windows that were similar in design to show-cases (see Figure 8).

Apart from placing goods behind glass, other display techniques were developed. Draping material and rugs over the rails of upper galleries was a method quickly imported from Paris. As the range of products sold in stores moved away from the historic core of drapery items, new display techniques evolved. Roberts of Stratford's *Santa's Grotto* of 1888 was emulated throughout Britain the following Christmas. Women's clothing had long been displayed on headless and armless mannequins which were gradually replaced in the 1890s with full-life wax figures.[19] The proliferation of departments, particularly furniture and household goods, posed new problems. One solution was simply to stand these objects on the floor and hope that they would sell themselves. The

Figure 8 A show-case shop front of 1909. As well as providing the allure of glass, the labyrinth of show-case windows also increased window space. By the 1930s the trade press was urging their removal claiming that they were being used at night by courting couples (*source*: British Library).

more innovative retailer chose to arrange these goods in room settings. Again Glasgow was in the van; Wylie and Lockhead, Buchanan Street's most up-market store, extended their floor-space in 1874 with the provision of 'flats' to display furniture. By the end of the century the store was pioneering the Scottish avant-garde art nouveau furniture style, producing many items in the firm's own factory, the largest of its type in Scotland. Kendal Milne in Manchester followed a similar path, with special furniture showrooms being built as part of the Deansgate improvement scheme. By 1882 the store was displaying Morris and Company's fabric and wallpaper and provided an interior design service.[20]

Glasgow's burgeoning West End, with its proliferation of middle-class tenements, obviously inspired the Wylie and Lockhead displays, but by the turn of the century young middle-class London couples were increasingly beginning married life in similar accommodation. Ardern Holt wrote an interesting article, 'How to Furnish a Flat with Economy', in the *Lady's Realm* of March 1905 which gives an account of flat displays in a London store. The article was in no doubt about the store's potential customers: 'When less than a hundred a year will provide a home with taxes and "tout compris", and £100 down will go a long way towards furnishing, many a young couple are tempted to Providence for the future.' According to Holt the store displayed the hundred pounds' flat with all items 'clearly enumerated' and for this sum the purchaser gained:

> A flat of ... modest description [consisting] of a hall, dining- and drawing rooms, a bedroom and servant's bedroom, bathroom and kitchen well supplied with the necessary utensils, china, glass, electro-plate, and cutlery. Linen and blankets are all included; and when you come to consider the sum, it is perfectly wonderful what you get for your money, bearing in mind that the furniture is up to date and so pretty that the owners need never be troubled by any sense of want of beauty or inappropriateness.[21]

Facilities for the comfort of customers increased during the late nineteenth century. Toilets, restrooms, cafés and tea-rooms were commonplace by the 1890s, amenities which not only made shopping more comfortable but also functioned as the major urban rendezvous for many women.

A Convenient Rendezvous!

We are pleased to find that many Ladies make our Warehouse a place of meeting in 'Town'. It is very central, and in any case a place of call, and it is big enough to be private! Of course, the *spot of meeting* should always be named – the The 'Blouse' Room! The 'Millinery!' The 'Flower and Perfume' Gallery! The 'Ladies Outfitting' Room! The 'Tea Room' any other of the magnetic points in our Huge Emporium.

Bainbridge & Co. Ltd[22]

Home delivery services were an early facility. Kendal Milne possessed a substantial fleet of wagons which required the stabling of fifty horses. Lewis's Liverpool Bon Marché fleet were painted in the same livery as its Parisian namesake and by 1906 Harrods owned 410 horses, 10 motor vans, 157 despatch vans and 52 removal vans.[23] Indeed many firms offered a home removal service, often combining it, like Whiteley's, with an estate agency. Department stores were quick to learn the commercial benefits of synchronising their services to their customers' housing cycle. By the 1890s the fleets of delivery vans owned by department stores throughout Britain were usually painted in the firm's livery and provided an early form of mobile advertisement and an opportunity to enhance the emporium's image. This service formed the tentacles of the store that could stretch into distant suburbs, nearby towns and villages. The customer, spared the responsibility of getting the goods home, was further enticed into the store, while the arrival of the delivery van announced in gilt lettering the good taste of the recipient. The birth of the GPO telephone system in 1902 provided another novelty. Goods could be ordered from afar, the equipment in the store for public use attracted much attention and store owners were quick to realise the potential for the image of the business by the acquisition of a good telephone number. Debenham's of Oxford Street, for example, could be contacted on Mayfair 1.[24]

By the late 1890s, the outside façades of the larger stores increasingly favoured the fashionable art nouveau style, often finished with terracotta tiles such as Doulton's Carrara ware.[25] Store-front windows became larger throughout the period thanks to the abolition of the glass tax in 1845 and the availability of cheaper and larger sheets of plate glass. Many stores, however, failed to realise the full potential of the new media of the large window; some, for example, preferred to leave the windows empty in order to gain the maximum benefit of natural light

Figure 9 The John Lewis Store, Oxford Street 1898. The fourth floor open-air tea-room gallery was an architectural feature that emphasised the growing importance of customer services (*source*: British Library).

provided by large areas of plate glass. Others packed their windows with a vast assortment of goods usually displaying large price tickets but with little regard to the aesthetics of display.

In truth Britain was beginning to lag behind other countries in retail innovation. France, Germany and the USA possessed commercial art colleges that taught and developed display techniques in the very early years of the present century and window display was a recognised craft in America with its own trade organisation.[26] Even the lessons of the Bon Marché proved difficult to digest in Britain. The *Draper's Record*, in a lengthy article in June 1888, questioned the wisdom of the Parisian system of the walk-around store, drawing attention to the moral threat to women customers, shoplifting and the tendency of male customers to become too familiar with women assistants.[27] As mentioned above, when Fenwick of Newcastle introduced Parisian methods to Newcastle in 1901 a local controversy ensued. Britain was slow in absorbing French techniques despite a steady flow of information in the trade press, but by the early 1900s Paris had been superseded as the city of retail innovation. The trade press in the 1890s carried an increasing number of articles on American stores. These commented not only on the vast size of the American emporiums but also on the revolution of store organisation and display pioneered by Macy's, Wanamaker and, above all, Marshall Field of Chicago.

Since the glittering World's Colombian Exposition of 1893, partly organised by Marshall Field, the store became as synonymous with Chicago as the stockyards, the Ferris Wheel, Midway amusements and, thanks to the writings of W.T. Stead, prostitution. When Gordon Selfridge took an office in London in 1906 and began excavating his site in Oxford Street the following year, British store owners were dumbstruck. Selfridge, for many years the manager of Marshall Field's, brought with him the reputation of America's greatest retailer. The Chicago store sold goods that were determined by the policy of the merchandise manager, not the buyer. The smooth running of the establishment was achieved by the efforts of the operations manager and above all customers were lured into the store by the world's most skilful window display artists. The London stores panicked as opening day approached for the new store. The *Draper's Record* monitored the situation by featuring the frenetic activities that took place in the windows of his rivals and London waited eagerly to glimpse the tableaux designed by the Chicago artists. But before we can assess the impact of Selfridge on British stores, time needs to be spent surveying and analysing this new revolution.

Notes

1. Lambert, *The Universal Provider*, 1938, p. 163.

2. For a survey of the Whiteley fires see Lambert, Chapter 5, *passim*.

3. For an interesting analysis of late nineteenth-century lighting see W. Schivelbusch, *Disenchanted Night. The Industrialisation of Light in the Nineteenth Century*, Berg, Oxford, 1988.

4. Moss and Turton, *A Legend of Retailing*, 1989, p. 44; p. 49.

5. Ibid., pp. 366–71.

6. Ibid., pp. 294; 321.

7. A. and J. Airey, *The Bainbridges of Newcastle*, 1979, p 114.

8. Moss and Turton, op. cit., p. 54.

9. Ibid., p. 57.

10. *Draper's Record*, 5 November 1898.

11. Moss and Turton, op. cit., p. 58.

12. *Draper's Record*, 17 September 1887.

13. Briggs, *Friends of the People*, pp. 66–7.

14. A. and J. Airey, op. cit., p. 109.

15. Moss and Turton, op. cit., p. 58.

16. Schivelbusch, op. cit., p. 153.

17. E.S. Abelson, *When Ladies Go A-Thieving. Middle Class Shoplifters in the Victorian Department Store*, Oxford University Press, New York, 1989, Chapter 3, *passim*.

18. See Sage's obituary in the *Draper's Record*, 8 October 1989.

19. For a fascinating account of the emergence of the shop window mannequin, see W. Leach, 'Strategists of display and the production of desire', in S. Bronner (ed.), *Consuming Visions, Accumulation and Display of Goods in America, 1880–1920*, Norton, New York, 1989, pp. 111–14.

20. Moss and Turton, op. cit., pp. 368; 344.

21. *Lady's Realm*, March 1905.

22. *Bainbridge Calendar*, 1910.

23. Moss and Turton, op. cit., pp. 344; 64; Briggs, op. cit., p. 37.

24. Corina, *Fine Silks and Oak Counters*, 1978, p. 73.

25. Ibid., p. 67.

26. Leach, op. cit., pp. 113–19.

27. *Draper's Record*, 30 June 1888.

CHAPTER FOUR

THE DRUMMER FROM THE LAND OF OZ

In the second half of the nineteenth century a number of large department stores emerged in the United States which, by the turn of the century, were to supersede the European *grands magasins* in both size and retail innovations. In New York, A.T. Stewart began as a small draper's in 1823; by 1842 the store could boast a marble front, but still sold a narrow range of textiles. By 1863 Stewart dominated New York's fashion trade and he was reputed to be New York's richest man whose annual tax bill approached two million dollars. Rowland Macy's enterprise began in 1858 catering for a more popular clientele, John Wanamaker pursued a similar path in Philadelphia, Filene in Boston and Potter Palmer in Chicago.[1] Generally American stores in the 1860s lagged a decade or so behind their European counterparts. Diversification into non-textile areas was slow and they were all close followers of the whims of Parisian fashion. Indeed Macy's historian has noted of the period, 'What [store proprietors] seem to have brought back from Paris is not so much their diversification of merchandise as certain physical features which appealed to the patron's desire for comfort and elegance, typically French contributions to life on the higher plane, but not the essence of the department store.'[2]

This conservatism was washed away in the tide of economic activity that accompanied the Civil War. Macy's offers a typical example. Along with Lord and Taylor, Macy's claimed to be New York's first department store, in terms of the range of goods sold, in 1874. Most of Macy's diversification was inspired by Margaret Getchell, the founder's relative and the first woman superintendent of a major American store. By 1869 the store had 12 departments and, under Getchell's influence, the range of goods such as sports equipment, picnic furniture, velocipedes, gardening sets and beach goods began to reflect the diversification of middle-class consumption.[3] The rapid growth of American emporiums in the last quarter of the nineteenth century is well known, but Chicago and Marshall Field's offer the quintessential example of the American contribution to the world of department stores.

In the second half of the nineteenth century Chicago was America's fastest-growing city, reaching its peak in the 1880s when it virtually doubled in size in ten years from 503,000 to 1,090,000. Chicago's growth was largely fuelled by its position. Being at the centre of the American railroad system it was able to dominate the meat and distribution trade.[4] A mere village in the 1830s, Chicago's expansion proceeded with few of the niceties of eastern society. Its reputation as a centre of crime, trickery and prostitution rose as rapidly as its population. It was inevitable that as Chicago prospered it would define itself in novel form, be it skyscraper architecture, elevated railways, Moody and Sankey circus tent religious gatherings, or the new science of sociology.[5] Cultural barriers were also less important than in older American and European cities. Dreisser's novel *Sister Carrie* charts the rapid rise up the city's social ladder, from shoe factory to the theatre set, of the book's main character.[6] James Gilbert's recent brilliant analysis of Chicago in the 1890s highlights the emergence of the Midway amusement park, replete with Ferris Wheel, in the heart of the 1893 Exposition, an event that purported to display the 'good taste' of the city.[7] The iconoclastic nature of Chicago attracted international notoriety. W.T. Stead's account of his visit to the city, *If Christ came to Chicago!*, clearly expresses the anxieties of the God-fearing of the Gomorrah of the Midwest. His denunciation of the city's bars, brothels and gambling dens also features a venomous appraisal of Marshall Field and his millionaire neighbours in Prairie Avenue: 'Marshall Fields and all that class ... loom up before the eyes of their fellow-men because they have succeeded in ascending a pyramid largely composed of human bones'.[8] This is strong stuff on the quietly spoken store owner, local philanthropist and main instigator of the exposition. But Stead was in no doubt that the Chicago emporium was the despoiler of female morality, the cause of sweated industry and the wrecker of numerous small businesses. For Stead, Field was the very essence of Chicago, ruthless and showy in a way that shocked his European sensibility. Yet how was Marshall Field's different from its counterparts in Europe and indeed other department stores in America?

Field's store began life as Potter Palmer's dry goods store in 1854. In 1865 Field along with Joseph Leiter became partners. Field's genius was to increase sales during the difficult post-war years by branching out into 'notions', the American equivalent of 'novelties', such as umbrellas

'It is written, My house shall be called the house of prayer ; but ye have
made it a den of thieves.'—MATTHEW xxi. 13.

Figure 10 The frontispiece to the 1894 edition of Stead's book shows Christ chasing
the modern-day money-changers from the Temple against a backcloth of the
Colombian Exposition. The cowering figure with the large moustache is clearly
based on Marshall Field.

and accessories. Palmer left the firm to concentrate on property speculations which culminated in the laying and setting out of State Street.
Palmer persuaded his old partners to move to a purpose-built store on

the new development in 1868. Field and Leiter's rivals followed suit and State Street became the most concentrated retailing street in the world.[9] Yet Field's, like most other major Chicago stores, was predominantly a wholesale establishment with retailing being a virtual sideshow in the warehouse. Chicago in this period rapidly became the hub of American distribution. The great mail order firms of Sears Roebuck and Montgomery Ward were based in the city, selling by catalogue to the United States' rapidly growing western hinterland.[10] Firms such as Field's increasingly depended for their trade on a vast growing army of travelling salesmen, often referred to as 'drummers', who sold the merchandise of the Chicago wholesalers to stores in rural areas. The 'drummer' was very much a liminal figure in the popular consciousness of rural America, with a reputation for trickery and moral laxity. The main character in Dreisser's novel is tempted to live in sin with and is deflowered by a Chicago drummer.[11] Despite the considerable business that was reaped by this system, many Chicago stores found that the city's exploding population also presented opportunities. Marshall Field's, as the store was known after Leiter's departure in 1881, benefited from this development.

Nevertheless Field was a reluctant retailer; his background and business instincts were essentially those of a wholesaler. Yet his retail showroom had one advantage over his rivals: class. Field had a finely tuned sense of the Midwestern woman's desire for European fashion; 'with a steady parade of exquisite gowns and "chic" bonnets, many in their original Paris boxes ... the firm was soon setting the style leadership of Chicago'. The State Street showroom became a magnet for the 'cream of the avenues' including Mrs Palmer, Chicago's leading socialite, and President Lincoln's widow. Field, however, was reluctant to expand into areas other than women's fashion, preferring to use his 'classy' reputation to drive the wholesale business.[12] Field's conservatism, however, was ultimately undermined by the skilful tactics of Gordon Selfridge, the manager of the retail division.

That such a conservative house as Marshall Field's became one of America's most innovative department stores is largely explained by the policies pursued by Selfridge in the two decades prior to his dramatic departure in 1904. Selfridge started his career at Field's as a stockboy in 1879 on the recommendation of Field's cousin, a former employer. Twyman describes Selfridge in this period as: 'A handsome, dashing young man, complete with long carefully trimmed sideburns and a gracious smile, he fascinated people by his presence. His superabundance of energy enabled him to participate actively in civic affairs and the highest society and, at the same time, foment small revolutions in the store.'[13] Field soon recognised Selfridge's qualities and transferred him to the more public but then less important retail section. Selfridge at this point was the senior 'drummer' for Indiana, and it was highly probable that he transferred to 'Retail' on the understanding that promotion was a probability. By 1887, three years after starting work in 'Retail', Selfridge was general manager of the section. Selfridge, known in the store as 'mile-a-minute Harry', updated the department in his own image.

> Always dressed in the latest style, he wore a frock coat and, 'the tails of it', everyone agreed, 'would whisk, stand out behind as he'd fly through the store'. Whether it was a plan for tearing out old counters and shelving, rearranging the display of goods, putting in a new system for marking sales slips, remodelling the main entrance to the store, developing a different kind of newspaper 'ad', putting in telephones and pneumatic tubes, or building an entire new building, Selfridge was in favour of it if it was new, sounded practical and stimulated sales.[14]

In a very short period 'mile-a-minute Harry' transformed Field's into a true department store, catching up on the innovations of east coast rivals Macy's and Wanamaker's. Over one hundred new departments were added by Selfridge, and 'Retail' overtook 'Wholesale' in importance. Selfridge, ever the Chicago drummer, with his finely tuned antennae to local life, transformed the basement into a permanent bargain sale which soon accounted for a quarter of total turnover, and greatly widened Field's customer base. By 1889 Selfridge was earning the then enormous salary of twenty thousand dollars a year, was made a junior partner to Field and lived in style on the avenues with his mother acting as his hostess.[15] His wedding the following year was the highlight of the social calendar. The ceremony was the embodiment of both Selfridge and Chicago. Held in the Central Music Hall, one of Moody and Sankey's favourite venues, the wedding was staged by Selfridge in the same manner as an annual sale. The thousand guests entered the rose and chrysanthemum filled hall to the sound of a large choir accompanied by organ, strings and harp.[16] Some thought it vulgar but in Chicago society it was Selfridge who increasingly made the weather.

Selfridge had risen through the ranks of Chicago drummers, that caste of men with the reputation for being the great seducers of Midwest young women, flashy dressers, but acutely aware of the 'bottom line'. He was no respecter of traditional niceties, especially if it threatened profit and turnover. The drummers were also notorious for the creation of desire amongst their customers by their clever display of swatches of material and other items carried in their travelling bags. Selfridge brought this aspect of merchandising to Field's at a critical time in Chicago's history.

In an extremely insightful essay, 'Strategies of Display and the production of Desire', the American historian William Leach has analysed the transformation in retail culture that took place in the 1890s. The Parisian method of letting the customer walk around the store at liberty and hoping that the sight of the goods would be enough to produce sales was becoming redundant in the United States. As real estate prices rose dramatically, buildings were becoming far taller and the 'dead space' of the central light well was bridged with floors, a process assisted by new developments in building technology particularly the use of re-inforced concrete.[17] Fierce competition from other stores presented another set of new circumstances. By the 1890s the problem facing the American store boss was how to get the customer to enter the store and once inside how to persuade them to the upper floors. Chicago was uniquely poised to solve these problems.

In the run up to the Colombian Exposition of 1893 Chicago was a hive of activity. The series of Great Exhibitions since 1851 produced a situation where each fair tried to better the previous one in attractions and novelties. Chicago, having won the right to stage the fair after stiff competition from other cities, was anxious to promote a good face and also show its uniqueness. The fair, with its organising committee of men from commerce, including Marshall Field, was also to be the most commercial. Thus the organisers had little compunction in promoting the 'Midway' amusement area, replete with Ferris Wheel, to help pay for 'palaces of art'. This juxtaposition of 'high' and 'low' entertainments was meat and grist to Chicagoans, who saw no contradiction in Moody and Sankey's use of popular tunes to accompany their sacred lyrics and had looked on with enthusiasm at Selfridge's wedding ceremony. The fair, and Chicago's iconoclastic culture, attracted as well as repelled. W.T. Stead was certainly amongst the latter but, as Leach has shown with much skill, those who were attracted to Chicago in the early 1890s had an ultimately more powerful message to sell.

Of all the liminal characters attracted to Chicago, the most liminal of modern cities, the most important was L. Frank Baum, the future author of the *Land of Oz*. Baum came from a wealthy New England oil family; as the son-in-law of Matilda Sage, the leading feminist, he was himself a committed feminist all his life. Leach has described Baum as:

> among the earliest architects of the dream life of the consumer age; he wrote in a new language tailored to consumer aspirations, and he created the first literature on display in the world. He articulated the new ideas on display, urging merchants to rid their windows of clutter and crowding to treat their goods aesthetically, to immerse them in colour and light, to place them in the foreground and single them out and to make them come 'alive'.[18]

When Baum arrived in Chicago he possessed a wealth of showmanship experience, having run his family's string of theatres where he had experimented with electric lights, the new generation of bright colour dyes and coloured glass. He applied this new arsenal of display techno-logy to his new china and glass store in Chicago. Baum's advice was soon sought by other merchants and his techniques were quickly absorbed by Chicago retailers. Leach has perceptively noted that in the 1890s the words 'display' and 'colourful' entered the language of retailing. The new language gained a wider acceptance with the publication of Baum's display theories and his magazine *Show Window* in 1897, the first periodical ever devoted to the subject.[19]

With Baum's work and the experience of the exhibition, the dis-tinction between art and commerce, greatly cherished by East Coast and European elites, disintegrated in Chicago. Harris, in an important essay, has explored the competition for the public eye between the three key institutions of display that came into existence in the second half of the nineteenth century: the exhibition, the museum and the department store. His conclusion, that by 1914 the department store offered the supreme visual experience, reflects the triumph of retail innovation in the 1890s, a process that enjoyed its most important stage in Chicago during the decade of the exposition.[20] East Coast commentators who feared that the exposition in Chicago would be 'only an enlarged agricultural fair with fat cattle and prize pigs galore' were silenced by the widespread acclaim bestowed upon the event. Yet the wide variety of architectural styles and the fairyland ethos of the White City, caused concern amongst some art critics. Claude Bragdon noted: 'All was simulacrum: the buildings, the statues and the bridges were not of enduring stone but lath and plaster... the crowds were composed not of free citizens of the place, but the slave ... of the Aladdin's lamp of competitive commerce.'[21]

For many visitors it must have been difficult to sense where the fair ended and Chicago began. Field's and the other major stores had information desks for the fair inside their stores and the magical effects created in the store interior by electric lighting rivalled the displays of the exposition.[22] Goods from the fair were on show in the store windows and Field's new annex building of 1893, erected as a major extension to the retail building, mirrored the fair in its audacious Italian renaissance style. Another striking feature was the new show windows, Field's first purpose-built set.[23]

Selfridge, a keen student and admirer of Baum, experimented with a series of display artists to dress the windows before giving the task permanently to Arthur Fraser in 1895. Fraser, who is widely regarded as the greatest ever window artist, worked on the State Street windows for 49 years.

> Fraser was not only clever with design and color but had a marked flair for showmanship. Since the curtains of the window displays were always lowered during Sunday anyway as a gesture of religious reverence, Fraser would start changing his windows on Saturday night. The curtains on several windows would then sometimes remain closed for several days. Finally, like the opening of a new show, the unveiling would suddenly take place to receive the admiration of the crowds of people passing by. Fraser's displays were usually tied together with some central theme. In 1897, for example, six of his largest and most conspicuous windows were all devoted to the display of only one color (red) because it was to be the fashionable color that season. On another occasion a whole series of display windows was given over to the portrayal of an exact reproduction of the interior of a large hall or gallery in a seventeenth-century English mansion in order to suggest the high standards of the interior-decorating section of the store. When the Retail expanded in 1902, and a long array of big windows was added, thirty to forty full-time trimmers were placed under his direction and Fraser was able to give free play to his talents. At Christmas time and during the numerous 'grand openings', his windows never failed to draw almost as much attention as the attractions on the inside.[24]

Fraser's great talent was his ability to forge 'an immediate relationship between these settings and the commodities', and often: 'The colors mimicked exactly the colors of the merchandise to form integrated color pictures that made "a most wonderful effect that one can never tire in looking at".[*] Leach locates Fraser's displays as being of seminal importance to the creation of the desire of consumption which emerged in the United States during the 1890s.[25] The windows of State Street were soon emulated in other American cities and the new urban pastime of 'window shopping' attracted thousands of participants day and night.

To the men and women on the streets drawn to what Dreisser described as the 'stinging quavering zest [of their] display', the new windows represented both the arousal of desire and the vanishing of the distinction between art and commerce.[26] Selfridge, like many other store managers, had long experimented with 'artware'. This usually took the form of a picture gallery where original paintings and prints were sold. Other goods of an 'artistic nature' such as the products of Morris and Co., were displayed in Marshall Field's Morris Room.[27] The impact of Baum and Fraser was to break down these spatial barriers and to integrate art and commodities into a seamless web. The windows were just the beginning of this process which continued inside the store.

The 1893 annex was just the start of a building scheme that was to last fourteen years, culminating in Louis Tiffany's giant stained glass cupola, the largest structure of its type in the world. Adjoining properties, including the Central Music Hall, were acquired and by 1907 the rebuilt twelve-storey steel and granite building, covering thirty-five acres of floor-space, was the largest department store in the world, overtaking its New York rivals. The main entrance to the new store led to 'a sumptuous vestibule with mahogany panelled walls, red marble floors, and specially designed chandeliers weighing over twelve hundred pounds apiece'. Entering through the Randolph Street entrance, the visitors saw stretched before them 'for the entire length of the building a spacious central arcade formed by parallel rows of classic white Grecian columns ...' [illuminated by] completely electric Tiffany chandeliers'.[28]

The new building started in 1902 represented a more confident Chicago. No longer did architecture mimic European themes, rather the new structure was a superb example of the new Chicago School; 'the simplicity of its lines has given it a less dated appearance ... so that it appears today [1954] almost as modern as when it was built'.[29] No sooner was it open than plans were already under way to link the various stores into a complete structure by purchasing more property. The new unified retail store of 1907 completed the process begun by Selfridge in the early 1890s. Yet Marshall Field's building programme was more than a modernising expansion. Despite the availability of great architectural talent and new building techniques, aspects of the store looked back to the beauty of the late nineteenth-century Parisian stores and at the same time announced its importance as Chicago's most important social institution. The most striking feature of the 1902 scheme is, without doubt, the great open light well reaching through twelve floors to the huge skylight and onto which the intervening floors opened like galleries. This was more than a store, combining as it did all the spectacle and drama of expositions and museums. The five thousand people who daily used the store's dining facilities enjoyed the finest restaurant settings in Chicago, and many looked upon the store and its services as a haven of order in the merciless *laissez-faire* world of Chicago's Loop.[30]

Undoubtedly the finest vestige from the Selfridge era was, and is, the Tiffany-illuminated vault between the fifth and seventh floors of the 1907 building. Designed in 1902 and taking its theme from Blakeian mysticism, Louis Tiffany considered it the 'acme of his most artistic work'. The dome consists of over one million pieces of Tiffany favrile glass and took two years to erect. Its pattern of three concentric circles intended to convey the illusion of open-ended space, of a heavenly domain without limits, is, according to Leach, 'the perfect symbol for this consumer setting'.[31]

In the fourteen years between the Colombian Exposition and the completion of the dome, the new consumer culture, based on the creation of desire through the new technology of display, came to maturity. The travelling showmanship of L. Frank Baum of flashing electric lights and coloured glass was now an integral part of American life. Display artists were respected professionals whose skills were now valid subjects on the college curriculum. The Selfridge-inspired Marshall Field's department store was central to this process. In 1893 visitors from the east were relieved to find not prize pigs but a large display of Tiffany products at the fair; this stand was one of the exposition's most popular attractions.[32] In 1907 Marshall Field's was illuminated by the master glassmaker's chandeliers and housed his greatest achievement. In the following decades, an array of leading artists and designers used department stores as sites for their talents, including Joseph Urban, Ann Estelle Rice and Boardman Robinson.[33] John Rost, Louis Sullivan and Frank Lloyd Wright were amongst the distinguished architects who worked on department store design;[34] while, in Europe, Willem de

Kooning began his artistic career working on the windows of an Utrecht department store.[35]

Just as these developments were taking form and becoming the norm in major American cities, their most important entrepreneur had left for Europe; indeed Selfridge left Field's in 1904, two years after commissioning the dome from Louis Tiffany. Selfridge's resignation from Field's is shrouded in mystery. One theory suggests that he left because Field refused to let him have his name over the door by turning down his request to be made a senior partner. Another, perhaps more plausible, explanation points to the poor share allocation that Selfridge received when the business was incorporated in 1901. For whatever reason, Selfridge resigned in 1904 – an event that made front-page headlines in the national press.[36] After a brief attempt to run his own business at another State Street store he sold up and retired at the age of forty-eight. His retirement did not last long. By 1906, at the age of fifty, 'mile-a-minute Harry' had based himself in London and formed a partnership with Sam Waring of Waring and Gillow's, the furniture manufacturing and store company. In June Selfridge announced his plans to build a one-million-pound giant store in Oxford Street which would be designed and operate on American principles. The news created a sensation in the press and the trade immediately became awash with speculation on the proposed venture.[37]

In the months before the announcement by Selfridge the trade press was rife with rumours and reflected the unease in the department store industry at the prospect of having to compete with the creator of the 'world's greatest store'. British traders were well aware of Selfridge's talents. Marshall Field's death in January produced lengthy obituaries and detailed descriptions of the State Street store in the *Draper's Record*. Field, it was claimed, was the twentieth richest man in the world, whose Chicago store often saw two hundred thousand customers pass through its doors daily and readers were told that 'the New York stores compare as villages to a fair size town'.[38] Field's death and speculation over Selfridge's plan initiated a major debate in the trade on the differences between British and American department stores and sales methods. Commentators generally agreed that stores on the American scale could not be built in Britain because of geography and market size. The debate instead focused upon two issues: store organisation, particularly labour relations; and sales policy and technique.

The arrival of Selfridge fuelled a debate that had been smouldering since the 1890s on the 'living-in' system (see pp. 125–8). Margaret Bondfield of the shopworkers' trade union made the telling point that in the larger French and American stores the 'living-in' system was unknown. Scottish readers of the *Draper's Record,* perhaps bemused by the panic in the London trade, drew attention to the fact that apart from Jenner's in Edinburgh the system was not practised in Scotland including, of course, the prosperous Buchanan Street area of Glasgow.[39] This unease in the industry was exacerbated by the election of a Liberal government, supported by the new Labour Party, whose future reforms it was rumoured included a new Truck Commission. The reliance on the 'living-in' system and the fining of employees for misdemeanours were the mainstays of industrial relations and neither were practised in America. Instead, Selfridge had developed his famous 'system' of staff relations, which involved workers being taught the firm's 'system' by a 'systems man', and the meticulous documentation of workers' performance in their individual record files.[40]

The relative backwardness of British stores was at its most glaring in the area of sales policy and customer relations. With the noble exception of a few northern stores, most notably Fenwick's of Newcastle with their famous 'silent sales assistants' introduced at the turn of the century, Britain had failed to develop the French-style walk-around shop. The trade press, many of whose readers had a vested interest in the maintenance of traditional methods, had long expressed hostility to the French system. Indeed, what information we have suggests that London stores in particular were becoming more formal as they increased in size. The floor-walker, whose craft of 'treading the boards' was questioned in the late 1880s and who had become a major subject of popular humour, owed his salvation to his ability to 'spot the tabbies', female customers who demanded attention but never bought.[41] This fear of the 'tabbies' and the need to control them politely, however, raised a deeper, more ingrained problem. Primitive methods of stock control and merchandising gave rise to the tendency to 'flog up' slow-moving items. This involved controlling the movement of customers towards slow-selling stock and aggressive selling by the assistants. The fear of shopping, the very progenitor of the early department store, was becoming ever present in the early Edwardian department store, an institution whose birth had promised the removal of such apprehension.

In truth British retailing had enjoyed a long period of organic expansion and individual department stores had carved out their

prosperity based on geography and social class. The big battles with
small proprietors had been won and there was minimal competition
between the large stores. Yet the more astute observer would be well
aware that retailing, just like manufacturing, was susceptible to foreign
competition. After all, a decade earlier Britain almost lost its footwear
industry with the invasion of American retailers aggressively selling cheap
Massachusetts boots and shoes.[42] This unease was underlined by the
increasing complaints of foreign visitors to London about British shopping methods. Foreign customers were becoming increasingly important
and London had long envied the Parisian *grands magasins*'s international
clientele. Despite these fears, many shopwalkers took a pride in showing
independently-minded American customers the door. The problem
culminated in a series of articles in American magazines, perhaps partly
prompted by rumours of Selfridge's intentions, on the backwardness of
London stores. Chief amongst these was a lengthy piece by Elizabeth
Hubert Clark in the American press. She complained bitterly about the
absence of 'walk-around' stores, being importuned by overbearing
shopwalkers and assistants pressurising customers into buying unsuitable
goods. The *Draper's Record* took up the defence of the British trade:

> The truth of the matter seems to be that American women as a result of
> general social conditions that prevail in the States, are more masculine in
> temperament than English women are. The former always show a disposition
> to resent civility from the male sex because in their view it constitutes a
> suggestion of feminine inferiority, a view of the situation against which they
> are always protesting.[43]

The article went on to praise the Englishwoman's civility and appreciation of service. Little wonder that Selfridge had pronounced the
London stores to be 'curiously backward'.

A further contribution to the debate came from an unexpected
quarter. Owen Owen of Liverpool, then with wide interests in London
store property, returned from a fact-finding American tour in the midst
of the controversy. Owen made a placatory gesture to his colleagues by
pointing out that he found British staff more civil than those in America,
but went on to discuss the more innovative features of American stores.
He was particularly impressed with the sophistication of American
advertising, techniques of which Selfridge had been in the forefront.
He also warned that in the USA advertising generally accounted for
between three and five per cent of turnover, while in Britain one per

cent was considered extravagant. He also marvelled at the American policy on 'sales'. These, he noted, were held at the beginning of the season, not at the end as in Britain, and together with the 'bargain basement' greatly improved stock velocity. 'Americans don't have sales, they have advertising campaigns', uttered the sage from Machynlleth, forewarning the trade of what to expect from the new Oxford Street emporium.[44] This unease over the American challenge and its perceived threat to British shopping manners could only have been amplified when a few weeks after the Owen article the first sales death was reported from St Joseph, Missouri, where, when a department store opened for its new season sale, 'thousands rushed through the doors and fought desperately for the best position. Many of them lost their temper and struck savagely at each other with their umbrellas ... one woman was crushed to death ... the store was eventually closed by police.'[45]

Another important component in the American method, window display, had been singled out by the trade press in Britain as an area where improvement could be quickly and cheaply implemented. As a source of trade intelligence, window novelties had featured in the *Draper's Record* since the late 1880s. In the earlier period, however, this was largely confined to seasonal features, particularly Christmas. By 1906 the *Record* was conducting a crusade for brighter, more artistic window shows.[46] Selfridge's patronage of Fraser was well known and it was generally expected that the new store would have highly innovative displays. By the middle of 1906 the *Record* printed photographs of what it considered the best of British window-dressing. Keddies of Southend frequently featured with its model elephants and dreadnought battleships constructed out of wire and handkerchiefs. Yet the truth is British display was slapdash and amateurish in comparison with American techniques. It is a telling point that Keddies's much-praised windows were produced by Mr A. Maitland Keddie, a member of the firm's family, in pursuit of his hobby, rather than by professional, trained window-dressers. In late summer, with a note of despair, the *Record* reported on the high-quality window displays in the major German department stores, which had quickly absorbed American techniques and 'were far superior to [those in] London'.[47]

The nerves of the London trade were further unsettled as Selfridge's plans began to unfold. The headline in the *Draper's Record* for 30 June confirmed this unease: '£1,000,000 Drapery Shop for London'. The accompanying interview with Selfridge was prefaced with a reminder to readers of his achievements at Marshall Field's and the financial clout that Selfridge and Waring could muster. After outlining the proposed store's policy to customers, he indicated the broad appeal on which the store was to be based. 'We will stock the finest goods and the range will be completed in the more moderately-priced qualities until it reaches a point where desirability and reliability alike end. At this point we shall stop.' The article was concluded with a laudatory section on Selfridge's employees' 'Book of Rules' at Marshall Field's, the lack of the 'living-in system' in the new store and his plans to employ two thousand workers without recourse to 'fines'.[48] The main fear of the London trade, however, was how much Selfridge was going to affect their profits. Department store share prices made heavy gains during the Edwardian period and dividends were historically high; D.H. Evans were paying 22½ per cent, Peter Robinson 18 per cent and Owen Owen 16 per cent. Little wonder that the London trade was disturbed by Selfridge's arrival from the USA where stores pursued turnover rather than high mark-ups and dividends were significantly lower.[49]

Selfridge soon found that building a store in London was very different from Chicago. His original drawing was drafted by Frank Swales, an itinerant American architect student who also produced the famous Selfridge pound and dollar monogram. Selfridge was enthusiastic over Swales's 'beautiful drawing' and sent it to D.H. Burnham, the prestigious Chicago architect. Burnham, whom Selfridge called 'Uncle Dan', had designed the Colombian Exposition, the rebuilding of Marshall Field's store and the Field Museum. Burnham worked on the Swales drawing and prepared detailed plans.[50] We can only speculate on whether or not the Swedenborgian Burnham had visions of Tiffany glazing the proposed dome with Blakeian themes! But this was the Borough of St Marylebone, part of the London County Council and not the Chicago Loop. The proposed dome was the first victim of building regulations which stipulated a maximum height of eighty feet. The Swales-Burnham plans were redrafted by Frank Atkinson and Sir John Burnet to comply with London building laws.[51]

The Atkinson-Burnet drawing was a scaled-down version of the Swales-Burnham design, but it nevertheless represented a major departure in the architecture of central London. 'Has the Parthenon pupped?' commented Waring on seeing his new partner's building plan.[52] Waring's own building company began excavations but he soon became unnerved as Selfridge's expensive dream took shape. Waring withdrew suddenly from the partnership, leaving Selfridge to contemplate his 'million-dollar hole'. Other department store proprietors predicted bankruptcy, but the scheme was saved when John Musker, a tea broker and part owner of Home and Colonial Grocery Stores, took over Waring's shares. At the peak of construction, over 1,000 workers were employed at the Oxford Street site. Steel girders had been used in construction for some time in Britain but never on the scale of Selfridge's. The concrete foundation walls were twenty-seven feet thick, necessary to support the massive girder frame. Selfridge employed a band of musicians on the site to speed up work and in one period of less than three weeks an entire eighty-foot corner section was erected. Selfridge also proposed to tunnel under Oxford Street into Bond Street Underground Station which he wanted renamed Selfridge's. Unfortunately this request was turned down.[53]

As well as building the store, Selfridge had to plan the internal organisation, recruit staff and buy merchandise. Many in the London trade were convinced that the new store would be American run and American staffed. To the surprise of all he only brought three former colleagues from Chicago, but more astute observers would recognise their significance. C.W. Steines became controller of merchandise; W. Oppenheimer organised layout and furnishings, and, perhaps of most importance, Edward Goldsman, designer and window artist, brought Chicago display techniques to London.[54] Steines's post also represented a major change in the organisation of stores in Britain. Selfridge, along with other American store bosses, had trimmed the plenipotentiary powers of the buyers at Marshall Field's and subordinated them to the Merchandise Manager. Buyers had often run their departments like separate empires which could result in two adjacent departments selling goods to very different types of customers. Buyers could also be extremely obstinate in protecting their space within the store that prevented the expansion and contraction of departments in line with seasonal demands. Staff training was also often the preserve of the buyer and could result in a variety of sales techniques within the store. Finally, buyers were also responsible for their department's layout and display which often resulted in a visual mishmash and clash of styles. By centralising these functions Selfridge was able to introduce thematic unity to the sales floors, respond with flexibility to seasonal demand and attract a broader customer base.[55]

The important task of staff training was dealt with by Selfridge. With no 'living-in system' and the absence of 'fines', Selfridge introduced revolutionary methods into the Dickensian world of British department stores' industrial relations. Selfridge had introduced formal staff training for all employees at Marshall Field's in 1902, conducted by 'education officers' within the store school. This house training was followed by specialist training on the merchandise being sold in the worker's individual department.[56]

Advertising was another area where Selfridge took personal charge. From the 1880s at Marshall Field's up until his departure, he had developed a highly innovative advertising style. Selfridge had to build on to the pattern of advertising established by the store's founder. This had emphasised class and an unwillingness to engage in sensationalism. Goods in sales were described as 'less expensive' rather than 'cheap'. The jumble of claims and prices that typified the newspaper advertisements of rivals was a stark contrast to the subdued prose of Marshall Field's.[57] Selfridge experimented with more white space in his copy and employed professional writers. Moreover, he introduced what is now referred to as the institutional advertising style where the store itself is given more prominence than the goods. The combination of Field's conservatism and Selfridge's flair resulted in the most modern newspaper advertisements in the USA, paradoxically made more effective by their less frequent appearances than those of rival establishments. Marshall Field's generally spent approximately half the advertising/turnover ratio of their competitors but nevertheless with an advertising budget approaching a quarter of a million dollars in 1904, Selfridge had employed this medium on a scale far in excess of his London rivals.[58]

As opening day in 1909 approached, other London stores found it hard to contain their anxiety. Harrods found it particularly difficult and they were the first to panic. In February they announced their Diamond Jubilee festival to coincide with Selfridge's opening. The festival events included grand afternoon concerts featuring the London Symphony Orchestra and the Band of the Grenadier Guards. Controversy, however, was aroused when Harrods announced that a Territorial Army promotion at the festival was to be opened by Haldane, the Secretary for War. Draping the store in the flag was considered the height of bad taste and the *Draper's Record* commented on this 'lapse from the recognised path of British retailing'. Haldane was forced to withdraw and the trade press reported on the lack of interest over the Knightsbridge festivities with Oxford Street enjoying the centre stage.[59]

On 13 March the *Draper's Record* published a detailed floor plan of the new store which highlighted the then novel feature of placing a perfume counter by the main entrance. Nothing highlighted the difference, however, between the old and the new more than the illustrations found in Figures 11 to 14.

The first illustrations (Figures 11 and 12) show the public faces – the windows of Selfridge's rivals during the opening week of the new store. The crammed, cluttered jumble was a stark contrast to Selfridge's highly modern themed displays. Inside, the store was fitted with new-style low counters and the total lack of floor-to-ceiling display gave a strong feeling of spaciousness. The press noted the sparseness of the window displays and the lack of prices on the items: 'the windows don't sell but act as a subtle invitation card'. The *Draper's Record* also wondered 'will the lady shopper be content with the absence of the polite enquiry as to the department required, as against the direct inquiry by herself, as under the Selfridge regime?'[60] Selfridge had, of course, solved this problem in the early 1890s when the 'carnationed usher', the American equivalent of a floor-walker, was replaced in Marshall Field's by an information desk.[61] The new store contained a Bureau of Information as well as 'a library and Silence Room, a First Aid Ward, a Bureau de Change, Patriotic Rooms ... Railway Steamship and Theatre Booking Offices, Parcel and Cloak Check desk – with gratuities neither expected nor allowed ... a Post and Telegraph Office, a Savings Bank, a Luncheon Hall, a tea garden open to the sky ...'. All these facilities and services in Selfridge's 'Community Centre' also had the beneficial effect of preventing 'the "tabby" who on occasions of this kind did not have the opportunity to air her graces'.[62] A week later the trade press prophesied that the 'Selfridge system would end the days of the shopwalker'.[63] Slowly British stores were learning the lesson of Fenwick's and Selfridge's that it cost far less to give the customers, including the 'tabbies', the run of the establishment than trying to police them. A year earlier the 'drummer from the Land of Oz' had been privately investigating the methods of London stores. In one establishment he was accosted by a shopwalker enquiring if he intended to make a purchase. Selfridge's negative answer met with the response 'Op It' and he was shown the door. Selfridge was to have the last laugh.[64]

Despite the great publicity, business proved slow in the first few weeks. Customers came more out of curiosity than to buy. But Selfridge was well aware that as long as the store contained a crowd, sales would

Figure 11 Harrods, 20 March 1909 (*source*: British Library).

Figure 12 Whiteley's, 20 March 1909 (*source*: British Library).

Figure 13 Selfridges, 20 March 1909 (*source:* British Library).

Figure 14 Selfridges, 20 March 1909 (*source*: British Library).

eventually follow. A month after opening, the trade press were calling the store a 'nine-day wonder' and it at times appeared curiously empty.[65] It was at this point that Selfridge played his trump card: showmanship. Selfridge had been present at the birth of the 'Midway' and was a master of its techniques. In early May he exhibited all the pictures rejected by the Royal Academy for their Summer Show on the third floor. Selfridge claimed that they were not at the Summer Show because of 'lack of wall space in Burlington House' and they included 'true works of genius lying hidden'.[66] Clever advertising also raised the store's profile, and in the summer George Grossmith's successful revue show was set in the beauty parlour of 'Pelfridges'. His greatest early coup was undoubtedly the display of Bleriot's plane in the Oxford Street store the day after the famous flight. More than one hundred and fifty thousand people came to see the flying machine in just four days. This event was followed by Trafalgar Day and Empire Day festivals and the following year Selfridge usurped Whiteley's with his external decorations to mark the death of the king and the subsequent coronation.[67]

Selfridge never quite managed to realise his ambition of creating London's premier department store. The battle for that title during the decline of Whiteley's was won by Harrods under the skilful management of the Burbidge dynasty. But the genie which he unleashed in 1909 could not be put back in the bottle. His competitors were forced to take notice and adopt his American managerial methods. The days of amateurish *ad hoc*-ery in the major stores were coming to an end. Many leading stores quickly followed Selfridge's lead. The historians of the House of Fraser have noted that 'the long rows of mahogany counters were ripped out and the main floors converted into salons with nicely decked glass cases'.[68] The prosperous years of 1913 and 1914 witnessed a boom in the shop-fitting industry as stores from Regent Street to Sheffield reacted to the Oxford Street revolution. Much of this investment came from the consumer boom amongst the upper classes during that much commented-upon period of conspicuous consumption. This expansion of the luxury trade, however, came to a rude end with the declaration of war in 1914.

The appeal by the government for economy in spending and the expression of patriotism through saving was quickly heeded by the better-off. The introduction of a 33.3 per cent import duty on foreign clothing in September 1915 consolidated this retreat from luxury. Those London stores which had a traditional up-market clientele were hit hardest. Yet the war also brought benefits of profound importance to many stores, particularly those which had cultivated customers amongst the upper echelons of the working class. Stores in the prosperous industrial centres such as north-east England and Clydeside did particularly well. High working-class wages boosted by a proliferation of well-paid female employment dramatically altered the pattern of shopping. High inflation accompanied high wartime wages but as in most periods of rising prices and incomes the velocity of consumption increased as consumers feared that goods would soon be out of their reach. The sober nature of wartime fashion may have dampened women's external attire but stores enjoyed a dramatic expansion of the luxury lingerie market.[69] At a more mundane level, working-class families increasingly patronised the furniture sections of the more popular department stores such as Lewis's in Liverpool. The *Report* of the Liverpool Settlement for 1917 noted that many Liverpool housewives had 'tasted the joys of home-making for the first time during the war'.[70] By 1920 department stores enjoyed between 3 and 4 per cent of total retail trade as compared with 1½ to 3 per cent in 1910.[71] The wartime economy was obviously the major cause of this growth but we also need to keep sight of the contribution made by Selfridge: by making stores more customer-friendly, the Oxford Street revolution assisted this process of expansion.

In many ways the wartime economy continued until 1920 with rising income and prices. The early 1920s, however, brought an abrupt halt to these conditions and the department store boom which had continued unabated since the Edwardian period came to a sudden end. By 1922 real income per head had dropped to the level of 1903 and the problem faced by department stores was not how to achieve expansion but how to survive. This was a very different Britain from that which had fired Gordon Selfridge with optimism in 1906.

Notes

1. The early history of American department stores is best approached from the three classic studies of major firms: R.M. Hower, *History of Macy's of New York, 1858-1919*, Cambridge, MA, 1943; R.W. Twyman, *History of Marshall Field and Co, 1852–1906*, University of Pennsylvania Press, Philadelphia, 1954; H Gibbons, *John Wanamaker*, Harper and Bros., New York, 1926.

2. Hower, op. cit., p. 143.

3. Ibid., pp. 60; 103.

4. On the development of nineteenth-century Chicago, see W. Cronon, *Nature's Metropolis, Chicago and the Great West,* Norton, New York, 1991.

5. These aspects of Chicago are analysed with great subtlety in J. Gilbert, *Perfect Cities, Chicago's Utopias of 1893,* University of Chicago Press, Chicago 1991.

6. T. Dreisser, *Sister Carrie,* 1900, reprinted by Oxford University Press, Oxford, 1991.

7. Gilbert, op. cit., Chapter 4, *passim.*

8. W.T. Stead, *If Christ Came to Chicago!,* Review of Reviews, London, 1894, p. 63. Field had already gained a notorious reputation amongst Liberals and labour leaders for his role in blocking the commutation of the death sentences of the Haymarket Anarchists in 1887. Field's involvement in this affair is discussed in P. Avrich, *The Haymarket Tragedy,* Princeton University Press, Princeton, NJ, 1984, especially pp. 364–7.

9. Twyman, op. cit., pp. 1–22.

10. Cronon, op. cit., Chapter 7, *passim.*

11. Ibid., pp. 329–30.

12. Twyman, op. cit., pp. 27–30.

13. Ibid., p. 105.

14. Ibid., p. 106.

15. Ibid., p. 107.

16. G. Honeycombe, *Selfridges, Seventy-Five Years, The Story of the Store,* Park Lane Press, London, 1984, pp. 25–6, has an account of the wedding.

17. Pasdermadjian, *The Department Store,* 1954, pp. 24–7.

18. Leach, 'Strategists of display', in Bronner (ed.), Norton, New York, *Consuming Visions,* 1989, pp. 106–10.

19. Ibid., p. 109.

20. N. Harris, 'Museums, merchandising, and popular taste: the struggle for influence', in I.M. G. Quimby (ed.), *Material Culture and the Study of American Life,* pp. 140–74, Norton, New York, 1978. See also R. Lewis, 'Everything under one roof: world's fairs and department stores in Paris and Chicago', *Chicago History XII* (Fall, 1983), pp. 28–47.

21. Lewis, op. cit., p. 44.

22. Ibid., p. 41.

23. Twyman, op. cit., p. 155.

24. Ibid., p. 153.

25. Leach, op. cit., pp. 118–19.

26. Ibid., p. 99.

27. Twyman, op. cit., p. 107. The relationship between 'art' and the department store is analysed in R.G. Saisselin, *The Bourgeois and the Bibelot,* Rutgers University Press, New Brunswick, NJ, 1984, especially Chapter 3.

28. Twyman, op. cit., p. 156.

29. Ibid.

30. Ibid., p. 126. By 1907 the State Street store's restaurants had a seating capacity of 2,800.

31. Leach, op. cit., p. 102. Twyman, op. cit., p. 159, has an account of the building

of the dome. It is also worth noting that the building's architect, Dan Burnham, was a practising Swedenborgian. Gilbert, op, cit,, p, 38.

32. Lewis, op, cit,, p, 44.

33. Leach, op, cit,, pp, 120–27.

34. Ibid., p. 123. Wright's famous office for Kaufmann's Pittsburgh store, which now forms the Victoria and Albert Museum's Frank Lloyd Wright room, was followed by the building of Fallingwater, his masterpiece for the Kaufmann family. See D. Hoffmann, *Frank Lloyd Wright's Fallingwater*, Dover, New York, 1978.

35. D. Waldman, *Willem De Kooning*, Thames and Hudson, London, 1988. Interestingly, de Kooning's 'Excavations', regarded as one of his finest works, was donated to the Art Institute of Chicago by Edgar Kaufmann, Jr, the heir to the Pittsburgh department store fortune.

36. Twyman, op. cit., pp. 162–4.

37. *Draper's Record,* 30 June 1906.

38. Ibid., 20 January; 27 January 1906.

39. Ibid., 28 July 1906.

40. Selfridge's system was discussed in detail in an interview with the entrepreneur published as the leading article in the *Draper's Record*, 30 June 1906.

41. Ibid., 24 December 1887.

42. B. Lancaster, *Radicalism, Cooperation and Socialism*, Leicester University Press, Leicester, 1987, p. 40.

43. *Draper's Record*, 28 April 1906.

44. Ibid., 21 June 1906.

45. Ibid., 18 August 1906.

46. Ibid., 6 January 1906; 17 February 1906.

47. Ibid., 29 September 1906.

48. Ibid., 30 June 1906.

49. Honeycombe, op. cit., p. 14.

50. Ibid., pp. 31–2.

51. Ibid.

52. Ibid., p. 33.

53. Ibid, pp 32–5.

54. Ibid, pp 166–8.

55. Pasdermadjian, op. cit., p. 38. The *Draper's Record*, 13 February 1909 published a feature on the functions of Selfridge's merchandise manager.

56. Twyman, op. cit., p. 80.

57. Ibid., Chapter 11, *passim*.

58. Ibid., p. 149.

59. *Draper's Record*, 27 February 1906; 6 March 1906.

60. Ibid., 20 March 1906.

61. Twyman, op. cit., p. 123.

62. *Draper's Record*, 20 March 1909.

63. Ibid., 27 March 1909.

64. *Draper's Record*, 30 January 1906.

65. *Draper's Record*, 1 May 1909.

66. Honeycombe, op. cit., pp. 38–9.

67. Ibid., pp. 39–43.
68. Moss and Turton, *A Legend of Retailing*, 1989, pp. 95–9.
69. Ibid., pp. 111–16.
70. Briggs, *Friends of the People*, pp. 135–6.
71. Ibid., p. 136.

CHAPTER FIVE

THE DEPARTMENT STORE 1920–39: MERGERS, REALIGNMENT AND GROWTH

Our images of the interwar department store are essentially benign: art deco façades, Palm Court terraces, roof-top cafés, daredevil Swedish women diving down stairwells into small pools of water, Clarice Cliff and her 'Bizarre Girls' painting bright coloured pottery in display windows and radio dance concerts broadcast from store restaurants. The period is firmly fixed in the popular psyche as the 'Golden Age' of the large store when Selfridge's vision of the grand emporium functioning as a community centre was realised. Yet these images are essentially from the late 1920s and 1930s and they exclude the troublesome period of the earlier 1920s when the very existence of the department store was threatened.

The collapse of income levels in the early 1920s was accompanied by a range of other ominous forces that bore upon the Queens of the High Street. The proliferation of chain stores undoubtedly posed the major threat. This phenomenon was far from new. Since the 1850s much of the footwear trade had been increasingly dominated by Leicester manufacturing retail firms such as Oliver's, Stead and Simpson and, during the 1880s, Freeman, Hardy and Willis.[1] W.H. Smith had established the famous chain of newspaper and bookshops during the same period and, of course, food multiples had long been a feature of British life. Woolworth's brought the concept of the unit price store from the USA when they opened their first branch in Liverpool in 1909.[2] None of these operations posed much of a threat to department stores. Even Woolworth's was to have its greatest impact on those indigenous traders who concentrated on the bottom end of the market such as the Marks and Spencer chain of market stalls. Marks and Spencer's response to the Woolworth invasion is one of the great success stores of twentieth-century Britain. The erstwhile market traders abandoned their low-price trade and dramatically repositioned the company in the market-place by concentrating on quality goods aimed at upper working- and lower middle-class customers.[3] This was a serious challenge to department stores, as the items central to Marks and Spencer's new image, women and children's clothing, formed a core area of department store business. This threat was compounded by the emergence on the High Street of other clothing chains such as C & A and British Home Stores.[4]

The chain stores enjoyed key advantages over department stores. First, they were able to reap the benefits of centralised buying during a period when most department stores were still independent concerns. Second, a far higher proportion of their staff was directly employed in sales and the chains did not need the sophisticated and costly managerial and bureaucratic structures essential to the smooth running of department stores. Third, display and layout were centrally controlled and uniform to all branches, which resulted in economies of scale and lower over-heads. Fourthly, by concentrating on particular items such as women's clothing, the chains could poach markets already developed by depart-ment stores and avoid the costs of having to stock slower-moving goods. Finally, the chains generally did not have to bear the heavy overheads of customer services that were a major hallmark of department stores. Besides the clothing chains, multiple furniture stores proliferated during the interwar period. The number of furniture stores with ten or more branches increased from 12 in 1920 to 29 in 1939. More impressively, the number of branches of these stores grew from 196 to 688 in the same period. Given the higher margins on furniture, this trend was extremely worrying for department stores.[5]

The decline in disposable income during the early 1920s was also accompanied by the emergence of new mass-produced goods competing for a share of the consumer's purse. Chief amongst these was the motor car.[6] Paradoxically, the motor car in the Edwardian period had brought benefits to the department store, providing new markets such as clothes and sundries for the motorist. But in the pre-war years, the motoring fad was only pursued by the very wealthy, although stores in towns such as Bath and Chester prospered from this clientele. The 1920s, however, saw the mass production of vehicles by companies such as Austin, Morris and Standard aimed at the lower middle-class market.[7] Department store proprietors were uneasy at the prospect of customers forgoing the purchase of clothing and household goods to ease the cost of family motoring. Some firms, most notably Howell's of Cardiff, responded by developing car retailing, but the majority of stores lacked the funds and expertise to participate in the new market.[8] Another important threat posed by the motor car was its impact on urban geography with the development of road building to accommodate the growing number of vehicles. This problem was exacerbated by the tendency of British stores to own the freehold of their sites. This rendered them far less mobile than, for example, their American counterparts, who not infrequently abandoned old and leased new buildings as they followed the crowds. Snowball's of Gateshead is a particularly tragic example of urban realignment created by increased traffic: the trajectory of the A1 trunk road was moved in central Gateshead with the building of the new Tyne Bridge, a shift which resulted in Snowball's being isolated from the rest of the town centre. Other stores, however, benefited immensely from road building. Bentall's of Kingston enjoyed remarkable rates of growth during the interwar years thanks to the Kingston Bypass which turned the town into a major subregional shopping centre. Developments in south-east London such as the building of Purley Way had similar effects on Croydon department stores.[9]

An even larger 'big ticket' item than the car, which was perceived as a threat by department stores, was the growing trend of home-owner-ship, already apparent in the early 1920s. With the benefit of hindsight, we can see all too clearly the boost to consumption that owner-occupation produced. But to the nervous eyes of retailers in the 1920s things looked very different. One fear was that mortgage payments would take a larger slice of the family budget than rent. Another was that home-ownership might produce a profound shift in consumer mentality. For example, in a period of rising unemployment and eco-nomic instability, home-owners could be expected to cut back on consumption and save in order to secure mortgage repayments. Rather than go to a department store and fully equip the new dwelling, like the man on less than a hundred a year in 1905, the new home-owner might choose to keep furnishings to a minimum, buy second-hand and make do and mend.[10]

Even those consumers who continued to rent presented problems. The boom in spending between 1914 and 1920 and the accompanying inflation caused many people to spend up to their limit or even above. This could result in customers having no extra disposable income to spend at sales and promotions which in many ways had become the life-blood of many department stores. Moreover, if stock was not moved at sales, turnover rapidly slowed down and replenishing the store with fresh goods became difficult.[11]

Slow-down in turnover was particularly problematic in the 1920s with the rise in popularity of manufacturers' branded goods. The rise of the 'brand' is well documented but what concerns us here is the impact, real or potential, on the fortunes of the department store. The most important effect of branded goods was their tendency to take control away from the store. Up until the 1920s, despite the rise of registered trade marks, the stores themselves created the ethos of the goods sold. The department store with its displays, services and, most important, tradition, functioned as the brand. 'This is a Harrods hand bag' ... 'Fenwick's dress' ... 'Arding and Hobbs curtains' were testimony to the department stores' centrality to the retailing process. The rise of the 'brand' threatened to remove stores' control of their own destiny.[12] Furthermore, the growing trend for manufacturers to fix retail prices removed another important tool from the department store.[13] It is true that customers might prefer to buy a brand in the comfortable surroundings of a department store at the same price as elsewhere, but the department store still had the burden of high overheads and little flexibility on the margins of branded goods.

A final threat came from the co-operative movement which had traditionally been the scourge of the small shopkeeper rather than the department store. Co-operative stores, with the exception of the two London middle-class co-operatives, the Army and Navy and the Civil Service, whose co-operative credentials were questionable, were generally located in mining villages and factory townships. The co-operative retail societies had traditionally eschewed city centre premises and exceptions to this pattern, such as Leicester, were usually in town centres with a large adjacent working class and a structure of backward retailing; Leicester, for example, lacked a large department store. Moreover, these few city centre co-operatives retained a system of separate units. Leicester again provides a good example; with its large imposing High Street facade, the Co-op remained a row of discrete shops.[14] This is not surprising – the co-operative movement had always emphasised economy and rational consumption, and the department stores with their 'frivolous displays' and inducements to impulse purchasing were anathema to co-operative principles. Yet the co-operative movement was also modern and highly innovative. It possessed a well-oiled centralised buying agency, the CWS, and owned a network of large, well-equipped factories, producing a vast array of consumer items. Moreover, with four and a half million members each spending on average fifty-six pounds in 1920, it was by far the largest trading organisation in the world. Department stores were therefore highly concerned when the Co-operative's Special Congress met in 1920 to consider the recommendations of the Survey Committee. Their endorsement of the Committee's proposal 'that neighbouring Societies should join hands to establish large "emporia" or department stores in the centre of big towns, and that Societies should imitate the methods of multiple chain stores by adopting uniform design of branch shops and systems of packing and wrapping Co-operative goods', could only have confirmed the fears of department stores and chains.[15]

This co-operative vision of centralised buying linked to uniform 'large emporiums' had long been mooted by some in the department store milieu. Selfridge in the 1890s had plans for a chain of Marshall Field stores, a vision that was met with hostility by Marshall Field and contributed to the final rupture of relationships between the two men.[16] Lewis's of Liverpool had early on embarked on the path of multiple outlets with stores in Manchester in 1877, Birmingham in 1885 and Sheffield in 1884.[17] Lewis's, specialising in the popular market, particularly mass tailoring and cheap foodstuffs, catered for an emerging working class which, according to Hobsbawm, was entering its period of homogenisation.[18] Lewis's trade of cheap suits, textiles and tea to the mass market of provincial industrial England was more predictable than the more up-market stores with their highly fashion-conscious customers. Moreover, these customers had been nurtured to expect a particular style of shopping environment and service that was usually unique to an individual store, and proprietors were extremely wary of breaking this mould. Bobby's, with their chain of seaside and resort town stores, enjoyed a similarly predictable market, catering for the needs of holiday-makers and tourists. Marshall Wilson, which became Marshall and Snelgrove in 1848, opened branches in fashionable Scarborough and Harrogate in the 1840s, but these stores only opened during the season and were later sold by the parent company. Too lengthy lines of communication were an obvious problem. An early attempt by a London fashion house, Clark and Debenham's, to establish a branch in the elite spa town of Cheltenham, Cavendish House, and a similar store in Harrogate was abandoned in 1888 when the Cheltenham store was allowed to 'go its own way'.[19]

These early efforts at branch trading were, with the noble exception of Bobby's and Lewis's, essentially London elite stores following their 'exclusive' customers on their country jaunts. The circumstances of the early 1920s presented far more serious problems than the temporary absence of customers. The majority of stores, which had been built or expanded in the nineteenth and early twentieth centuries, had been neglected and often poorly maintained during the war years. Investment and refurbishment were desperately needed, especially as shoppers were now being tempted by the smart new chain stores. Some luxury stores had experienced serious disruption to trade during the austere war years and emerged into peacetime burdened with serious debts. This phenomenon produced its own process of amalgamation when Debenham's, thanks to its large wholesale business, which was used by many of its rivals, found itself the major creditor of several indebted stores. As early as 1916, Debenham's and Marshall's were linked by the formation of Textile Securities, a trust that was essentially established to keep Marshall and Snelgrove trading during the war. By 1919 Debenham's had formally taken over its old rival and was negotiating the purchase of Harvey Nichols of Knightsbridge, which was also heavily indebted to Debenham's.[20]

Harrods began their acquisitions even earlier. Dickens and Jones of Regent Street found itself bereft of heirs with an interest in running the business in 1914 and was forced to conclude a friendly take-over with Harrods.[21] Similarly, John Barker of Kensington High Street acquired the neighbouring store of Pontings when the latter was forced into liquidation by an overambitious expansion scheme in 1907. Barker's completed its domination of Kensington High Street when it took over Derry and Toms in 1920. Yet Barker's did not pursue a policy of uniformity, rather it continued to concentrate on 'high class lines and Pontings and Derry and Toms [to] cater for the multitude or good middle class lines'.[22] Harrods continued this process of picking up ailing giants when it acquired Kendal Milne of Manchester in 1919, Swan and Edgar in 1920, D H Evans in 1928 and Schoolbred's of Tottenham Court Road and the Civil Service Co-operative Society of Haymarket in 1931. The latter two were immediately closed and their stock sold off.[23] At a less notable level, Binns of Sunderland acquired sick regional neighbours during the same period and eventually built up a chain of small department stores on the north-east coast and in southern Scotland.[24]

Not surprisingly, Selfridge was also a key player in the take-over free-for-all of the 1920s. The now ageing entrepreneur, urged on by the success of his Oxford Street store and his need to finance his playboy life-style of gambling, young women and air travel, entered a period of frantic acquisitions. Selfridge was joined by Jimmy White, a former Lancashire bricklayer who had a penchant for both spotting ailing stores in need of a white knight and boosting Selfridge's already expanding ego.[25] White acted as middleman in a series of take-overs which earned him a hefty personal commission. Selfridge, during the 1920s, bought a chain of London and regional stores which became Selfridge Provincial Ltd. This quickly assembled chain eventually totalled 19 stores including the Bon Marché of Brixton, South London, Pratts, Quin and Axtens, Jones Bros. and John Barnes. Outside London, Selfridge bought stores in Dublin, Liverpool, Leeds, Sheffield, Peterborough, Northampton, Gloucester, Windsor, Watford and Brighton. The culmination of this activity was the take-over of Whiteley's, after secret negotiations by White, in late 1926 and early 1927.[26] It is difficult to conclude that anything other than vanity and ego were Selfridge's main motive for taking over the famous Bayswater premises. Queensway had long been in decline and Whiteley's had been in serious financial difficulties for some years. There is also an ironic symmetry in that the womanising Selfridge should eventually own the store of the philandering 'Universal Provider'. Selfridge's agreement to pay Whiteley shareholders dividends of 25 per cent for 15 years was a rash mistake that would eventually be a major contributor to his downfall.[27] Overall, the Selfridge chain was never very profitable; Gordon Selfridge's hectic social life and the demands of Oxford Street, together with his failure to manage adequately his provincial empire, forced the company to sell the bulk of the stores to the John Lewis Partnership in 1940.[28]

An apparently more systematic attempt at establishing a group of stores with the express aim of reaping the benefits of centralised buying was put together by the City financier, Clarence Hatry and his Austin Friar Trust. Hatry, a former City insurance underwriter, had been involved in the flotation of British Glass Industries and the merger of several steel companies. He soon gained a reputation as a brilliant manipulator of company stock and his talent for putting together groups of companies matched the atmosphere of protectionism in British business in the 1920s; a decade which saw the formation of Distillers, Imperial Chemical Industries, United Alkali and other large combines.

Hatry's company established the Drapery and General Investment Trust in late 1925 with the purpose of bringing together a large number of stores.[29] Selfridge was also busy in the same period, building his provincial empire, and there was often fierce competition amongst these two predators. Hatry, however, had an advantage over Selfridge in that he allowed the existing management structure of each store to remain intact and his promise of economies of scale from his proposed central buying unit often clinched the deal. By 1927, Hatry's empire consisted of sixty-five stores with 11,000 employees including the Bobby Group, the Bon Marché of Gloucester, Handley's of Southsea, the three Midlands stores of Smiths and Kennards of Croydon.[30] The Trust, however, also consisted of many smaller stores and even a few credit drapers. The financing of these acquisitions was largely based on a rising mountain of paper shares manipulated by Hatry. Profits of £600,000 in 1927 were boosted by the capture of Swan and Edgar which became the group's flagship. Yet Hatry failed to establish his central buying agency and by late 1927 he was negotiating a reverse take-over with Debenham's.[31]

The deal was highly complex and controversial. Debenhams Ltd. bought 75 per cent of the Drapery Trust shares at thirty shillings per share plus a commission of one shilling and four pence per share to Hatry. The acquisition cost Debenham's £2,350,000 which was financed by Hatry's Austin Friar's Trust purchase of £1.6 million of Debenham shares and the creation of millions of new Debenham shares. In 1929 the Hatry empire collapsed in what was described as the biggest failure since the South Sea Bubble. Hatry was convicted of fraud and sentenced to 15 years' penal servitude. Debenham's emerged unscathed from the fiasco but had to write off almost two-thirds of the company's issued capital, an act which did not endear the firm to the City of London.[32] Nevertheless Debenham's entered the 1930s with Britain's largest group of stores, then numbering 70, a centralised buying agency, Debenham's Limited Manufacturing and Supplies and perhaps of most importance, a fortuitous tranche of outlets in the prospering Midlands and southern manufacturing towns. Moreover, Debenham's decision to retain some of Hatry's federal managerial structure with the creation of the group 'C' provincial stores gave free rein to the entrepreneurial talents that the company had inherited. It was these provincial managers who created the rising profits of the 1930s and subsidised the operations of the increasingly expensive central London flagships.[33] Their brash methods may have been unpopular with the West End traditionalists, but these were the true children of Selfridge who were creating a new 'Golden Age' in department store history.

Notes

1. J.B. Jefferys, *Retail Trading in Britain 1850–1950*, Cambridge University Press, Cambridge, 1954, pp. 21–7.

2. Ibid., pp. 69–70.

3. G. Rees, *St Michael. A History of Marks and Spencer*, Weidenfeld and Nicolson, London, 1969; Chapter 6, *passim*.

4. Jefferys, op. cit., p. 70.

5. Ibid., p. 62.

6. Pasdermadjian, *The Department Store*, 1954, p. 52.

7. R. Church, *The Rise and Decline of the British Motor Industry*, Macmillan, Basingstoke, 1994, p. 34.

8. Moss and Turton, *A Legend of Retailing*, 1989, p. 333.

9. R. Bentall, *My Store of Memories*, W.H. Allen, London, 1974, p. 148.

10. Moss and Turton, op. cit., p. 126.

11. Ibid., p. 119.

12. Pasdermadjian, op. cit., p. 47.

13. Jefferys, op. cit., p. 38, discusses the origins of RPM.

14. Part of the Leicester Co-operative premises was even used as a producer's co-operative for the manufacturer of hosiery. B. Lancaster, *Radicalism, Co-operation and Socialism*, Leicester University Press, Leicester, 1987, p. 137.

15. G.D.H. Cole, *A Century of Co-operation*, Manchester, 1944, p. 295.

16. Honeycombe, *Selfridges*, 1984, p. 26; Twyman, *History of Marshall Field*, 1954, pp. 162–4.

17. Briggs, *Friends of the People*, 1956, Chapters 3 and 4, *passim*.

18. E.J. Hobsbawm, *Worlds of Labour*, Weidenfeld and Nicolson, London, 1984.

19. Adburgham, *Shops and Shopping*, 1981, pp. 45–7. Corina, *Fine Silks and Oak Counters*, 1978, p. 99.

20. Corina, op. cit., p. 77; p. 84.

21. Moss and Turton, op. cit., p. 326.

22. Ibid., p. 284.

23. Ibid., pp. 328–9.

24. Ibid., p. 292.

25. Honeycombe, op. cit., pp. 59–60.

26. Ibid., p. 60.

27. Ibid., p. 75.

28. Ibid., p. 190.

29. Corina, op. cit., p. 92.

30. Ibid., p. 94.

31. Ibid., pp. 100–1.

32. Ibid., pp. 103–4.

33. Ibid., pp. 113–14.

CHAPTER SIX

THE MIDWAY COMES TO
THE HIGH STREET

As the economy improved in the 1930s, particularly in the Midlands and the South, and living standards rose, for those in work, as a consequence of falling prices, department stores faced new challenges. Not least of these was the decision of the Lord Chancellor's Committee of 1930 that resale price maintenance was to the consumer's benefit.[1] This surprise verdict from a Labour Party government confirmed a trend that had been under way since 1912. In that year, J. and P. Coats, the large thread manufacturer, and the Bedstead Manufacturers Association had introduced fixed retail prices.[2] This process had been disrupted by heavy discounting in the bleak years of the early 1920s but by 1930 it was being applied to a large range of branded goods. Department stores therefore found themselves without control over prices and bearing far greater overheads than the small retailers. Moreover, the rising popularity of branded goods, many of which were assiduously publicised by manufacturers employing quickly maturing advertising agencies, was eroding the merchandising power of the large stores. In short, the manufacturer was gaining the upper hand in the realm of retailing.

One response to the challenge of the 'brand' was for stores to establish their own; a practice that was proving highly successful for the chain stores such as Marks and Spencer with their St Michael label. Indeed, many stores still had manufacturing facilities from the days when many combined production and retailing. But these production units were rapidly being phased out as they failed to compete with the large manufacturers employing new mass production techniques in purpose-built factories. Department stores could, however, thanks to the size of their market, negotiate with manufacturers for the production of goods bearing store labels that were usually of slightly less quality than their branded equivalent. Debenham's popular provincial stores sold furnishing fabric under their 'Vereston' label and women's underwear bore the 'Golden Dawn' label.[3] Lewis's of Liverpool, who now possessed an extremely efficient central buying department, introduced the 'Standex'

Figure 15 The Newcastle Co-operative Society's Newgate Street department store. Designed by the Co-operative Wholesale society architect, L.G. Elkins in 1929 (*source:* Co-operative Union).

and 'Wilwer' labels and John Barker's sold a wide range of items under the 'Kenbar' brand. Harrods likewise found that its own label coupled to its exclusive image was a highly successful marketing device.[4]

Department store labels could not on their own stop the rising tide of branded goods and the tendency for a large number of customers to go shopping 'already sold on a particular article'. Furthermore, the co-operative movement was beginning to implement the recommendations of their Survey Committee by building large city-centre department stores. Many of these stores, such as London Road, Brighton, and Newgate Street, Newcastle, were highly impressive, purpose-built structures. Indeed the Newcastle department store is arguably the north of England's finest art deco building (see Figure 15). The danger that these stores presented was that the co-operative 'divi' culture could spread to city centres.

A further blow was added in 1930 when the National Government imposed a 50 per cent tariff on many foreign fancy goods which had long enjoyed a department store market.[5] Department stores, facing all these threats, were forced to develop more innovative and aggressive marketing tactics. Department store managers had long known the benefits of crowd-pulling events; Christmas grottoes, toy fairs and sales had been popular since the last quarter of the nineteenth century. Since 1909 Selfridge had led the way in staging highly popular events starting with his display of Bleriot's flying machine. Surprise followed surprise as the Oxford Street entrepreneur waged his battle of the pavement. During the interwar period Selfridge's Chicago tactics of display and theatre were designed to draw the crowds into the department store carnival. 'Customer services' became novel in the extreme with the introduction of a free wart-removal service, cricket bat oiling and umbrella rolling at the Oxford Street store.[6] These ideas were increasingly utilised by other department store proprietors. It was, after all, the best way of creating distinctiveness in the increasingly homogeneous world of branded goods. But once started, the show had to continue and constantly change. Provincial and suburban stores led the way as they battled with the chains for the expanding purse of working Britain.

Next to the new Kingston Bypass, Gerrard Bentall entertained southwest London. Beginning in 1930 with the engagement of Albert Sadler and his Palm Court Orchestra in the store's Tudor Restaurant, events accelerated with the appointment of Eric Fleming, formerly of Gammages, as Publicity Director.[7] Bentall and Fleming quickly spotted the potential population growth with the completion of the bypass and decided to confine all their efforts to this rapidly prospering area. 'Why go to the West End – when there's Bentall's of Kingston' was an early slogan used by Fleming in publicity material.[8] Such slogans were highly effective in new expanding communities which were putting down roots and seeking a sense of geographical identity. By 1932 Bentall's were stealing a march on Selfridge when they displayed Sir Malcolm Campbell's *Bluebird* which had just won the world land speed record. Twice daily mannequin displays drew crowds of over 500, while the store's Bonny Baby competition attracted over 3,000 entries. Judging these suburban infants was undertaken by Bentall's customers; up to 10,000 completed ballot forms being counted by a team of staff gave the store a general election atmosphere.[9] Bentall's search for the novel knew no bounds; the floral decorations from the Royal Box at Ascot were bought annually by the store, displayed in the vestibule and sold to the public. Sewing exhibitions were given a touch of glamour by the arrival of Marjorie Knowles, the Lancashire Cotton Queen from Nelson, who, in

> full regalia ... was installed on a special dais. Film stars were brought in to dispense the prizes to lucky winners of Bentall's many competitions and film fans were given a further treat when the store set up a movie camera and operator and also hired a make-up artist. The result of such a screen test was then shown to the customer. And all for 2s 6d.[10]

Bentall's arranged visits for over a thousand schoolboys to Southampton to view the Queen Mary, then the subject of the store's window display, and each was provided with a Bentall's tuck box.[11] Fun for the children reached its peak at Christmas when along with the annual toy fair Bentall's staged an in-store circus. The store held a menagerie of animals for this event, including elephants and a lion, which was housed overnight in the lift shaft. No wonder a local schoolboy, when asked what was the most important place in Surrey, promptly replied, 'That's an easy one, Sir. It's Bentall's.'[12]

Adults at Bentall's were kept amused by mannequin displays, the Bijou theatre set, daily performances by the 'Goblin Cabaret' and even a peep-show featuring 'Marsana the long-necked woman'.[13] In the linen department, 'Bilton's Marionettes' gave a continuous show while 'on the escalator platform were the gaily attired figures of Alfredo and his Gipsy Band'; this group alternated weekly with Mounkman and his Czardas Band.[14] Well-known sports personalities gave demonstrations and newly-weds were given lectures on 'Mothercraft' and 'Fathercraft'. The star performance at Bentall's during the thirties was undoubtedly Anita Kittner:

> The forte of Miss Kittner, a young Swedish woman, was to dive from a great height into a small pool of water, an act she performed in the escalator hall twice daily for a fortnight. The balconies of the upper floors were as packed as the ground floor on every occasion. In bathing costume and hat, and to the accompaniment of music, Miss Kittner climbed up a ladder held by stunts until she reached the top of the well, her head nearly touching the glass roof. As the music stopped and the customers held their breath she would take off her shoes and throw them down. Then she would climb on all fours out

along a diving board and perform a handstand at the end of it. And finally
with a blood-curdling scream she leapt. ... As Miss Kittner plunged 63 feet
into the tank of water she put tremendous pressure on the floor so that we
had to shore up the ceiling of the lower ground floor beneath. On a more
personal level there was great pressure exerted on her costume – so much so
that on one occasion it split in two. No doubt to the disappointment of
some, one of our electricians, Mr Tom Bliss, was nearby to snatch up a towel
and wrap it round her.[15]

By employing such theatrical techniques Bentall's were able to with-
stand the trading pressures of the 1930s. A large new store was built and
the company enjoyed record profits. Department stores also greatly
benefited from the new consumer products that were mass-produced
during the period. Electrical goods in this era, when specialist electrical
shops were few, found their greatest market in the department store. As
we saw above with the 'Goblin Cabaret', these new manufacturers
recognised the importance of department stores and participated in the
new marketing techniques. Selfridge, reflecting his Chicago origins, had
long been fascinated with the new and the novel. Radios, gramophones
and the new 'Brunswick Radiogram' joined Selfridge's stock of 124,000
Edison Bell records. Nearby, Baird transmitted television pictures from
his workroom to a screen on Selfridge's roof.[16] Bentall's had great success
with their 'Radio Bentall Exhibition' which also included television
demonstrations, whilst downstairs the vestibule was dominated by 'a
vacuum cleaner, built by Hoover, at twenty times the normal size. What
is more, it actually worked; at intervals someone would come along
and throw confetti around which the monster gobbled up as customers
looked on.'[17]

The demand for these new products grew rapidly, particularly
amongst the lower middle and better-off working classes. The problem
was their relatively high price. The solution to this obstacle was the
adoption of the hire purchase system by many department stores. The
history of credit is probably as old as human society. It was certainly
commonly used by 'Scotch traders' and pedlars in the early nineteenth
century and it was, of course, the norm in upper class drapery shops.
The lower classes had typically used the credit system to buy everyday
items such as hardware and textiles from itinerant traders, but the system
took a new turn in the mid-nineteenth century when northern jewel-
lers and silversmiths formed 'clubs' for the purchase of the first major
item of working-class 'conspicuous consumption', the pocket watch.

The 'watch clubs', generally confined to skilled workers, developed into 'cutlery clubs' and later, full-blown mail order businesses. The bicycle boom of the late nineteenth century and early twentieth century was another development that boosted popular credit and introduced many new customers to hire purchase, with payment schemes often organised by manufacturers widely advertised in the press. Similarly, the growth of 'cheque trading', which originated in Bradford with the Provident Company formed in 1880, opened up yet more avenues of credit.[18]

Many small drapery businesses expanded on the credit system during the second half of the nineteenth century and some, such as Affleck and Brown of Manchester, Parish's of Newcastle, and Shepherd's of Gateshead, developed into department stores. These stores could be highly innovative in organising their credit systems. The Tyneside stores, for example, employed a network of neighbourhood agents which rivalled those of the 'cheque traders'. Similar to firms such as Provident, these stores issued 'cheques' which could only be used in the originating store where, upon the first transaction, the customer received change in the store's plastic and die-cast currency to spend in other departments. Credit always comes at a price. The 'cheque traders' charged the customer five per cent, usually one week's payment out of twenty, and the shopkeepers who accepted the cheques paid the company a further 15 per cent. Not surprisingly, the goods offered in these outlets were often inferior to, but priced the same as, well-known brands. Despite these drawbacks, credit trading expanded during the slump years, particularly amongst the poorer working class in the depressed areas. Parish's of Byker in Newcastle rebuilt their store as a mini-Selfridge's, Shepherd's became one of the largest stores on Tyneside and opened up branch stores in the mid-1930s, including one in Jarrow.[19]

The scale of credit trading is extremely difficult to assess in the interwar period. The sociologist J. Hilton, writing in 1938, estimated that:

> The volume of Hire Purchase dealing probably increased by twenty times between 1918 and 1938. The proportion of goods sold in 1938 was as nearly as I can tell, furniture 50 per cent; radio sets 70 per cent; bicycles 90 per cent; sewing machines 85 per cent; motor cars 40 per cent to 50 per cent; gramophones 60 per cent. ... Two-thirds of all mass-produced, repetition-manufactured goods sold to householders are sold 'on the nod'. ... At any given moment in a normal trading year the public owes on deferred payment agreements £50,000,000 to traders in respect of goods for which they have

signed on the dotted line; and £30,000,000 of that is 'laid off' if I may so express it, by the traders on to Finance Houses.[20]

Such growth naturally gave rise to concern, particularly in poorer areas. Helen Wilkinson, MP for Jarrow, introduced a Bill to control the credit trade in 1938. The Bill became the Hire Purchase Act and one contemporary noted 'That Parliament should have found it necessary, in a period when a Conservative and therefore supposedly 'Capitalist' Government was in office, to pass an Act codifying case-law and regimenting the activities of hire-purchase firms is *prima facie* evidence that the social consequences of the system, as operated in practice, have been deleterious.'[21] Much of this concern was directed against door-to-door salesmen selling vacuum cleaners, unscrupulous small dealers and the heavy-handed collecting practices of furniture stores such as Drage's. Drage's methods even found their way into popular song. The following are a few verses from the *Drage Way*, recorded about 1930:

> I've only just got married, and I'm on the rocks and broke.
> He said 'Don't let that worry you, why money is a joke!
> Why, we only run our business to oblige you sort of folk,
> And we always lay your lino on the floor!'

> 'But Mr Drage' my Missus said, 'Our neighbours know we're new,
> And when they see your van, they're bound to say a thing or two.'
> He said 'They won't: we send it round in vans as plain as you,
> And we always lay your lino on the floor!'

> So five hundred pounds in furniture, she spent, did my old Dutch;
> 'What deposit, Mr Drage' said I 'would you require for such?'
> He simply smiled, and said 'Would two and sixpence be too much?
> And we'll always lay your lino on the floor!'

> I said 'That's very generous, but no reference I've got.'
> He said 'We do not want them, they're a lot of tommy-rot.
> Why you needn't even give your name, if you would rather not,
> And we'll always lay your lino on the floor!'

> 'Well thank you Dr Drage,' I said 'You've really been most kind,
> But what about the payments?' He said 'That's as you're inclined.
> Pay half a crown a week, and if you can't, well never mind –
> For we'll always lay your lino on the floor!'[22]

Missed payments to Mr Drage, however, could have serious consequences. The *Hackney Gazette* of 23 December 1935 reported the experience of one such customer in arrears: 'A van called for the goods; one of the men with it was an ex-boxer, a regular brute, just the type of bruiser for the job. Mrs—, judging what their errand was, had not let them in; but they used force. Mrs— screamed, and a neighbour came to her aid. The boxer promptly floored him and the man made off with the goods.'[23]

Department stores generally avoided such publicity-drawing tactics. Their customer base tended to be the middle and employed well paid working-class and were therefore more credit worthy. Large stores had quietly introduced the monthly account system to their better-off regular customers in the last two decades of the nineteenth century, a period when stores greatly expanded customer services. In the interwar period, department stores were forced to offer hire-purchase schemes which were becoming very common in the furniture and electrical chains. They were, however, usually more careful than the multiples, insisting on higher deposits and references and they were also vocal in their criticism of the high-powered techniques that were often found elsewhere in the retail industry.[24] In truth, the move into hire-purchase trading was unavoidable for department stores during this period. New products, particularly electrical goods, were a high growth area of the market and it would have been suicidal for many stores to stand aloof from these developments.

Besides electrical goods a few imaginative manufacturers of traditional products joined in the fun. Colley Shorter, the flamboyant pottery manufacturer who owned three factories in Stoke-on-Trent, sent his star designer, the young Clarice Cliff and a team of paintresses, the 'Bizarre Girls', on a tour of department store china departments. Customers could watch these young women painting the highly-coloured art deco ware that earned Cliff her reputation as one of Britain's most important decorative artists of the twentieth century (see Figure 16).[25] Even the seemingly mundane 'Babies' Linen' department was livened up by 'Bilton's Marionettes', who produced a constant chorus for Bentall's customers.[26]

Over at Croydon, at the beginning of another arterial road, Purley Way, Kennards were providing similar fare to Bentall's for the prosperous outer suburbs of south-east London. *Bluebird* was carted across South London to repeat its Bentall's display, Dorothy Marno's Bohemian orchestra entertained diners in Kennards' restaurant and they even staged a 'Wild West Shoot Out between Two Gun Rix and Ranger Cliff

Figure 16 A hand-painting demonstration at Waring and Gillow, London, in August 1928. This was the first in-store promotion of Bizarre Ware which had been introduced early in 1928. On the extreme right is Clarice Cliff (*source*: courtesy of Mr L. Griffin, Clarice Cliff Collector's Club).

Norman'.[27] Kennards was managed by the Australian Jimmy Driscoll and was part of the Debenham 'C' group. Driscoll was part of a team of lively managers controlled by Fred Pope whom Debenham's acquired with the Bon Marché of Gloucester. Pope's team of managers were enthusiastic advocates of the new retail showmanship. Plummer's of Hastings entertained customers with performances by 'Koringa and her Crocodile' and Bobby's flagship store at Bournemouth presented musical acts and a wide range of demonstrations.[28]

Debenham's did not develop the same efficient central buying service as Lewis's, owing to the diverse nature of the group, but the provincial stores did develop new forms of management. Traditionally, stores had relied on the skill, flamboyance and hunches of the founder or his offspring. This to a certain extent continued within Debenham's federal structure. The role of Fred Pope, however, marked a new departure for Debenham's. Pope encouraged his managers to experiment with the new methods but more importantly his frequent group meetings and constant touring of the stores in the group facilitated the rapid exchange

of ideas and the introduction of 'best practice' management methods.[29]
Lewis's of Liverpool had, of course, been following a similar path for
many years. Note the confidence of Frederick Marquis, Lewis's
managing director, in his Memorandum to the Board of Trade on the
British Pavilion at the Paris Exhibition of 1937:

> The flooring I thought was a mistake. It really is no use wasting money
> putting down beautiful flooring in an exhibition, because the public never
> sees what they walk on: if we want to exhibit tiles then they ought to have
> a special show, railed off, if it is to have any value.
>
> The lighting of the exhibition was probably its worst feature. Those
> responsible had not realised that light can be used to isolate special features
> in an exhibition.
>
> *Display.* The major criticism that I have to make of the exhibition is that
> the display was not designed to meet the purpose of an exhibition. It was an
> intimate display, and designed for people who were careful students of goods,
> whereas in an exhibition there are great masses of people, probably footsore
> and mind-weary, whose eyes can only take in things that are shown with
> some dramatic force. There was very little that was dramatic about the displays
> in the British Pavilion in Paris.
>
> I think it would be a mistake to assume that this is a new technique that
> we have to learn. Exhibitions are not new and if those who had chosen the
> merchandise had handed the exhibiting of it over to competent people we
> should have obtained a much better result than we did: but these people
> would have to be people accustomed to exhibition work or accustomed to
> the somewhat strident appeal of the shop window that caters for the million...
> The commissionaires on duty had all the smartness that we associate with the
> British Services: I think we might have emphasised this a little more had we
> brought in a show of heraldry and a little more national colour into the
> entrance hall.[30]

Marquis was the spokesman for an industry that had had a 'good'
recession unlike many of the industrial exhibitions. It is surely of no
surprise to find this consummate shopkeeper being appointed Minister
of Production during the war rather than an industrialist.

Despite the uncertainties of the 1920s, department stores prospered
well during the interwar period. Table 2 clearly illustrates this success.
This growth was also reflected in the number of stores which rose from
a tentative estimate of 175-225 stores in 1914 to about 475-525 in 1938.[31]
Much of this increase was produced by the rise of the suburban and
outer suburban stores. Keddies of Southend, Stones of Romford, Bentall's of Kingston and Kennards of Croydon all stepped over the threshold

from large drapers to fully-fledged department stores during these years. This reflected the growth of suburbia and its tendency to decant the middle classes from their central heartland to the new arterial developments.

Table 2 Estimated percentage share of department stores in total retail sales 1900–39

Year	Percentage
1900	1.0–2.0
1910	1.5–3.0
1920	3.0–4.0
1925	3.0–4.0
1930	3.5–5.0
1935	4.0–5.0
1939	4.5–5.5

Source: Jefferys, *Retail Trading in Britain, 1850–1950*, Cambridge, 1954, p. 61.

The expanding world of the department store also indicates that the threats present in the 1920s had been largely overcome. The Co-operative movement's challenge was not seriously mounted and the few stores that were opened were handicapped by the traditionalism of co-operation. Co-operatives also faced the hostility of brand manufacturers, particularly of new high-priced goods such as radios, to allowing their products to be sold on the dividend system, which they saw as a breach of price maintenance. Department stores, however, were increasingly given volume rebates from manufacturers which did not affect the price, but helped pay for the store's high overheads.[32]

Chains presented a far more serious challenge. Firms such as Littlewoods and Marks and Spencer developed their own brands and concentrated on fast-moving lines. The share of multiples of total retail sales in the key area of clothing and footwear rose from 9.0–11.0 per cent in 1920, to 13.0–15.5 per cent in 1939. The number of firms with more than one hundred branches also rose from twenty-eight in 1920, to forty-seven in 1939.[33] Yet surprisingly, this growth appears to have incurred little damage to department stores. The chain stores tended to concentrate on a narrow range of goods at the low end of the market, allowing department stores to continue to enjoy the higher profits from a more prosperous clientele. But there were some ominous signs emanating from the high street chains by the late 1930s. The challenge of the clothing multiple had been partly offset by the department store's quick adoption of the new electrical consumer goods: by the late 1930s, however, firms such as Curry's, a former bicycle multiple, Stones and Lloyds Retailing, were expanding rapidly.[34]

By 1939, the department store could look back over the previous decade with satisfaction. Largely the product of the Victorian period, the *grand magasin* in Britain continued to prosper, unlike many of its industrial counterparts that were born in the same period. This is one area of the British economy where the complex managerial structures which had organically developed over the previous half century, readily adapted to the so-called 'Fordist' era of mass-produced consumer goods. Moreover, it had rapidly risen to the challenge of the retailing equivalent of the new industrial structure: the multiple chain store. The salvation of the department store was its finely tuned antennae to shifts in living standards and consumer taste. This sensitivity had been nurtured for almost a century. Fads and fashions come and go, as do their retail equivalents; but underneath this frothy surface of the novel and the sensational, the vast majority of consumers continue to 'shop': a process that involves the exercise of the customer's free will and the retailer's attempt to create a new desire. No side ever wins this socio-economic wrestling match, evidenced by the constant rise and fall of retail types. The department store was the pioneer of mass consumerism; it had long learnt the lesson of the necessity of combining an alluring environment with choice, and the economic rationale of a bargain price. Customers were never fools; their limited disposable income was always the subject of competition between the retailers and providers of goods and services. This process is further complicated by the constant shifts in social structure and the income levels of the various classes and status groups. The department store was a product of a seismic movement in the class system with the rapid nineteenth-century expansion of the commercial and industrial middle class. Stores in industrial areas had also long nurtured customers from the higher levels of the working class. Most stores were acutely aware that modern industrial society is an ever changing myriad of classes and status divisions whose changing tastes could be met, provided they were affordable. The high-class stores of London could possibly survive on rich customers willing to pay high prices on exclusive goods, but the majority of department stores were dependent on low mark-ups and high turnover. Despite the nostrums of puritanical Jeremiahs from various points of the political spectrum, spending and consuming is an enjoyable and creative process. Department stores emerged and prospered because their owners and managers recognised and catered for this intrinsic human experience. But consumer choice and taste had to be met and cultivated by those who controlled and developed these retail Leviathans. It is this group of people to which we must now give our attention.

Notes

1. A full discussion of this report is presented in H. Levy, *Retail Trade Associations. A New Form of Monopolistic Organisation in Britain*, Routledge and Kegan Paul, London, 1942, especially Chapter 13.

2. Moss and Turton, *A Legend of Retailing*, 1989, p. 102.

3. Corina, *Fine Silks and Oak Counters*, 1978, p. 115.

4. Briggs, *Friends of the People*, 1956, p. 173; Moss and Turton, op. cit., p. 285; p. 182.

5. Moss and Turton, op. cit., p. 141.

6. International Association of Department Stores (IADS) *Newsletter* 23.4.47.

7. Bentall, *My Store of Memories*, 1974, p. 147.

8. Ibid., p. 148.

9. Ibid., pp. 149–50.

10. Ibid., pp. 151–2.

11. Ibid., p. 159.

12. Ibid., p. 169.

13. Ibid., p. 167.

14. Ibid., p. 168.

15. Ibid., p. 166.

16. Honeycombe, *Selfridges*, 1974.

17. Bentall, op. cit., pp. 141–2.

18. *Provident's Ninety Years of Service*, Provident Clothing and Supply Co. Ltd., Bradford, 1970.

19. *Shepherd's Ltd.,* 1949. Privately published, copy in Gateshead Library.

20. J. Hilton, *Rich Man Poor Man*, George Allen and Unwin, London, 1938, pp. 133–4.

21. A. Vallance, *Hire Purchase*, Nelson, London, 1939, VIII.

22. I am indebted to my colleague, Mike Sutton, for providing these verses. Every attempt has been made to ascertain the copyright but it remains unknown. The publishers would be be grateful for any information and will update any future editions.

23. Vallance, op. cit., p. 68.

24. J.B. Jefferys, *Retail Trading in Britain*, 1954, p. 426.

25. L. Griffin and L.K. and S.P. Meisel, *Clarice Cliff, The Bizarre Affair*, Thames and Hudson, London, 1988, p. 67.

26. Bentall, op. cit.
27. Corina, op. cit., p. 118.
28. Ibid.
29. Ibid., p. 114.
30. B of T 57/19/36.
31. Jefferys, op. cit., p. 59.
32. Ibid., p. 407.
33. Ibid., p. 65.
34. Ibid., p. 407.

CHAPTER SEVEN

PEDLARS, NONCONFORMISTS AND SCIENTIFIC MANAGERS: DEPARTMENT STORE ENTREPRENEURS

Retailing is Britain's largest area of economic activity; it is also one of the few areas where the British have been highly successful in terms of international comparison. Yet the pioneers of modern retailing remain unsung heroes. How many A level students, or for that matter history undergraduates, have heard of Emerson Muschamp Bainbridge or Messrs Kendal, Milne and Faulkner? These men, after all, have had as much impact on the shaping of modern society as their industrial counterparts. Shopkeeping, we must suppose, did not figure largely in the Victorian psyche with its emphasis on grandiose engineering and large manufacturing industry. Samuel Smiles is certainly silent on the subject. Perhaps this is because shopping, to the male-dominated Victorian mentality, was too closely associated with women. With a few noble exceptions, scholars have perpetuated this indifference. Indeed, it has been remarked that they consider shopkeepers 'to contain an essential element of unworthiness, a blend of the sinister and the ridiculous'.[1] It appears that as a nation we have spent nearly two centuries trying to deny Napoleon's jibe. The 'sinister' and the 'ridiculous' have long been allied with deeply held notions that retailing is essentially parasitic, an area where 'value' is produced by trickery and deceit and affronts the world of hard work and honest toil of manufacturing Britain. A sensible survey, however, of nineteenth-century industrialisation would surely conclude that the rise of modern manufacturing industry was inextricably linked to a revolution in the distributive processes. One is forced to wonder whether the expansion of the textile and clothing trades, which were central to Britain's industrialisation, would have been halted in their tracks if they were dependent on the old shopocracy.

The proximity of innovation in the drapery trade to the Reformed Corporation Act of 1835 is worth noting. Winstanley has explored the politics of shopkeepers in this period, concluding that the 1835 Act 'thrust tradesmen to the fore locally in the reformed corporate boroughs'.[2] The majority of shopkeepers in these towns generally supported the Liberal or Radical cause. It is difficult to chart accurately the connections between political enfranchisement and retail innovation; the vote may have added to the shopkeeper's confidence, whilst the widened electorate resulted in the shopkeeper being less vulnerable to commercial coercion. These must, of course, remain speculations, but the Liberals' championing of the free-trade cause was an issue close to the shopkeeper's heart. Moreover, clearly marked prices, low margins, high turnover and the freedom to buy from the most advantageous source are the retailing realities of Manchester economics. Further, the insistence on cash payment removed the element of the decent useful classes subsidising the credit facilities of the idle.

What is also inescapable is the political allegiance of department store pioneers to the Liberal cause. Bainbridge was allied to both Liberalism and temperance; Whiteley was Bradlaugh's paymaster, the Beales of Bournemouth and the Browns of Chester dominated local politics in their respective towns. Owen Owen and D.H. Evans were Lloyd George's principal backers; he in turn served as their solicitor. The radical Binns family saw one of its members imprisoned as a physical force Chartist. Henry Brown of Brown, Muff was three times Liberal mayor of Bradford; Tom Baker, co-owner of Dingles, also served as Liberal councillor and mayor of Plymouth. The Jollys of Bath served a function in local politics similar to that of the Browns of Chester; indeed, the list of political involvement and support for Liberalism is an almost universal attribute of department store proprietorship. It is not surprising when we consider that the late Victorian department store was the most concrete and visible realisation of the doctrine of free trade, and their owners the veritable personification of 'The Triumph of the Entrepreneurial Ideal'.

Opposition to the department store in Britain was ineffectual and spasmodic. Whiteley's battle with the drapers of Bayswater is the best documented, with hints that a neighbouring trader may have been responsible for an arson attack on the store. There is no concrete evidence to support this claim, and by the 1890s the small shopkeepers of Queensway and Westbourne Grove prospered, thanks to the crowds attracted to the district by the 'Universal Provider's' anchor site.[3] Winstanley has noted the tendency for tradesmen to support the Liberal cause with the exception of those linked to British agriculture, such as butchers selling native meat, and publicans.[4] Moreover, the entrenchment of craft consciousness amongst traders had been diminishing since the decline of the guilds in the eighteenth century. Indeed, the 'art and mystery' of much production in the textile and clothing trades had been undermined by Britain's long experience of 'proto-industrialisation'.

Department stores in Britain did not create the political activity that occurred elsewhere in Europe. In France, for example, the department store was the focus of intense political debate. The 'ligue syndicale du travail de l'industrie et du commerce' boasted over 140,000 members at its peak in the 1890s.[5] This shopkeepers' protest movement has attracted the attention of historians; Crossick, for example, highlights the slow political integration, in comparison with Britain, of the lower middle class and the strong rural connections of the French *petite bourgeoisie*.[6] Miller analyses the phenomenon of the 'ligue' in terms of an old *petite bourgeoisie* being replaced by a new, larger, more bureaucratic elite. The department store was perceived as a challenge, not only to the small trader, but also struck at the heart of community values: the organic relationship between customer, trader and community.[7] Nord's study continues this theme by locating the small trader department store protest in the wider process of Parisian urban transformation.[8] The 'ligue's' right-wing nationalism was to prove a harbinger of subsequent fascist movements. Similar sentiments were vented in Wilhelmine Germany where department stores attracted criticism from Social Democrats and small traders, the latter often combining anti-Semitism with their protest. These are vividly described in Marguerite Böhme's novel of 1912; processes which adumbrate themes from the 1920s and Hitler's promise in his programme to 'socialise' the department store.[9] Shopkeeper protest in some European countries further reflected the political power of the small trader, with serious restrictions imposed upon department stores in Luxembourg, Switzerland and Yugoslavia.[10]

The American scene was much closer to Britain. Competition between large stores defused any charges against monopoly during the period of Anti-Trust political campaigns. Indeed many department stores championed consumer rights against restrictive practices. Macy's, for example, broke the price maintenance system imposed by American publishers after a lengthy legal battle in 1913.[11] Marshall Field led a similarly high profile campaign to win 'port' status for Chicago. Midwest retailers had long suffered delays with imported goods at New York, particularly with customs procedures. It was claimed that this gave an unfair advantage to New York traders, especially in the marketing of French fashion goods. Led by Marshall Field, Chicago lobbied the Government, and Chicago was declared a port of entry with its own customs facilities in 1870.[12]

Nonconformity was another attribute shared by many department store proprietors. Bainbridge came to Newcastle in the 1830s steeped in the Methodist tradition of the lead-mining districts of the Durham dales. He was a lay preacher at the Brunswick Chapel, a benefactor of the local Methodist building programme and a leading member of the Newcastle temperance movement. His son continued this tradition, becoming chairman of the Federation of Free Churches, and he was secretary of the Moody and Sankey organisation in Britain.[13] The Bainbridges's fellow dalesman, J.J. Fenwick, was equally active in northern Nonconformity. He was the Sunday School Superintendent at the Brunswick Chapel and the two store owners financed a new Methodist church in the suburb of Jesmond.[14] In nearby Sunderland, the Binns family were devout Quakers and the Welsh department store owners, Owen Owen, James Howell and D.H. Evans and the Cornishman, Edward Dingle, were all Nonconformist.[15] William Whiteley, however, was an Anglican, but in his youth he devoted his leisure time to 'Bible class work ... falling evidently at this stage of his life under Evangelical influences'.[16]

There is also a certain uniformity in the social background of these men. Virtually all made vast fortunes during their lifetime but none truly conform to the 'Rags to Riches' myth that was a popular feature of Victorian discourse. Nevertheless, most of them climbed a great number of rungs on the economic ladder. The most common background was from various forms of shopkeeping. Bainbridge and Fenwick came from the world of small shopkeepers in the North Dales, Frank Bentall came from a shopkeeping family in Maldon, Essex, and James Jolly came from a similar background in Norfolk.[17] The Binns' firm began life as a small drapers in late eighteenth-century Bishop Wearmouth and Brown, Muff likewise originated in late eighteenth-century circumstances as saddlers and drapers in Bradford.[18] Others came from outside shopkeeping: John Barker was the son of a Kent carpenter and brewer who could afford to educate his son privately before he embarked on a drapery apprenticeship. Thomas Dickens of Dickens and Jones was the son of a York coal merchant and James Howell the son of a Fishguard farmer. The first Hugh Fraser came from a family of

Figure 17 The Brunswick Place Methodist Chapel and the Fenwick Newcastle store remain tied together by bricks and mortar. Both Fenwick and Bainbridge were leading officers of the Brunswick Place Chapel during the late 19th century (*source*: collection of the author).

innkeepers, his colleagues in Glasgow, Wylie and Lockhead, had backgrounds in the hair and feather and the undertaking trades. In Edinburgh, Robert Maule took the unusual path of opening his store for the sale of wool and tartan shawls manufactured in his own factory.[19] Beale's of Bournemouth crossed the divide of the excursionist/tourist resort trade when he abandoned the 'bucket-and-spade' market which he entered in 1881 with his 'Fancy Fair' shop, to pursue the wealthy purses of the quality visitors.[20]

The original ownership of the Bon Marché in Brixton which, when opened in 1877, claimed to be Britain's first purpose-built department store, resulted from bizarre circumstances. James Smith, a printer and owner of the *Sportsman*, entered his horse, Roseberry, for the Cambridgeshire and Cesarewitch Stakes in 1876. Roseberry was the first horse to win this double and Smith's prize of £80,000 was spent on building the Bon Marché as a secure future for his sons.[21] Fenwick of Newcastle was able to branch out with his own store, thanks to a similar, but much smaller, windfall. Sacked by his employer, the local well-to-do silk draper Braggs and Company, for running an insurance agency alongside his shop duties, Fenwick sued for unfair dismissal and was awarded £1,000 damages. This money, helped by a good marriage to the daughter of a leading local tailor, financed the opening of his own shop in 1882.[22]

More typical recruits came from within the trade. Owen Owen belonged to a dynasty of Welsh drapers and began his business life working in the family's large store at Bath.[23] The Chiesman brothers were sons of a wholesaler's accountant; both D.H. Evans and E. Dingle came from the managerial ranks of the drapery profession; and the Yorkshire store founders, Schofield of Leeds and Walsh of Sheffield, were buyers before embarking on their own account. Harrods' origins as pork butchers from Cable Street, Stepney, is well known, but the real growth and success of the company was achieved after the Harrod family had left the business. This success was largely the work of Richard Burbidge, Whiteley's former manager.[24]

None of these men found too much difficulty in starting their own businesses. Most had either access to various amounts of family money or had accrued savings from employment at managerial level. Moreover, the initial investment in the new venture was quite modest. Premises were usually rented and thanks to their owners' reputation in the trade, most stock could be obtained by credit from suppliers. Owen Owen's bank manager reported to his head office in May 1868: 'New account opened with Owen Owen, Draper, London Road. This party has only commenced business within the last week. It will be a cash account and always be in credit. The turnover he expects will amount to £3,000 per annum.'[25] Owen Owen's trading policy of low margins, fast turnover and expansion into other lines, soon achieved his business projections. Moreover, the insistence on cash payment allowed such men to pay their suppliers more quickly than normal, a system that attracted a discount. Indeed, once established, such men often found the retailers' 'philosopher's stone' of being able to borrow money from banks at a considerably lower rate than the discount they received from suppliers.[26]

Quick profits facilitated expansion, usually in the form of acquiring the freehold of the original and surrounding properties. The building of the department store in Victorian and Edwardian Britain often resulted in the proprietor becoming as skilful in property matters as he was in retailing. Owen Owen's involvement in property has already been mentioned. Others were equally astute, if on a less grandiose scale.

Bentall's at Kingston were quick to exploit their position in Clarence Road, having had the foresight to recognise the area's potential with the expansion of the town centre.[27] Others made the weather in the growth and realignment of city centres. Fenwick, for example, pioneered Northumberland Street as Newcastle's main thoroughfare, while his son Frederick 'made it his hobby in life to add to the sprawl of the Northumberland Street premises'. Some hobby! The Newcastle store now dominates an area which boasts some of the highest property prices in Britain.[28] Similarly, James Beale was extremely active in the Bournemouth property market and his dealings produced not only a major department store but also the Carlton Hotel – Europe's only remaining independent five-star hotel, which is still owned by the Beale family.[29] There were, however, some casualties in the property market, most notably D.H. Evans, who died penniless in 1928 after a series of disastrous speculations on property, no doubt trying to emulate the example of his friend, Owen Owen.[30]

During the period when the process of mass production of consumer goods was far from complete, it is no surprise that many department store proprietors were also drawn to manufacturing. Clothing was the obvious area for these activities, with virtually all stores employing workers to make up and adjust clothing and soft furnishings in their own workrooms. Lewis's of Liverpool were major manufacturers of boys' and men's clothing, particularly suits; Bainbridge employed over a thousand workers in his Leeds factories making garments and boots and shoes.[31] At a more diverse level, Owen Owen entered market gardening, no doubt with an eye to a future property deal, while Bentall's employed their construction knowledge gained in the incessant rebuilding of their premises in the local building industry. The Kingston store built interwar council housing estates for the local authority, modernised hotels and stately homes, and was famous for its best-selling wooden bungalow which the building department manufactured and erected on the South Coast and in the Essex and Kent countryside.[32]

These activities are characteristic of the enterprising individualistic entrepreneur of the Victorian period, yet the store owners shared much in common and established their own business and social institutions. Levy, in his study of retail trade associations, correctly locates the first formal institution to represent the interests of department stores in the formation of the Retail Distributors' Association of 1919. There had been, however, an active informal associational life amongst store proprietors well before 1919.[33] The 'Twenty Club' existed from at least the early 1890s to provide a social and business venue for department store bosses. By 1897, Owen Owen was a member and he soon became chairman, with Edwin Jones of Dickens and Jones as president.[34] It was at the 'Twenty Club' that Owen Owen negotiated many of his property deals for London store owners. Another important form of contact was provided by the Linen and Woollen Drapers' Institution and Cottage Homes. This charity provided accommodation for newly retired workers and by the turn of the century was dominated by the owners of the large stores, reflecting the size of their contribution to the organisation's funds. The regular meetings and annual dinner of the 'Cottage Homes' increasingly gave vent to common concerns and during wartime the government held informal meetings with the charity to discuss issues related to distribution.[35]

By the 1920s there were strong social links between department store entrepreneurs. One of the most noticeable was the growing tendency for the sons of entrepreneurs to spend at least some time with another large firm at the beginning of their career. Rowan Bentall spent a period at Harrods, an arrangement sealed by his father in a Winchester pub where he used to meet Sir Richard Burbidge when the two store bosses drove down to the New Forest home of Selfridge for social occasions.[36] Most male members of the Fenwick family served similar apprenticeships, often in stores belonging to the Harrods group. These social links even produced the occasional marriage. Rowan Bentall, for example, married Adelia Hawes, whom he had 'known for quite a time as I had been a schoolfriend of her brother Bernard as well as working with her father, the director of Frederick Sage and Co.'. Similarly, in Newcastle, the 'marriage of the year' in 1934, was between George Bainbridge and Pamela Fenwick.[37]

A more secretive form of contact was provided by the Mutual Communication Society. This organisation began in a London coffee house in the early nineteenth century for the purpose of exchanging information between traders on the credit status of customers. By the 1920s, the Society was largely controlled by big store owners; A.E.W. Cowper, Selfridge's 'Manager, Systems', was a leading officer and announced at the annual dinner of 1920 that '100,000 ordering enquiries went through the Society's central office. In the period January to November, there had been a rise of 2,000 in "special" inquiries. Agents throughout England, Scotland and Ireland (not Wales) undertook debt inquiries in return for subscriptions to the MCS. A central register of information blacklisted certain people, particularly "passers of bad cheques and people placing fraudulent overseas orders".[38]

Despite these impressive formal and informal networks, the trade still lacked a central co-ordinating body that could speak on behalf of the large stores. This deficiency was overcome with the formation in 1920 of the Retail Distributors' Association to deal exclusively with department store issues. Writing in 1942, Levy noted that the Association was 'widely known on account of the statistical and general information services which it performs for its members, relating to statistics, labour questions, legal and parliamentary questions, and of late, war problems'. Levy is emphatic in his categorisation of the Association as a 'type of association ... [where] the general interests of the members, needing collective representation, are covered by the activities of the association, while the individual member's decisions about his individual business activities remain untouched'.[39] Wartime experiences and the worsening economic climate of the early 1920s were obvious stimuli to organisation amongst department stores. Another important factor, however, was the growing science of management in American business. Scholars of 'scientific management' have generally focused upon the attempts to apply the ideas of F. W. Taylor to manufacturing industry and have tended to ignore the wider 'managerial revolution' that was underway in other sectors of the economy. Retailing first encountered these new techniques with Selfridge's new methods of store management which he introduced to London in 1909. American stores were in the vanguard of these developments which gathered apace in the 1920s under the influence of Edward Filene, chairman of the Boston store bearing his name.[40]

A key feature of the new managerialism was the importance of gathering and sharing business information and the importance of emulating 'best practice'. Despite the competitive nature of the market, department stores generally had little to fear from each other. In truth, few stores were in direct competition with their neighbours, individual stores tending to cater for particular market sectors. Co-operation was further enhanced by the growth of large groups, which was usually accompanied by the dilution of entrepreneurial control and the increasing importance of professional managers. Even privately-owned stores conformed to this trend with the introduction of non-family members to the board. Pasdermadjian, in his classic study, has summarised the achievements of managerial innovation in this period as follows:

the introduction of the retail inventory method (or cost and selling system), which makes it possible to obtain at the end of every month and without the obligation of taking a physical inventory the two basic figures represented by the gross margin and the value of stocks; the development and application of a standard classification of the expenses with a dissection into natural and functional divisions; the application of departmental accounting; the introduction of modern methods of merchandise and assortment planning; the use of statistical merchandise control; the development of methods for the control of slow selling and old merchandise; the introduction of an increased functional and merchandise specialisation; the improvement of grouping of the merchandise lines by more rational classification and the suppression of confused and heterogeneous assortment of goods; the control of the production and of the expenses of non-selling departments by the selection of units of performance and the determination of unit costs; and the use of market and customer research.

Dry language perhaps, but few areas of manufacturing industry could boast such a sophisticated system of control.[41]

Many of these techniques originated in the USA which had a head start down the path of managerialism with the formation of the National Retail Dry Goods Association in 1911 and the Retail Research Association in 1916.[42] These developments took on an increasingly international dimension with the formation of the International Management Institute in 1927, one of whose leading members was Edward Filene, who encouraged retail research which culminated in the International Association of Department Stores the following year.[43] The IADS originally consisted of one member per company from a number of European countries and it has published a monthly newsletter of business intelligence since 1936. The Association, over the years, has employed a number of distinguished scholars amongst its research staff including H. Pasdermadjian and J.B. Jefferys at its Paris headquarters.

The world of department store management was also influenced by other ideas that were becoming popular in the interwar period. An inner circle of the Retail Distributors' Association led by F.J. Marquis (later Lord Woolton), President of the Association and managing director of Lewis's Ltd, and L.E. Neal, managing director of Daniel Neal and Sons Ltd, was formed in the late 1920s. The group, according to Marquis, were 'the new generation ... whom the schools and universities of this country have had a hand in moulding: but they have been through the further process of education which comes from occupying positions of control in business life. With minds trained in accurate thought, they have looked on the world of business and found it sadly confusing.'[44] The research of 'the new generation' was published in a book written by Lawrence Neal, *Retailing and the Public*, which was published in 1932. The volume is heavily tinged with the language of the planning ideal that became influential in the 1930s. Neal called for greater co-operation and co-ordination between manufacturers and retailers and the elimination of 'overlap'. He was also scathing about the poor quality of design of many products which resulted in the multiplication of similar items.[45]

Indeed the 'standardised' high-quality product was Neal's ideal and he envisaged a system of trade boards imposing controls of quality, style and size on products.[46] Neal was particularly keen to point to the advantages achieved by Lewis's with their somewhat uniform market amongst the northern industrial classes, selling mass-produced products of reasonable quality and achieving low levels of overheads. He was also heartened by the amalgamation of luxury department stores into the Harrods group, claiming that similar economies of scale could be achieved. The main thrust of Neal's argument, however, consisted of an attack on the inefficiencies of small traders and the need for a system of town planning. Zoning schemes, the removal of redundant and in-efficient retail outlets would, Neal argued, reduce distribution costs and facilitate concentration. This would boost the trade of the department stores, chains and the efficient local grocer, facilitate a more rational advertising industry and ultimately lower prices.[47]

This vision of the 'new generation' of standardisation and redundancy schemes for small shopkeepers was challenged by contemporary commentators. Hermann Levy, a scholar of trusts, monopolies and cartels, ranging from the 'Newcastle Vend' to the 'Syndikats' of 1930s' Germany, attacked Neal in a Fabian publication, *Retail Trades Association*. Levy was concerned at the monopolistic tendencies of the Neal proposals and its somewhat bullying attitude to small entrepreneurs. Moreover, Levy was quick to point out some of the contradictions in the department store industry. In a subsequent book, *The Shops of Britain*, Levy ironically quotes Neal's historic account of the rise of department stores from the ranks of small traders and wondered, if Neal's scheme had been in place in the nineteenth century, if the department store would have emerged at all.[48] Furthermore, Neal was also proposing a scheme that would deny new blood entering the trade. Finally, Levy points his finger to the 'overlap' of department stores in such areas as Kensington High

Street and Oxford Street. Levy, of course, chose to ignore the point that Barkers, Pontings and Derry and Toms catered for slightly different markets, but under Neal's 'standardisation' scheme, such distinctions would disappear.[49]

The Neal-Marquis study group were advocating the views of popular market department stores. This was undoubtedly the growth area of the 1930s but could they be sure that it would continue? Other more shrewd operators chose to persist with the more conservative formula of combining the 'carriage trade' with the bargain basement. In the USA, the drive to standardisation and the reduction in the number of lines stocked had gone much further than in Britain. 'Starve the Stocks' was the slogan of the new retail management philosophy, yet Marshall Field continued with such techniques as stocking a brand of 'toilet soap which was infrequently, but steadily purchased by a handful of custom- ers: a cost conscious model stock plan would have eliminated it, but Marshall Field kept it on the shelves as a testimony to its concern for the exceptional customer'.[50]

Clearly two managerial strategies emerged during the 1930s. On the one hand the modernisers, usually based in the large new groups such as Debenham's, Selfridge Provincial and Lewis's, preached the gospel of lean stock, reduction of lines, staff training and market research. In many respects this strategy is both a response to the competition from the chains and a move towards their competitors' methods. On the other, we have the more empirical techniques of the numerous in- dependent department stores and small groups. This category covered an extremely wide range, from the luxurious yet distinct stores in the Harrods group, to the somewhat different 'carriage trade' store of Brown, Muff catering for bourgeois Yorkshire taste, intermingled with Bradford's sophisticated and prosperous European immigrant community. Stores such as Fenwick's of Newcastle continued their democratic luxury tradition by serving both the upper and middle classes of the region and the wives of pitmen and shipyard workers; a very different managerial strategy to that pursued in the company's up-market Bond Street store. This large number of stores, accounting for approximately three hundred of the 475-525 department stores, was in size more important than the groups.[51] These 'independents' cultivated their local market, sometimes serving their third generation of customer. They were part of an integral urban world which they themselves had helped create. The reputation of the house, the presence of family members on the management team and a deep knowledge of local conditions served to ensure customer loyalty.

Despite the growth of homogeneity in goods and marketing during the 1930s, the autonomous store continued to prosper. Even the groups, with the exception of Lewis's, chose to allow the majority of their stores to retain much autonomy. It was not so much that the Neal-Marquis crusade of scientific management was preaching in the wilderness but rather that many of the technical improvements that they advocated had been gradually adopted to meet local conditions since their arrival with Selfridge in 1909. The more ambitious policies outlined by Neal found little currency in the wider world during the 1930s; they were, however, to re-emerge in more ominous form, for retailers, during the nationalisation crisis of the late 1940s.

Up until 1939 the personality of many stores was largely the product of the individual managers and owners who operated them. Even the modernisers still shared personal and family links with stores in the amalgamated groups. Frederick Pope, the boss of the Debenham 'C' stores still retained a personal interest in the Bon Marché, Gloucester, a product of Debenham's complex federal structure.[52] Marquis of Lewis's was joint managing director of the group, alongside a member of the Lewis-Cohen family.[53] Arthur and Frederick Bobby remained at the helm of the family stores that were part of the Debenham's empire and strove to retain Bobby's 'popular to good' market.[54]

The huge number of independents continued the tradition of family involvement. The enduring habit of staff in these stores to refer to the owner-manager as 'Mr John' or 'Mr Trevor' is testimony to the persistence of dynastic control over many stores. The longevity of family control is an interesting feature of the department store world. This phenomenon is, of course, found elsewhere in British industry, but perhaps not on the same scale. The highly successful Fenwick group is, in 1994, still a private family company. The Bentalls still exercise much control over the Kingston-based group. The Bainbridge store in Newcastle was managed continuously by family members from 1837 until 1974, despite the fact that the company became part of the John Lewis Partnership in 1953. Four Hugh Frasers headed the company from 1815 until 1982 and similar examples of enduring family interest can be found elsewhere.

Family involvement often served to shape a store's image of being 'reasonable and sensible'. Fraser's reputation in Glasgow owed much to the family's charitable work and campaigning for Scottish business interests. The Beales of Bournemouth and the Browns of Chester were virtually synonymous with their respective towns. The Burbidge dynasty of Harrods presented a social veneer that reflected the pomp and circumstance of the Knightsbridge establishment. Yet the behaviour of store owners and family members did not always reflect the firm's personality.

Rumours of Whiteley's sexual involvement with some of his female assistants did much to fuel the Victorian fear of the department store as a place of moral danger. Gordon Selfridge's womanising and much-publicised gambling scared off potential creditors and led to his downfall.[55] A similar fate was met by Sir Hugh Fraser in the early 1980s.[56] Even the somewhat staid image of Bainbridge's was spiced up in the 1930s by the social activities of Jack Bainbridge, Newcastle's premier playboy and much commented upon host to numerous chorus girls and actresses. Jack's activities in Newcastle were so notorious that the Fenwick family for a time opposed the marriage of their daughter to a Bainbridge on the grounds that their prospective son-in-law came from 'a wild and dangerous family'.[57]

Such flamboyant social behaviour was rare amongst owners and bosses. Selfridge's downfall is still talked about in department store circles. One store director recently told the present writer that 'The day Gordon Selfridge walked up to a till and removed a fiver to pay for his and his girlfriend's lunch was the day he was finished as a trader'. Such behaviour has an obvious effect on staff, whilst the publicity that surrounds high living and a 'frivolous life-style' raises important and potentially dangerous questions in the minds of customers. Stores are glamorous places, often designed to induce impulse purchase of luxury items but their success is still firmly grounded in their Victorian founders' claim of pursuing fair prices and low profits.

By 1939 the department store manager could take pride in his achievement. Most stores had come through the depression unscathed, sales were steadily increasing and managing the organisation, despite its growing sophistication, was becoming more efficient. Few industries born in the early Victorian period could make similar claims. This success was largely the product of the adaptability of department store managements to change and innovation, as well as their willingness to learn from each other through their associations. This laudable flexibility achieved more than higher profits – it also produced a dramatic shift in both popular perceptions and the reality of workers' conditions. When Leonard Bentall and his wife returned to Kingston after their world tour in 1937, they attended a Ball of 1,200 employees in the store, organised by the workers acting on their own initiative:

> As my mother and father entered the store, there was a fanfare by trumpeters of the Coldstream Guards and they were greeted by members of the committee ... Miss D.W. Webb of the Millinery department presented my mother with a bouquet of pale mauve orchids and lilies of the valley. To tremendous applause my parents entered the ballroom where they walked under a canopy of flower-bedecked poles held aloft by 16 girls while rose petals were strewn at their feet and the band played 'There's a Long Long Trail A-Winding' and 'Home Sweet Home'.[58]

Paternalism is often regarded by labour historians as a nineteenth-century system of industrial relations, but its most successful application was the twentieth-century department store. Bentall's Ball of 1937 is a far cry from the concern voiced by many commentators during the early years of the century on the misery of store conditions. It is to this transformation to the world behind the counter that we must now give our attention.

Notes

1. P. Scott, *Geography of Retailing*, Hutchinson, London, 1970, p. 11.
2. M.J. Winstanley, *The Shopkeeper's World 1830–1914*, Manchester University Press, Manchester, 1983, p. 19.
3. Lambert, *The Universal Provider*, 1938, p. 217.
4. Winstanley, op. cit., pp. 19–30. Winstanley does note, however, that shopkeepers did have reservations 'about the uncontrolled operation of the market'.
5. P.G. Nord, *Paris Shopkeepers and the Politics of Resentment*, Princeton, 1986, p. 7. Nord's study offers the fullest account of this phenomenon.
6. G. Crossick, 'The emergence of the lower middle class in Britain: a discussion', in G. Crossick (ed.), *The Lower Middle Class in Britain*, Croom Helm, London, 1977, pp. 41–2.
7. Miller, *The Bon Marché*, pp. 207–11.
8. Nord, op. cit., p. 100.
9. Marguerite Böhme, *The Department Store, A Novel of Today*, D. Appleton, New York, 1912.
10. IADS *Newsletter*, 24.9.37; 2.12.37.
11. Hower, *History of Macy's*, 1943, pp. 349–60.
12. Twyman, *History of Marshall Field and Co.*, 1954, pp. 27–8.
13. A. and J. Airey, The *Bainbridges of Newcastle*, 1979, p. 105.

14. Pound, *The Fenwick Story*, 1972, p. 11.

15. Moss and Turton, *A Legend of Retailing*, 1989, pp. 287; 310; 333. D.W. Davies, *Owen Owen*, (nd), p. 48.

16. Lambert, op. cit., p. 17.

17. Pound, op. cit., p. 3; A. and J. Airey, op. cit., pp. 32–3; Moss and Turton, op. cit., p. 337.

18. Moss and Turton, op. cit., p. 287; p. 293.

19. Ibid., pp. 281; 305; 332; 26; 351.

20. *Dictionary of Business Biography*, 1984, Vol I, p. 227.

21. Adburgham, *Shops and Shopping*, p. 169.

22. Pound, op. cit., pp. 11–15.

23. D.W. Davies, op. cit., p. 14.

24. Moss and Turton, op. cit., pp. 302; 309; 315; 356; 360; 321–3.

25. D.W. Davies, op. cit., p. 22.

26. Pasdermadjian, *The Department Store*, 1954, p. 22.

27. Bentall, *My Store of Memories*, p. 47.

28. Pound, op. cit., p. 84.

29. *Dictionary of Business Biography*, 1984, Vol I, pp. 226–9.

30. Moss and Turton, op. cit., p. 316.

31. Briggs, op. cit., p. 30; A. and J. Airey, op. cit., p. 109.

32. Bentall, op. cit., p. 163.

33. Levy, *Retail Trade Associations*, 1942, p. 2.

34. D.W. Davies, op. cit., p. 82.

35. Moss and Turton, op. cit., p. 164.

36. Bentall, op. cit., p. 131.

37. Ibid., p 126; A. and J. Airey, op. cit., p. 181.

38. Corina, *Fine Silks and Oak Counters*, pp. 87–8.

39. Levy, op. cit., pp. 2–3.

40. S.P. Benson, *Counter Cultures. Saleswomen, Managers and Customers in American Department Stores 1890-1940*, University of Illinois Press, Urbana and Chicago, 1988, pp. 64–5.

41. Pasdermadjian, op. cit., pp. 87–8.

42. S.P. Benson, op. cit., pp. 49; 54.

43. IADS, *Handbook*, 1988, p. 3.

44. L.E. Neal, *Retailing and the Public*, George Allen and Unwin, London, 1932; p. vii.

45. Ibid., p. 160.

46. Ibid., pp. 185–7.

47. Ibid., pp. 187–91.

48. H. Levy, *The Shops of Britain*, Routledge and Kegan Paul, London, 1947, p. 28.

49. Ibid., pp. 28–9.

50. S.P. Benson, op. cit., p. 66.

51. Jefferys, *Retail Trading in Britain*, 1954, pp. 59–60.

52. Corina, op. cit., p. 114.

53. Briggs, op. cit., p. 139.

54. Corina, op. cit., p. 115.
55. Honeycombe, *Selfridges*, 1984, p. 75.
56. Moss and Turton, op. cit., pp. 229; 238.
57. A and J Airey, op. cit., pp. 160–3; p. 182.
58. Bentall, op. cit., pp. 160–1.

CHAPTER EIGHT

BEHIND THE COUNTER:
WORKERS AND THE DEPARTMENT
STORE

The labour history of the department store in Britain is virgin territory. Bain and Woolven's major bibliography of British industrial relations cites only four minor studies on the subject.[1] Susan Porter Benson and Theresa McBride have, of course, done major work on American and French department store labour, but the absence of scholarly activity on British stores is both puzzling and at the same time indicative of British labour history's traditional concern with the world of production.[2] Department stores were, after all, major employers by the late nineteenth century. Metropolitan stores, such as Harrods, employed over a thousand workers, as did some of the major provincial firms such as Bainbridge's and Kendal Milne. These workforces were of the same scale as those in large mills, factories and shipyards yet they lack their historian. Several factors explain this paucity of scholarly interest. First, the record of industrial relations in department stores is a quiet, even harmonious one. Major strikes and industrial relations incidents have hardly ever punctuated the smooth running of the *grand magasin*. Secondly, department stores have a history of relative economic success which has rendered them unproblematic to economic and labour historians. The fact that stores for much of their history have been dominated by women workers has also put them beyond the gaze of the labour historian's usual concern for male workers. Moreover, the failure of trade unionism to establish itself in department stores has helped to compound the above factors. It must also be noted that the popular image of deferential assistants, obsequious floor-walkers and buyers full of their own self-importance, is hardly one of a class-conscious proletariat. Yet there is a history of the department store worker, a history that includes, arguably, the most successful example of labour management in modern industry and at the same time illuminates the complex mentality of workers employed on the front line of consumption.

Department stores, with very few exceptions, emerged organically from the drapery trade and this inevitably resulted in strong continuities in employment practice. Most notable of these was the persistence of the centuries-old tradition of the 'living-in' system. This method of employment was common to many trades in earlier periods – young workers indentured to an employer would reside with their master's family, sharing the table and not leaving the household until marriage. The economic expansion of the eighteenth and nineteenth centuries tended to separate household and workplace in many industries and the practice became obsolete in most trades. Retailing was the notable exception to this process. Long opening hours, the tendency for many people to shop late at night, the need for stock to be put away after trading and set out before opening time – all served to make the residential employee a desirable asset to storekeepers. Moreover, the combination of work and lodging kept labour turnover to a minimum, greatly assisted discipline, and the dependency of the worker upon the employer helped to create a deferential mentality, ideally suited, from the master's point of view, for polite service to the public.

By the late nineteenth century, however, the 'living-in' system was becoming a subject of major public concern. The idealised situation of master, family and assistants sharing the table, amiably bound together by mutual dependencies, had long passed. With the intensification of competition in retailing, the residential costs of workers were often trimmed to a minimum, particularly amongst the middling-size drapers who were being squeezed by the new department stores.[3]

P.C. Hoffman, the future shop assistants' union official and Labour MP, recalled his own experience at such an establishment as a fourteen-year-old in 1894. Hoffman was born to the trade – having been orphaned at the age of nine, he was brought up in the Warehousemen, Clerks and Drapers School in Surrey. The School placed him with the Holborn Silk Market. His first experience was traumatic:

> That night I found myself along with half-a-dozen other young shavers in a small dirty room with six beds packed very close together, covered with coarse red and black counterpanes. The ceiling was very low and could be reached easily by stretching our young arms. Both walls and ceilings were bare, grimy and splotched. The two windows, being curtained with dirt, needed no other obscuring. The naked gas jet had a wire cage over it. The boys undressed or dressed sitting or standing on their beds – there was so little room otherwise. But there was no bed for me; I had been overlooked.

The steward with one eye, who was one of the porters, said I must sleep with one of the others. I refused. I had never done that before. He brought up from somewhere a blanket and a pillow. I lay down with them on the floor between two of those crowded beds. The gas was turned out at the main at 11.15. One of the boys lighted a piece of candle and they hunted for bugs on the wall, cracking them with slipper heels. They stuffed cracks in the wall with soap. When standing about and above me they lifted up their nightshirts and asked will this pass? will this pass? I thought my sensitive heart would break. I sobbed through that dismal night.[4]

Lower down the retail ladder, young workers were often treated with similar harshness. John Birch Thomas, the son of a grocer, spent his childhood in London and Swansea. He moved back to London in the 1870s to work and 'live-in' at a hardware store in Hornsey. Thomas's first day at work was not as bug-infested as Hoffman's, but it was still a daunting experience:

The shop closed at nine and I had to start carrying all the things in at half past eight, and then put up the shutters. They gave me some bread and cheese in the kitchen and later on one of the ladies showed me where I was to sleep. It was a small bed in the corner of a front room where the young man slept. She said I could go to bed as soon as I liked and she would wake me at a quarter to seven and show me what I had to do before the shop opened at eight. I was very tired and soon went to sleep, but there weren't enough clothes on the bed. In the morning I had to clear out the ashes in the fireplace, blacklead the stoves and light the fires. Then the lady said, 'Clean yer master's boots', and after that I had to scrub the kitchen table. Then I had a wash and carried the things out on the pavement again, after taking down the shutters. By this time it was nine o'clock and they called me into the kitchen to have breakfast. I had a cup of coffee and three lumps of bread and butter. It was rather stale and leathery but I enjoyed it.[5]

The new department stores in the second half of the nineteenth century could not risk damaging reports on workers' living conditions. Bainbridge, Owen Owen and Whiteley all invested large sums in substantial, if not luxurious, property to house their workers who 'lived in'. This accommodation was also separate from the store, reflecting the growing value of prime retail space; and possibly the fear of upsetting the sensibility of the customers who may have found the idea of workers living upstairs objectionable. Department store owners also strictly segregated the quarters of men and women.[6]

A trawl of the census enumerators' books for 1891 tends to confirm

Figure 18 Westbourne Terrace: much of this property was used by Whiteley to house his female workers. The church at the end of the street adds to the air of solid middle-class respectability (*source*: British Library).

this picture. The major stores in the north-east towns of Newcastle and Sunderland appear to have provided accommodation for male members of staff only. Bainbridge of Newcastle, for example, in 1891 used Albert House in Ellison Place and another building in Jesmond Road.[7] These two premises housed a total of eighty men and boys aged between sixteen and thirty-seven. It also needs to be noted that both of these addresses were located in highly fashionable middle-class districts. Significantly, Bainbridge's no longer used the upper floor of their Market Street store for accommodating male workers which, according to census documents, had been the practice in 1881. The majority of these workers came from the North-East, particularly the lead-mining districts, and followed the Newcastle practice of favouring Methodists in their recruitment policy. Indeed local Catholics complained, at the turn of the century, about the unwillingness of local department stores to employ members of their congregation.[8] Sunderland largely followed the Newcastle pattern. Blackett's large store only accommodated males but, perhaps reflecting lower land values in Sunderland, continued to house these workers on the premises. Their neighbour and rival Binns had, by 1891, abandoned 'living in'.[9]

In Manchester, Kendal Milne housed only twenty-six male staff at a house in nearby St Anne's Square out of a total store workforce of five hundred and fifty. Affleck and Brown on Church and Oldham Street housed twenty-eight staff, mainly women, in adjoining premises and a further fourteen women were accommodated above the store.[10] It seems reasonable to surmise that in both Manchester and Newcastle, both pioneering centres of department stores, 'living-in' was in rapid decline by the 1890s. A similar picture can be seen in Scotland where, by the turn of the century, only Jenners of Edinburgh continued 'living-in'.[11]

The system was more prevalent in London, despite higher property prices. C.R. Fender, an early critic of 'living-in', noted in 1894 that fear of trade unionism, especially after the Dock Strike and the rise of New Unionism, accounted for many employers' reluctance to ease their grip on the control of workers.[12] Hoffman's account of the system's demise illustrates the willingness of large well-known stores to abandon 'living-in'. The union campaign to end the system was usually aimed at small and middle-sized establishments against a backcloth of large stores, with much publicity, announcing the 'setting free' of their workforce. Apart from bad publicity, especially from the death of young workers caused by fires, and the publication of H.G. Wells's novel, *Kipps*, the large stores were also beginning to realise that there were less damaging forms of workforce control. The smaller stores clung tenaciously to a form of labour discipline that was virtually medieval while the large department stores were moving rapidly to a highly modern industrial relations system.[13]

Like so many other facets of department store life, control of the workforce followed patterns established in the drapery trade. To the customer, the most visible form of discipline was the floor-walker. The enduring caricature of this 'pacer of the boards' is typically a male, intensely obsequious to customers and a bully to the staff. That this image still persists despite the fact that they disappeared from even small stores decades ago is testimony to their powerful impact on the retail experience of both customers and workers. The floor-walker originated in the larger drapery establishments as a buyer of particular lines, with responsibility for the total management of their department, including recruiting and training staff, pricing, display, stock control and sales. Hoffman gives a vivid portrayal of his boss at the Holborn Silk Market during the 1890s. Initially recruited into the counting-house, he was passed on to the silk department under the control of:

My buyer – I will call him Tommy Peters – had white hair and a long white beard. What sort of collar or tie he had on I could not tell you. I never saw them; I don't believe anyone else did. He had a habit of putting his gold-rimmed eyeglasses sideways but upright in his mouth, twiddling them to and fro. He was a bully, swore like a trooper, and knew the silk trade from A to Z.[14]

The larger department stores by the 1880s were separating some of the buyers' functions with a new division of labour. The need to visit national and international suppliers and trade centres, avail themselves of knowledge on fashion and product development, attend to travelling salesmen and keep up to date with display and merchandising techniques involved often lengthy absences from the shop floor. The floor-walker's role was to take over many of the buyer's front-line duties. In the stifling world of the late nineteenth-century department store, the floor-walker became both host to the customer and the NCO of the sales staff. Their overbearing presence often annoyed foreign customers, especially those used to the democratised stores of Paris and the USA, but their role was stoutly defended in the trade press. In 1887 the *Draper's Record* insisted on their necessity for the efficient running of large establishments and called for more training for 'young aspirants to the boards'. By December of the same year, however, the same journal began to concede that the walker was becoming a figure of popular humour. While still useful in 'spotting the tabbies', the *Record*, rather tongue-in-cheek, spoke of their tendency to lunacy manifested by walkers 'bowing to costume dummies and asking, "What can I do for you madam?"'.[15]

The staff controlled by walkers were bullied far more seriously than customers just wishing to browse. The practice in many stores of imposing a system of fines upon workers depended upon walkers for its operation. Hoffman recalled being fined for returning late from a meal break at the Holborn Silk Market. The fine was accompanied by 'the rasping tongue of Tommy who, walking after you, would say: "Damn your eyes, mister! Been on 'oliday, or did you 'ave a kipper for your tea, mister?"'. Tommy would also fine the young Hoffman for a long series of offences, including 'putting a wrong date on the duplicate; for putting the wrong department against each item of sale; for not putting on the amount tendered by customer; for wrong addition; for illegibility, etc.'.[16]

The most notorious system of fines was that operated by Whiteley during the 1880s. Even the trade press, often an admirer of the

'Universal Provider's success, found his method of staff discipline obnoxious. The *Draper's Record* in 1886 reported that Whiteley's new rule book contained 176 offences that carried fines and that some workers found that 'they had no wages to collect as they had all gone on fines'. The journal also noted that other stores imposed fines, but this income was paid into the staff benevolent fund. Whiteley, however, 'kept them for himself'. The 'Universal Provider' was reported to patrol his establishment 'like a rearing lion' and that instant dismissal had replaced one month's notice.[17] Whiteley's regime was widely regarded in the national press to be the cause of his frequent fires, started, it was claimed, by disgruntled staff. It is, of course, impossible to say whether or not these allegations were true. It is worth noting that when Hoffman joined the store as an apprentice in the late 1890s fines had been abandoned, but Whiteley's cutting wit and policy of instant dismissal remained:

As I have already stated (or as he did for me) they had no fines. Instead there was each day a 'late list' exhibited in a glass case. In this was given the name of the offender, with his department, his excuse, and Whiteley's comments scrawled thereon in red ink.

Name of latecomer	Excuse	Remarks
Jones (Cabinets)	Unwell	No, he is not – lazy fellow
Smith (Silks)	Illness at home	Clear him out
Robinson (Drapery)	Relation ill	Fine excuse
Williams (Hosiery)	Lost the train	Yes, and will lose head, too, if not careful[18]

Juxtaposed with the flow of critical reports on fines and other aspects of work conditions were glowing accounts of staff–employer relations in the Parisian *grands magasins*. Despite its unease over the 'democratisation of luxury' system of retailing, the *Record* was, nevertheless, a great admirer of the working conditions and staff benefits in such stores as the Bon Marché. It was reported that while Boucicaut's employees worked a twelve-hour day, they enjoyed 'very good meal and refreshment arrangements'.[19] A few weeks later, the *Record* carried an obituary on Madame Boucicaut and singled out her labour relations policy, profit-sharing and partnership schemes for favourable comment.

The major lesson that the Boucicaut system taught the wider world of retailing was, as Miller has pointed out, that the store encapsulated 'public virtues as well as private achievements'. Thanks to refined public relations skills, the Bon Marché 'portrayed a department store world far from the menace that many envisaged'.[20] This linkage between civic virtue and business, with its obvious economic benefits, could not be achieved by vicious methods of staff control like those used at Whiteley's. Reports in prestigious journals, such as the *Pall Mall Gazette,* on conditions at Whiteley's, promised to damage the entire industry.

The vast majority of major department stores avoided the undesirable publicity that Whiteley attracted. Their proprietors, from Bournemouth to Newcastle, were often the personification of local civic pride with their stores rivalling and complementing the new town halls in city centre dignity. Moreover, the important political and religious activities of many proprietors increased the department stores' respectability. The owners jealously guarded this reputation and were fully aware of its importance to economic success. Poor staff relationships and their attendant publicity could quickly shatter this veneer of civic respectability but it is worth noting that no important store proprietor with a major local profile, either political or religious, had his image sullied by strikes and labour scandals. They did not repeat the mistakes made by many of their industrial counterparts, usually Liberals, who had their political careers broken by labour disputes. The large stores also took the lead in reducing working hours, as Winstanley has pointed out: 'In the West-End, the Mecca of the affluent shopper, few stores remained open after 6.00 pm on weekdays and Saturday was accepted as a half-day by 1894. A similar situation existed in centres of other large cities.'[21]

Customers played an important role in establishing the Saturday half holiday. As early as 1860 a group of prominent society women advertised in *The Times* informing store owners that they had 'agreed to abstain from shopping after 2 o'clock on Saturdays, to enable trading establishments to close at an early hour, in furtherance of the Volunteer Movement'.[22] It is hard to establish whether or not the ranks of the volunteers were increased with young salesmen, but with leading personalities such as Charles Dickens actively supporting the Early Closing Movement, the large stores complied with the Saturday half holiday movement.[23] By 1886 the Select Committee on Shop Hours reported that the length of the working week in large London stores was as follows:

SCHOOLBRED'S (700 assistants)

Winter months	8.30 to 6
Summer months	8.30 to 7
Saturdays	Close at 2 P.M. all the year round

MARSHALL AND SNELGROVE'S (550 assistants)

Winter months	8.15 to 6.30
Summer months	8.15 to 7
Saturdays	Close at 2 P.M.

JOHN BARKER'S (400 assistants)

Winter months (six)	8.30 to 6.30
Summer months(three)	8.30 to 8
Other seasons	8.30 to 7 or 7.30

SPENCER, TURNER, AND BOLDERO'S (650 assistants)

All the year	8 to 7
Saturdays	Close at 2 P.M.

DEBENHAM'S (400–500 assistants)

Winter months	7 to 6
Summer months	7 to 7
Saturdays	Close at 2 P.M.[24]

The reality was that large stores found long hours to be unprofitable. Fixed overheads such as heating, lighting and staff meals soaked up whatever small advantage that could be gained by late closing. It is no surprise to find the department stores as major supporters and contributors to the Early Closing Association. This organisation, formed in 1842, was an amalgamation of concerned customers, political and religious figures and large storekeepers. Most of their battles were directed towards the small traders, often family businesses, that served a largely working-class clientele. These customers themselves often worked long hours and were dependent upon small stores that remained open late. Some even preferred to shop after the pubs and music halls closed: 'At six o'clock you could see crowds waiting to go in, the women taking their shopping bags with them. Then when they turned out at eleven they'd start their Saturday night shopping'.[25] But this market sector was far removed from the city centre department store, and the conclusion that the much-publicised membership of the Early Closing Association, by the large establishments, was mainly for public relations purposes is inescapable. Even the Holborn Silk Market deducted two-pence per week from workers' wages for the Association.[26]

Hoffman expressed exasperation at the deductions from his weekly wage of two shillings and sixpence. Apart from the Association levy, these deductions included twopence for boot cleaning, a service never provided, and a penny-halfpenny for the 'Library' which consisted of 'a few old books in the bookcase – Smiles' *Self Help*, and so on – never any additions'. Board and lodging was a major part of Hoffman's income; in kind, as we have seen above – the accommodation was far from desirable and the food appeared to be of a similar standard: 'all I got for breakfast and tea was bread and butter and tea from the urn'. When meat was served it was usually 'roughly and savagely served, and as savagely gulped by the young assistants'.[27] Life in the larger establishments was more comfortable. The fear of customer disquiet over being served by 'half-starved' assistants was ever present. Whiteley, hardly renowned for his generosity to staff, provided his workers with meals that may have mitigated to some extent the otherwise harsh regime:

> The dining-rooms at Westbourne Grove compare favourably with those of any other large house in London, and the comfort of the assistants who make use of them is much studied, even to the substitution of electric light for gas... In each dining-room there are from five to ten tables; each table is presided over by a professional carver, assisted by a waiter in a neat, clean uniform, and the meals are served with lightning-like rapidity – five minutes sufficing to supply the wants of the whole table. There are different joints on almost every table, and an assistant may send the waiter to any part of the room for a cut from the joint of his fancy... Each assistant is allowed a pint of good beer for his dinner, and another for supper. There are no calls upon him to serve customers during dinner hours... There are fresh joints for each party, and they are served smoking-hot from the ovens.[28]

Employers, even large ones, appear to have been less generous to their workers when it came to providing seats behind the counter. After the failure of Sir John Lubbock's Bill to restrict shop hours in 1871, a new organisation, the Shop Hours Labour League, emerged to campaign for state control of opening hours. Open to employers and workers on an equal footing, this body marked the beginning of the split in the Early Closing Movement between those who favoured voluntary restriction and those who perceived legislation as the only solution.

By the 1880s the League was becoming increasingly concerned with the health of shop workers. The League's president, Thomas Sutherst, pointed out that:

Incessant walking for twenty-four hours was considered one of the most unbearable tortures to which witches in former times were subjected ... The shop assistant in these days is obliged to submit to the intolerable fatigue of standing for periods, varying according to the locality, from thirteen to seventeen hours a day.[29]

The figures on the opening hours of the large London stores cited above suggest that Sutherst was primarily referring to smaller establishments. *Punch* and other journals campaigned for the provision of seats for assistants in the late 1870s and 1880s (see Figure 27) but the problem touched a deep nerve with employers. The Select Committee of 1886 noted:

The shopkeeper imagines that if a customer were to enter his establishment and find a number of assistants sitting down behind the counter, an impression would be engendered that the shop was not well patronized and did but little business.[30]

Workers were instructed to 'look busy' in order to maintain the ethos of a successful establishment. Some stores complied with the campaign for seats, which were visibly positioned so as to be sighted by concerned customers, but the Select Committee found their usage restricted. Some employers imposed a fine of sixpence for workers caught sitting down and it was reported that:

One very large establishment boasts of the seats it provides for its assistants, but anyone found sitting down is reprimanded the first time, and dismissed on a repetition of the offence. The assistant who worked there himself, added to this information that there were mirrors on all sides in which every movement was reflected.[31]

Workers did have some means of recourse against harsh working regimes apart from the sympathy of customers and social commentators. We have already noted the claims that Whiteley's fires were started by disgruntled staff. This could not be proved, but it takes little imagination to realise the impact of such allegations upon Whiteley and other store proprietors. A similar notoriously difficult area is the incidence of staff theft. Whiteley was an incessant prosecutor of both customers and workers caught stealing in the Westbourne Grove store. Some of his assistants were *habitués* of a gambling salon, The Monmouth Club, set up near the store in 1878. A sacked salesman of Whiteley's organised the theft of money and goods by workers who frequented the club, which was also used by a receiver. After a major legal case the club was closed in 1881 but staff theft continued. In 1886 a combination of young assistants defrauded Whiteley of large sums by manipulating documents and receipts. More major cases were uncovered in 1889 and throughout this period many staff were prosecuted for minor theft. One young man caught stealing small sums told the magistrates that he was recouping the losses that he had suffered from Whiteley's fines.[32]

Whether or not theft and fire constituted a guerrilla warfare campaign of industrial relations by Whiteley's workers is a moot point. We have no hard evidence of a 'Captain Swing' of Westbourne Grove apart from rumour and press speculation. Similarly, although labour historians have described the 'industrial relations of theft' in other industries, it is difficult to distinguish between organised or opportunistic stealing on the one hand, and the revenge of a harshly treated employee on the other.[33] What can be measured, however, is the softening of Whiteley's regime during the 1890s. Apart from copious amounts of meat served steaming hot by waiters, fines were abandoned and Whiteley paid increasing attention to the welfare and social well-being of his staff. As early as 1870 Whiteley formed the Kildare Athletic Club for his employees. Silver plate prizes presented to the winners of competitions were the main incentives along with an extra chop or steak at dinner for those in training.[34] The athletic club was joined by a rowing club in the late 1870s but it was in the late 1880s and 1890s that the firm's leisure activities were greatly expanded. The employees were given their own building in 1885, the Hatherley Institute, which became the home for the company's Musical Union and the Choral Society in 1896. A drama society was formed in this period; these new clubs were also used by both sexes which reflected the growing importance of women in the Westbourne Grove workforce.[35]

Whiteley was far from unique in the provision of staff social facilities. These organisations were in some respects an organic response to the problem posed by an increasing workforce, many of whom lived in. Bainbridge, in the same period, formed the Albert House Benevolent Society which provided sickness and holiday benefits for staff. Employees suffering from illness were often sent on a sea voyage and the firm funded numerous social clubs and paid for 'guest artistes' to entertain workers during the evening. The Newcastle store also boasted several football and cricket teams which often played early morning games before commencing work.[36] Jones Brothers of Holloway were frequently singled out for praise in the trade press for their progressive policy in the provision of staff social facilities. At the Peter Jones store staff conditions and facilities were so good that the firm experienced intense competition amongst would-be employees.[37]

The mushrooming of welfare and social facilities was eagerly reported and encouraged by the trade press. The *Draper's Record* had run many features on the large Parisian stores and held the Boucicauts in high regard. The Bon Marché, with its large workforce and impeccable public image, was the model to follow according to the *Record*.[38] The Boucicauts' formula of longish hours, but generous meal breaks and high-quality food, welfare benefits and profit-sharing moulded into an intensely paternalistic system, promised a loyal, hard-working labour force whose close identity with the company guaranteed first-class customer service, and were the store's best advertisement. The majority of large British stores quickly absorbed the Parisian lesson. In structural terms, the growth of stores' workforce size, over five hundred staff, was far from uncommon by the late 1880s, demanding new managerial techniques and policies. Moreover, the new forms of internal display which invited customers to wander, and the adoption by the early 1900s, in some stores at least, of the 'walk-around' principle, required sales staff to rely more on their own initiative, rather than being instructed by the 'walker'.

Previous writers on women shop workers have been somewhat ambiguous about the level of skill that the occupation required. The Cadbury investigation into women's work in Birmingham in 1906 found that 'some girls are apprenticed for one or two years ... They receive no wages, but the familiar "pocket money"'. There was a clearly defined hierarchy in Birmingham of women retail workers, the most skilled and prized by their employers being found 'in the costume departments of large shops. Here the assistants may receive about 30s per week'. Such high wages were paid only to this elite, but such levels of remuneration indicate that knowledge of textiles, fashion, good personal grooming and impeccable manners, were marketable skills.[39] Lee Holcombe has analysed the decline in the 'craft' nature of retail work from the mid-nineteenth century. The growth of large stores, the mass production of standardised products, advertising and branding – all served to deskill retail labour. There is much truth in this analysis. The 'craft' dealer, who cut, weighed, measured and finished much of his stock, was a declining figure in late Victorian society. Many store workers were, according to Holcombe, doing little more than 'keeping the stock tidy and showing merchandise across the counters and receiving payment'. Moreover, Holcombe has demonstrated, albeit from imperfect census data, the feminisation of the workforce after 1870.[40]

Much department store work, on the surface, would fit Holcombe's description. Yet the expansion of departments, new products and a greater range of merchandise, also created demand for new skills amongst the workforce. Customers, for example, would expect sales staff to offer advice on a wide variety of competing products in departments such as china, glassware and hardware. This would involve more than 'showing merchandise across the counter'. The trade press was certainly alert to this problem. In 1887 the *Draper's Record* was calling for a national system of technical education and in 1889 it was advocating John Wanamaker's system of staff management and training.[41] The absence of college courses tailored for the retail industry forced some stores to introduce their own training programmes. Debenham and Freebody, for example, had its own education department in 1898 which, apart from routine staff training, held three evening classes per week for young assistants on commercial affairs. By the beginning of the present century, Harrods was calling its young trainees 'students', and smaller provincial stores such as Eaden Lilley's of Cambridge would only recruit 'Grammar School' girls.[42]

This last point reaches the central feature of the department store industrial relations policy which emerged in the late nineteenth and early twentieth centuries. Young John Thomas, in the 1870s, relied on the situations vacant columns of the many newspapers that were available to unemployed assistants in London in the City News Rooms in Ludgate Circus. For a one-penny admission to this four-storey building, the unemployed hopefuls gained access to warmth, washing facilities, companionship, as well as employment news both verbal and printed. The *Christian World* was a particularly popular publication amongst shop assistants. Thomas recalls how:

> At the City News Rooms I first saw the paper called the *Christian World*. It had a lot of good reading and a large number of advertisements for assistants in the drapery and grocery trade. Some of the fellows agreed that it was a good medium for getting 'cribs', but the jobs were mostly in country towns and as leaving London was unthinkable the paper didn't interest them. One

chap said that the advertisers believed that if they engaged a young person through that paper they would get one who was religious and had no bad habits, and consequently would accept lower wages than a more worldly one would.[43]

In the late 1890s Hoffman claimed that thousands were attracted to city centre stores by advertisements in the *Christian World* and the Irish and Welsh press. But employers were becoming much more selective. Hoffman had his photograph taken for the purpose of 'cribbing' by post:

> It shows a clean-shaven, round, unsophisticated type of face with eyeglass on a black cord, with top hat, frock coat, umbrella. In that very long queue all of us were dressed like that. Not many with an unsophisticated type of face (I was to lose mine with time) and no other with eyeglasses and black cord, but certainly all with top hats, frock coats and umbrellas.

Hoffman's distinguished appearance and clothing provided by the Draper's School appears to have set him apart from the rest of the queue of unemployed assistants when he gained a position at Whiteley's (see Figure 19).

It is not surprising to find social commentators of the period expressing ambiguity about the social position of store assistants. Cadbury reported in 1906 that 'Shop assistants form a class by themselves for many reasons'.[44] Elsewhere in this survey they are grouped with schoolteachers and collectors and are referred to as 'the better class of women', along with clerks.[45] One store worker informed the Cadbury team that:

> You do not get such liberty in a shop as you do in a factory for the hours are much longer but sometimes you get amongst girls who use language they ought not to in a factory. It is not very often you hear it in a shop for the girls have to talk properly and this is another very good use which makes up for the extra hours.

Despite the hours, this worker noted the tendency amongst her colleagues for:

> dress and following the fashions of the world such as regular theatre-going and dancing and out somewhere every night of the week and if all the other girls in the shop follow these fashions you get a very trying life …[46]

Figure 19 P.C. Hoffman's 'Cribbing' photograph (*source*: British Library).

This informant clearly saw this life-style as a threat to both her deeply held Christian beliefs and the respectability of her profession and it was this ethos of respectability that formed the common ground between the worker and the employer.

Dropped aitches and expressions such as 'cor blimey' did not form part of the genteel language used by staff and customers in department stores. Before the 1920s the quality of the store defined the products sold, rather than brand names and labels. Proprietors assiduously nurtured an atmosphere of respectability which provided the common ground between the often wide variation in the class composition of customers. Staff were often recruited from diverse social backgrounds:

> Girls from every stratum of society were found serving behind counters, the daughters of artisans, of agricultural labourers, of skilled mechanics, of struggling and of prosperous shopkeepers, of clerks and of professional men.[47]

Holcombe further notes that for 'many young people of the working classes, becoming a shop assistant represented a definite step upwards in the social scale, while for those of the middle classes it opened the way of life of supposedly respectable work'.[48] This quest for respectability, particularly amongst women, presented employers with an abundance of potentially deferential and, because of their sex, cheap labour. It is doubtful, however, if many daughters of agricultural labourers made it to the counters of the larger stores. The cost of clothing that the new recruit had to wear and provide was prohibitive, and the Cadbury team despaired at the failure of trade unionism amongst shop assistants because of the large number of women workers who accepted 'pocket money' wages in return for respectable work.[49]

Indeed some families were willing to pay dearly to gaurantee their daughters respectable positions. Young Helen Roberts's parents paid £25 in 1917 for her premium apprenticeship at Folkestone's up-market Plummer Rodis store. Helen's wage was a princely one shilling per week plus board and lodging in the company's hostel. Her spirited sister was caught roller skating on Folkestone's municipal rink and was sacked, as 'nice Plummer's girls did not allow themselves to be seen in such a place as a public skating rink'. Helen persevered with Plummer's strict regime, which included having to be back in the hostel every night by 9.30 pm, under the watchful eyes of two Baptist manageresses. Nevertheless, on completing her apprenticeship, she was poached by another store as a showroom assistant on a salary of £60 per year.[50]

This increasingly feminine labour force was quick to absorb the house atmosphere. They were part of the store's public image, and its class and reputation was also theirs. If 'pocket money' wages were fairly common in Britain, a similar situation was present in the USA. Even Marshal Field's official historians noted the phenomenon of the State Street store's women workers accepting lower wages than Field's rivals because, in the words of John Shed, the store boss, 'the prestige of working there was worth the difference'.[51] As we shall see below, the same trend prevailed in Britain, but it was to take more than respectability and store image to secure a successful industrial relations system. The gentility of the store could be shattered by bad publicity on employment policy as witnessed by the young Margaret Bondfield's exposés of working life in large shops and small department stores that were printed in the *Daily Chronicle* in 1898.[52] Moreover, Hoffman and his comrades were actively attempting to recruit workers to the new assistants' union and both Bondfield and Hoffman were quick to realise that bad publicity was the Achilles' heel of retail employers.

The employers' response to the threat of a unionised workforce, in alliance with public opinion, was to institutionalise and strengthen the organic system of paternalism which had gradually been emerging since the 1880s. The social clubs and recreational organisations which had sprung up as a response to the problems of the 'living-in' system took on a new importance. Buildings and sports fields, relatively elaborate facilities and equipment, became normal benefits of department store workers throughout Britain. Yet for paternalism to be really effective, the visible presence of the *'pater familias'* was essential. In the early years of the department store, proprietors such as Owen Owen greeted both customers and staff as they entered the store.[53] As early as 1869 grateful employees presented Louis Cohen, the managing partner of Lewis's of Liverpool, with a medallion. Up until 1922 Cohen was the dominant personality of the Liverpool store. Briggs has noted:

> He was always the first customer each morning to visit Hill's the barbers, in Ranelagh Street, and then attired in frock coat and silk hat, he would make his formal entrance into the store. 'My pleasure is my business', he is reported to have said. 'I go down to business every morning at 8.45, and it pleases me very much to see my thousand hands come to business.'[54]

It is interesting to note that by early this century a 9.00 am start was becoming the norm for staff. At Brown's of Chester most workers arrived at half-past nine. The onerous task of starting work at 7.30 am to dust and lay out stock was, by early this century, reserved for young juniors, 'every other day taking it in turns'. But this was a temporary experience, ended by promotion into a hierarchical workforce where:

The male assistants always wore morning coats, black tie, white vest. Spats weren't allowed. No spats. And the female assistants always wore black. I really think they look smartest in black, but it's really because it makes such a background to any goods they are selling. If they are holding up a most beautiful gown, it shows the material up so well.

This old employee of Brown's, interviewed in the Mass Observation 1946 study, was obviously proud to be both a special effects prop as well as an actor in the theatre of the Brown's enterprise.[55]

The paternalistic regime of Brown's, by 1914, closely resembled the late nineteenth-century Parisian ideal of equating virtue with the department store. Chester was, by then, beginning to reap the benefits of its new economic role as a shire town retailing centre that had been defined and developed by the Brown–Harris dynasties. An article in the local press, which enthused on the luxury and style of the store, concluded with an appeal to a future of sumptuous surroundings and a polite, contented workforce:

> Perhaps also it may inspire Cheshire ladies with the local patriotism that patronises Cheshire shops, advances the prosperity of Cheshire trade and supports the employment of Cheshire Labour.[56]

The success of paternalism in department store organisation was dependent upon the continuation of family ownership. Despite the mergers and groupings of the 1920s, control tended to remain in the hands of trader dynasties. Even large groups such as Debenham's retained a federal structure of ownership and control which assured the survival of these entrepreneurial families. The highly centralised John Lewis Partnership, which bought Bainbridge of Newcastle in 1953, kept G.V.M. Bainbridge on as managing director up until his retirement in 1974. Members of these owner families, usually male, continued to be highly active in the day-to-day running of their stores. They prided themselves on their ability to address as many of their staff as possible by name; indeed one present-day senior executive told the author of spending every Saturday in the store from the age of eleven doing minor tasks and being quizzed every night by his father on the names of the employees whom he had encountered.

Rowan Bentall, whose recollection of his parents' return from a world cruise was cited in the previous chapter, continued his account of the staff reception which combined theatre with ritual:

The music was almost drowned by the ovation as my parents stepped on to the platform. At that moment the lights dimmed and behind them there was illuminated a huge map of the world on which the chief places of their tour lit up in succession while, over the top, brilliant red neon lights flashed 'Welcome Home'.

Obviously overcome with emotion, the charismatic 'Mr Leonard' gave an almost godlike address to his assembled employees:

You have all heard a considerable amount about 'A merchant venturer' and perhaps a little about 'the phantom king of Kingston' but in my heart I would rather you knew me as a friend, and a deep friend, of you all. The more I travelled the more I felt the necessity of keeping close to one another. I cannot do without any one of you, and I do not want any one of you to do without me, and if in the few years that remain to me as head of this business I can be of any added service to any one, or as many as like to take the advantage, I am determined to do so in every way which lies in my power.[57]

Bentall's neon-lit paternalism was not unusual. Many store histories detail similar events that took place in the 1930s. The workers of Bainbridge's, for example, were occasionally invited to the family's country mansion for various jubilee celebrations. This mansion, now a hotel, is still visited by Bainbridge's dwindling group of interwar employees who use the facilities for major family events.[58]

The longevity of family ownership and control served to cement the structure of department store paternalism well into the twentieth century. Labour historians such as Patrick Joyce have analysed the decline of paternalism in manufacturing industry caused by a widening share ownership and the withdrawal from business by the descendants of industrial magnates.[59] The reverse process seems to have been at work in the world of department stores. This must not be viewed as the clinging to traditional methods by rather amateurish managers. Rather it was a system of industrial relations that was constantly being refined. Indeed department stores were amongst the first industries to embrace scientific management and Edward Filene and the International Association of Department Stores served to nurture an extremely efficient and forward-thinking managerial culture. But treating workers as numbers whose sole purpose was the maximisation of profit could never be part of the department store milieu. Indeed the Association was highly critical of Henry Ford's labour policies during an era when the

Association promoted concepts of welfare combined with the tradition of paternalism.[60]

The *ad hoc* nature of staff benefits, ranging from free meals on rainy days to cruise tickets for favoured sick employees, gave way to a more systematic style of welfare provision. By the First World War many major stores retained the services of a doctor for workers.[61] At least one week's paid holiday became the industry's norm and staff discount began to replace commission on sales. Bainbridge, like many stores, started to phase out commission during the 1890s, a period when there was much concern in the industry over zealous assistants 'over-flogging' certain items. By 1898 the board of Bainbridge held monthly meetings with buyers and floor-walkers to determine the percentage of discount for staff for the following four weeks.[62] Staff discount was a highly effective benefit; it overcame the problem of disruptive rivalry between staff and departments that was endemic to the commission system; it promoted a sense of corporate loyalty amongst workers; and it allowed staff access to goods which otherwise could have been prohibitively expensive. Moreover, by facilitating greater access to the store's merchandise, the staff's identity with, and loyalty to, the company was much enhanced. 'House' journals and magazines which became synonymous with the larger establishments were common during the 1920s and 1930s and served a similar purpose.[63] British stores never matched the welfare provisions of the Parisian *grands magasins* analysed by McBride or even some American stores such as Kaufmans of Pittsburgh, whose workers were provided with holiday facilities at Bear Run, the future site of Frank Lloyd Wright's Fallingwater, built for the Kaufman family. But they were in advance of the majority of British industry in staff welfare.[64]

The new welfare systems operated alongside the idiosyncratic nature of paternalism. After all stores strove to keep and nurture their individuality and the personality of the owner-manager was central to this aim. Bentall's, the large Kingston store, furnishes a good example of this process. By the 1920s, Bentall's provided their staff with a clinic, pensions and preferential savings schemes. The firm even adopted a private family allowance system – every full-time employee with more than two children under the age of fifteen received an extra five shillings a week for a third child and an extra 2s 6d per week for each additional child. The matron of the clinic, Miss Clifton, was provided with a car to visit sick members of staff, who also received food parcels and new-laid eggs from the firm via the motoring matron.[65] Overarching these institutional benefits was the powerful personality of the managing director, Leonard Bentall. Known to all his staff as 'Mr Leonard' (a common feature in virtually all family-owned stores was to address the male members by their Christian names), he would pace the Kingston store dishing out discipline and largesse in consecutive sentences. One new worker, employed as a humble porter, was tapped on the shoulder by Mr Leonard soon after commencing employment and was told, 'I hear jolly good reports about you. Stick to me and you will never be out of work for the rest of your life.'[66] 'Mr Leonard's' son, 'Mr Rowan', has recounted an incident of his father's munificence that perhaps would not be so welcome today:

> my father was leaving the store through the despatch department; he noticed a driver holding the side of his face. 'What's the matter?', my father enquired. 'I'm afraid I've got toothache', the man answered. My father got the driver to open his mouth and examined his teeth – although I was never aware that he had any ability in dentistry! 'H'mm', my father said, 'come up to my office tomorrow morning.' By the time the driver presented himself my father had already made the necessary arrangements with a dentist. At Bentall's expense, the driver had all his teeth out and a set of dentures fitted.[67]

Even senior management were subject to Mr Leonard's individual attention. Geese and turkeys were dispensed to the higher ranks each Christmas. The geese came from Bentall's own flock and the turkeys from a local butcher. Each bird was individually inspected and labelled with the recipient's name by Mr Leonard, no doubt taking their year's performance into account.[68] We may pause for a chuckle at the activities of Mr Leonard, from free dentures to graded turkeys. Cynics may even scorn at supposedly outmoded, neo-Victorian management methods. Yet Bentall's never had a strike and their workforce appear to have been generally content. It is also worth reflecting that promises of 'a job for life' were not easily given by this dynamic, hard-working businessman. Moreover, his son's account of Bentall's development has many recollections of his father's ability to spot and deal with shirkers and unsatisfactory employees. It is more productive to view Mr Leonard's staff policies, both institutional and personal, as a sustained process of creating and maintaining a relatively happy, industrious workforce that was imbued with the firm's corporate identity. The existence of such a workforce was the only basis upon which promises of lifetime employment could be made. It is also worth remembering

that industrial sociologists have long been aware of the explosive potential for militancy that is latent within workers employed in paternalistic
regimes, a militancy that can quickly surface when workers experience
the betrayal of broken promises.[69] Bentall's skilfully avoided this potential
hazard, their workers enjoying the company's prestige as Kingston's
premier business institution. Indeed Bentall's recently realised the Boucicaut ambition of combining civic and business virtue when Kingston
named its new town centre shopping area the 'Bentall's Centre'.

One proprietor who experienced the wrath of his workers when he
broke the 'paternalist's promise' was John Lewis of Oxford Street. Similar
to other owners, Lewis had a reputation for prowling the floors of his
West End store, dishing out both discipline and generosity. Sales staff
who turned up for work 'with a ragged pair of shoes in wet weather'
would be sent to the shoe department for a new pair.[70] But Lewis,
who feared neither 'God nor Devil', failed to mellow with age. His
cantankerous managerial style, which included instant dismissal for no
apparent reason, became the hallmark of the eighty-four-year-old during
the difficult period immediately after the First World War. By 1920
Lewis had managed to retain the services of just fifty-four out of the
1914 workforce of four hundred and fifty.[71] Staff discontent was further
fuelled by rapid inflation and the success of the Shop Assistants' Union
in gaining a substantial wage increase at the Army and Navy stores in
the Autumn of 1919 after a short strike action. The Union, which had
previously failed to recruit significantly in department stores, organised
the Army and Navy workers, whose wages had been greatly reduced
by inflation.[72]

After a brief strike which won public support, probably because of
widespread disenchantment with the military high command, the gen-
erals and admirals who ran this pseudo-co-operative submitted to the
workers' demands. Lewis proved far more stubborn than the retired
officers of Victoria. After a bitter six-week dispute, the workers ended
the strike but refused to go back to Lewis's, many having found work
elsewhere.[73]

A similar strike at Beatties of Wolverhampton later in the year also
ended in defeat and by 1922 the Union had retreated from their toe-
hold in the larger stores. The fear of unemployment amongst shop
workers was to snuff out the brief period of confidence that followed
the Army and Navy settlement.[74] One noticeable feature, however, of
this upsurge in militancy was the organisation and leadership of the

strikes. Union officers such as Hoffman played a part, but the brunt of the campaign was orchestrated by floor-walkers and buyers. These two groups did not suffer the economic hardship experienced by sales staff, but they were responsible for mainstream discipline and upholding the 'house values'. The rapid decline in real wage levels tore the fabric of paternalism and made their position in the workplace extremely difficult. The need to retain the respect of those below them pushed them to the fore. The motion for the Lewis's workers to strike was moved by Mr Turner Thomas, a buyer, and seconded by a shopwalker.[75] The majority of Lewis's strikers never returned to the Oxford Street store, many following their buyers and walker to the more enlightened paternalistic regimes in Kensington High Street.[76] Lewis's obstinacy and the upsurge of anger amongst his workers shocked the wider world of department stores – the lesson that paternalistic systems of store management did have limits of worker tolerance was quickly absorbed by others, especially by John Spedan Lewis, the heir to the Oxford Street store.

Young Lewis took control in 1914 of the Peter Jones store in Chelsea which had been acquired by his father in 1905. The Sloane Square store had a reputation of being a model employer, but at the time of the Lewis take-over it was experiencing a poor economic performance. Spedan Lewis, perhaps reacting against his father's aggressive managerial style, experimented with the industrial relations system of Peter Jones after the First World War, which culminated in the introduction of an employees' profit-sharing scheme in 1920. By 1926 Spedan Lewis inherited the Oxford Street store where he introduced the profit-sharing system that was practised at Peter Jones's. Profit-sharing was formalised in 1929 when Spedan Lewis established the John Lewis Partnership Limited as a trust settlement.[77]

Lewis was as aggressive as his competitors in acquiring other stores. In the two decades after 1933, the Partnership bought Jessops, Nottingham (1933); Knight and Lee, Southsea; Tyrell and Green, Southampton (1934); D.H. Evans of Oxford Street (1935); the Waitrose grocery chain (1937); the fifteen stores of the Selfridge Provincial Group (1940); and Bainbridge, Newcastle (1953). All of these stores became part of the Partnership and all employees benefited from the profit-sharing scheme. Spedan Lewis was undoubtedly one of the most successful store owners of the twentieth century. His stealthy expansion avoided the financial pitfalls and damaging publicity that surrounded the growth of other groups, particularly Debenham's. Moreover, this expansion was thoroughly modern in the form that it took. Despite the retention of the original names of some stores, such as Knight and Lee, and Bainbridge, all the Partnership stores took on a clear corporate identity, and paternalistic management was supposedly replaced by employee participation.

The Partnership has long proved an enigma to industrial relations experts and market analysts. The Partnership ideal has presented to the public a different image from that of 'civic virtue', so long nourished by other stores. These images of happy workers enjoying a genuine five-day week, sharing in decision-making, and benefiting from the Partnership profits can be perceived as forming a portrait of 'corporate virtue'. Visually, the stores in the group are distinguished by their understated stylishness and lack of frivolity, a material rationality that is reflected in the group's economic slogan of 'Never Knowingly Undersold'. This vision of the rational, caring organisation was nurtured amongst the employees in the pages of the *Gazette*, the company journal which first appeared in 1918. Medical services, generous paid holidays and pension schemes were all established in the interwar period, which consolidated the image of a new Utopian organisation operating in a world of often rapacious capitalism.[78] Yet how far does the popular perception of the Partnership match the reality? Are the workers happier and better paid that their counterparts in other stores? And does the group operate a genuine form of industrial democracy?

Such questions certainly taxed the talents of Allan Flanders and his distinguished team of Oxford industrial relations experts when they studied the Partnership during the 1960s. The Oxford team were keen that 'The familiar distinction between ownership and control need not be laboured.' But while paying short shrift to this Marxist concept their evidence clearly shows that Spedan Lewis and his wife owned most of the group up until 1950.[79] They also discovered that:

> the Chairman's view of what is good for the business takes precedence over all other considerations. Indeed it would appear that the Chairman has greater power than either his counterparts in the more usual kind of private enterprise or the heads of the nationalised industries.[80]

Another point cited by Flanders, '[the Chairman] has no anxiety about take-over bids', is well worth pondering when we consider the frenetic climate of mergers in the department store world during the 1920s, the decade when the structure of the Partnership was established.[81]

Table 3 Staff Census: John Lewis Partnership, 1931

Mean weekly remuneration	Men and boys		Women and girls	
	Number	Average age	Number	Average age
Over £24	16	44	3	48
£18 to £24	5	35	3	40
£10 10s. to £18	20	42	13	39
£8 14s. to £10.10s.	7	39	10	40
£8 14s.	4	35	4	40
£8 8s.	1	28	1	53
£8 2s.	7	45	2	49
£7 16s.	5	39	9	37
£7 10s.	6	43	9	35
£7 4s.	–	–	4	49
£6 18s.	11	45	2	32
£6 12s.	9	41	6	32
£6 6s.	24	37	22	34
£6	18	35	4	32
£5 14s.	18	35	14	37
£5 8s.	22	42	4	43
£5 2s.	49	40	41	31
£4 16s.	16	47	6	34
£4 13s.	27	35	17	30
£4 10s.	7	32	7	36
£4 7s.	23	39	12	38
£4 4s.	25	35	36	31
£4 1s.	27	33	11	28
£3 18s.	25	37	23	34
£3 15s.	21	39	24	32
£3 12s.	33	36	56	30
£3 9s.	23	32	28	31
£3 6s.	10	36	58	31
£3 3s.	9	33	34	30
£3	13	30	86	28
£2 17s.	5	31	51	28
£2 14s.	14	39	70	32
£2 11s.	8	35	111	30
£2 8s.	14	24	145	28
£2 5s.	6	26	101	27
£2 2s.	9	21	126	27
£1 19s.	3	20	51	23
£1 16s.	18	24	107	23
£1 13s.	10	28	72	23
£1 10s.	24	19	91	20
£1 7s.	15	17	43	19
£1 4s.	17	17	42	21
£1 1s.	9	17	41	18
18s.	8	16	16	16
15s.	5	15	7	16
12s.	–	–	11	15
9s.	–	–	33	14
Total	**650**	**34 yrs**	**1,663**	**27 yrs**

Source: Draper's Record, 6 February 1932.

This may cast the Partnership in a somewhat conspiratorial and cynical light and we need to keep in mind that staff conditions were often well in advance of other stores and certainly most of British industry. Evidence does emerge, however, which challenges the Partnership's image of a caring, democratic institution. For example, in February 1932 the *Draper's Record* published the Partnership's staff census which included wages, the gender composition of the workforce and details of staff turnover (see Table 3).

Whilst wages and the age/sex profile of the company roughly comply to the industry's norm, the numbers of workers who left in the previous twelve months was fairly high. Out of 2,313 'partners' in 1931, 341 left and 241 were sacked. This represents over twenty-five per cent of the work-force leaving the Partnership in the depths of the Depression when unemployment was at its peak and jobs were at a premium. Moreover, 241 dismissals, over ten per cent of all employees, suggests that work in the Partnership's then two stores was no bed of roses and raises a question about the Partnership's ideology of industrial relations harmony. In truth the management of the Partnership was autocratic from the beginning. Spedan Lewis described the activities of his management team as performing 'what the Army calls "Staff Work"' and the Partnership for most of its existence has recruited its executives from the ranks of the military, the higher echelons of the civil service and a few academics.[82] By the 1960s, the Oxford team were able to report that 'employment relationships [were] positively attractive for most employees' but tempered this with their conclusion that 'there is very little real sharing of power in the Partnership as between management and rank-and-file'.[83]

The Partnership has never been an industrial democracy on the lines envisaged by the Utopian Socialists. At best it has functioned as a benign managerial bureaucracy and during Spedan Lewis's reign there were some occasions when he could act in an autocratic manner similar to his father. The International Association of Department Stores' *Monthly Newsletter* was somewhat bemused in July 1948 when it reported that all Partnership workers were required to sign an anti-Communist pledge, and in July 1952, partners who would not accept wage cuts were to be dismissed.[84] In a similar vein, the Partnership has never accepted trade unionism amongst workers, apart from a small minority of skilled service workers.[85]

Similar to most other stores in the industry, the John Lewis

Partnership did not pay fixed rates for similar types of work. Rather, partners received a wage that was negotiated individually with their manager. This method of individual bargaining was one of the major grievances found by the Oxford team – workers resented having to ask for an increase. One worker commented, 'My view is that working for a firm as big as this I shouldn't have to lower myself to go and ask for a rise.'[86] The secretiveness with which the Partnership management treated wage levels resulted in a lack of collective bargaining and a reluctance to use the Partnership's democratic channels to raise questions of remuneration. The system of personal wage rates for each worker bring into sharp focus the real nature of Spedan Lewis's business: it was a partnership of individuals managed by a highly-organised bureaucratic executive.[87] In reality, the Lewis system was not very different from that practised at other well-run stores. Buyers and floor managers continued to settle wage levels on an individual basis. Bainbridge's of Newcastle were slightly different. Here, workers had to put their request for a rise in writing and then be prepared to discuss the issue on their own with the board of directors. This method of individual bargaining can be interpreted as a managerial strategy of divide and rule and may account for the historic difficulties of unionising department store workers. It also provided an opportunity for continuing and reinforcing the tradition of store paternalism. Douglas, who worked in Bainbridge's grocery department during the 1920s, recalls how his several meetings with the directors to discuss his wages were always conducted with kindness and courtesy and he was addressed by his first name.[88] Douglas's claim, similar to the vast majority of such requests, was based on the prevailing rates in the local labour market and were rarely exorbitant. But the display of courtesy and reasonableness could serve to forge bonds of loyalty between managers and the individual worker.

The hundreds of thousands of individual wage contracts that were conducted during the interwar period defy generalisation. Some rates, particularly for long-serving employees with valued skills, appear generous in comparison with other industries. For example, as the John Lewis Partnership census shows, sixty-five per cent of male workers at the John Lewis Partnership earned between £3 and £8 per week in 1932 and thirty-two per cent of women employees received similar rates. As in other industries, young workers were paid much lower rates, with fourteen to seventeen-year-olds receiving between 9s and £1 4s per week. These figures only provide a snapshot, a rough measure of central London wages during the early 1930s. As we move away from the West End, we enter different labour markets and a wide variety of store types.

This complexity was explored by Joan Woodward in her 1950s' study of women workers in department stores.[89] Woodward, who later became part of Flanders' Oxford team, interviewed 205 women in four different department stores: Store A was a West End establishment; Store B was based in a London suburban centre; Store C in a provincial industrial town; and Store D in a rural provincial town.[90] These stores, with their pneumatic tubes and black and white uniforms, had changed little in organisational terms since the 1930s and whilst outside the main period of this study, many of the attitudes expressed by the workers were common throughout the twentieth century.

The variety of worker experience is the most striking feature of Woodward's survey. Staff in the West End store were the most dissatisfied with wage levels; they displayed little loyalty to their employer; few were interested in promotion and labour turnover was high.[91] The London suburban store was very different. Located in an area with few alternative forms of female non-industrial employment, this store's staff rejected factory work as 'not being respectable'.[92] Woodward was struck by the happy working atmosphere in this store which also had the lowest rate of labour turnover. The provincial industrial town department store was family-owned and the workers showed intense loyalty to the owners. The staff expressed high levels of job satisfaction and, perhaps reflecting the paternalistic style of management, wanted wage levels to be determined by length of service rather than ability.[93] The provincial rural town store enjoyed a high-class reputation and sent staff to residential courses on grooming. Woodward noted that workers in this store sometimes had difficulty in dealing with awkward wealthy customers. However, this did not result in any expression of class feelings. Indeed these workers claimed that a lack of trade unionism was a positive advantage. The buyers in this store still carried out staff management functions and Woodward underlined the fact that this saleswoman-buyer relationship was the best form of supervision encountered on her survey. These women experienced the highest levels of job satisfaction, but surprisingly had a relatively high level of staff turnover which, according to Woodward, was caused by a strong demand from London stores for women from this high-class establishment.[94]

Despite this variety, Woodward did find many common features amongst these women. They were generally 'status conscious', drawn to this form of employment by the reputation of department stores.[95] A common complaint in all stores was that wage levels did not reflect the status of the work.[96] Woodward also made an interesting distinction between young unmarried women and married women, on the one hand, and older unmarried women, widows and divorcees on the other. Woodward discovered that the first group had little interest in establishing a career and they did not possess strong economic motives. The second group were obviously more economically dependent upon their work. These women were far more motivated and interested in selling as a career, and whilst all workers accepted Saturday work as 'part and parcel of the job', single women over forty actually liked it. Woodward wryly commented that Saturday work 'saved them from a long, lonely weekend'.[97] Finally, the widespread indifference to trade unionism amongst all these women reflected the success of the employer's industrial relations practices, a system largely based upon paternalism.

Department store managers and proprietors during the twentieth century had learned the lessons of the mistakes of William Whiteley and John Lewis senior. In economic terms they created an apparently deferential, loyal workforce that assured the continued success of most stores. Lacking a formal labour history, it is easy to accept paternalism as the major factor in the continuation of labour harmony. Another important element in the labour relations of department stores is the increasing feminisation of the workforce during the period. Such a view would no doubt broaden its analysis to include glamorous surroundings, fashion and the lure of finery as contributors to the women's lack of militancy. It is hoped that Chapter 10 will demonstrate that such an approach is problematic and needs cautious handling. Another perspective can be drawn from the evidence presented in this chapter. Commentators from Cadbury to Woodward have spoken about the existence of an elite within the department store workforce. Woodward, in particular, drew attention to those unmarried women who clearly saw their jobs in career terms and it was the ranks of these workers which produced the senior sales staff and occasional buyer for most stores. It could be argued that this group formed a 'labour aristocracy' within the workforce; their value system was the same as the employer's, and they functioned to control and police the rest of the workforce. Most labour historians have rejected this somewhat conspiratorial usage of the concept and have, instead, urged the notion of a 'negotiated hegemony' between elite workers and employers.[98] This perspective has the benefit, for example, of explaining the role of buyers and shop-walkers during the Army and Navy strike, a period when 'hegemony' was undermined by rapid inflation. But in this early period the elite was largely male and the problem of apparent female quiescence remains. Susan Porter-Benson, in an American context, has drawn attention to the phenomenon of 'sisterly solidarity' across the counter between women assistants and customers.[99] This can be expressed by such simple acts as advising the customer quietly that the same product could be bought at a lower price elsewhere. It can be seen more clearly every day in all stores when we realise the element of personal service that assistants bring to transactions. This is most noticeable in the perfume and fashion departments. In these areas women advise women on products at an intimate level that can transcend the interests of the store. Such service obviously serves the long-term interests of the store, but this misses the point that the assistant is not just 'selling' but is being creative, using her own initiative, and achieving job satisfaction. The values of the customer, assistant and proprietor may coincide during this process but this is not inevitable. Moreover, such successful trans-actions usually hinge on the assistant's self-belief in the efficacy of her advice. Department store bosses have, of course, long realised the importance of the assistant appearing impartial, and have encouraged this aspect of the sales nexus. Yet this 'independence' of the assistant also serves to increase her sense of her own self-worth. It may boost store profits, but an unintended consequence of this process, at least for the employer, is that it also increases the life chances of the worker. Young Helen Roberts was a 'nice Plummer's girl' but it did not stop her moving to a better-paid job. Indeed, lacking a union and formal system of collective bargaining, mobility between stores has been one of the great defences of department store labour. The extremely high level of staff turnover at the classy provincial store in the Woodward study demonstrates that the well-groomed, beautifully-mannered assistant may reflect 'house values', but these qualities also reflect the assistant's high self-esteem and realisation of her enhanced life chances gained through employment in a department store. Above all, it was the 'elective affinity' of the workers with the store's public image, an image carefully nurtured by generations of entrepreneurs, that brought harmony to the industrial relations of the *grand magasin*.

Notes

1. G.S. Bain and G.B. Woolven, *A Bibliography of British Industrial Relations,* Cambridge University Press, Cambridge, 1979.

2. S. Porter-Benson, *Counter Cultures,* 1988; T. McBride, 'A woman's world: department stores and the evolution of women's employment', 1870–1920, *French Historical Studies,* Vol. X, Fall 1978.

3. C.R. Fender, 'A few facts about the "living-in system"', *Economic Review,* April 1894, summarises these concerns.

4. P.C. Hoffman, *They Also Serve: The Story of the Shopworker,* Porcupine Press, London, 1949, pp. 24–5.

5. J.B. Thomas. *Shop Boy. An Autobiography.* Routledge and Kegan Paul, London, 1983, p. 73.

6. A. and J. Airey, *The Bainbridges of Newcastle,* 1979, p. 115; D.W. Davies, Owen Owen, nd (1984), p. 94; R. Lambert, The Universal Provider, p. 149.

7. I am indebted to my former student, Nichola Jones, whose University of Northumbria undergraduate dissertation, 'The living-in system', analyses the census material upon which this discussion is based.

8. L. Edgar, 'Catholic life in Newcastle seventy years ago', *Northern Catholic History,* 6, 1977, p. 29.

9. N. Jones, op. cit., pp. 14–15.

10. Ibid., pp. 15–17.

11. *Draper's Record,* 28 July 1906.

12. C.R. Fender, op. cit.

13. P.C. Hoffman, op. cit., pp. 48–66.

14. Ibid., p. 25.

15. *Draper's Record,* 13 August 1887; 31 December 1887.

16. Hoffman, op. cit., p. 28.

17. *Draper's Record,* 13 August 1886.

18. Hoffman, op. cit., pp. 39–40.

19. Draper's Record, 29 October 1897.

20. M.B. Miller, *The Bon Marché,* 1981, p. 228.

21. M. Winstanley, *The Shopkeeper's World,* 1983, p. 57.

22. *The Times,* 9 July 1860.

23. R.S. Lambert, op. cit., p. 137.

24. Ibid., p. 140.

25. J.B. Thomas, op. cit., p. 157.

26. Hoffman, op. cit., p. 26.

27. Ibid., pp. 26–7.

28. R.S. Lambert, op. cit., pp. 149–50.

29. Ibid., p. 142.

30. Ibid.

31. Ibid.

32. Ibid., pp. 155–6.

33. The phenomenon of the industrial relations of theft is discussed in E. Nijhof,

'The consciousness of dockers in the port of Rotterdam', Conference Papers, Anglo-Dutch Social History Conference, Maastricht, 1982.

34. R.S. Lambert, op. cit., pp. 150–1.

35. Ibid.

36. A. and J. Airey, op. cit., p. 115.

37. *Warehouseman and Draper's Trade Journal,* 7 and 28 January 1888.

38. *Draper's Record,* 17 December 1887.

39. E. Cadbury, M.C. Matheson, G. Shaun. *Women's Work and Wages,* T. Fisher Unwin, London, 1906, p. 108.

40. L. Holcombe, *Victorian Ladies at Work,* Hamden, Archon Books, Connecticut, 1973, pp. 104–6. Data on the feminisation of the workforce is presented by Holcombe in Appendix 3.

41. *Draper's Record,* 19 November 1887; 20 July 1889.

42. Ibid., 1898; I am indebted to Janet Beardmore for this information on Eaden Lilley.

43. J.B. Thomas, op. cit., pp. 164–5.

44. E. Cadbury *et al.,* op. cit., p. 188.

45. Ibid., p 219; p 281.

46. Ibid., p. 117.

47. L. Holcombe, op. cit., p. 107.

48. Ibid.

49. E. Cadbury, op. cit., p. 129.

50. M. Corina, *Fine Silks and Oak Counters,* pp. 80–81.

51. L. Wendt and H. Kogan, *Give the Lady What She Wants. The Story of Marshall Field and Company.* Rand, McNally, Chicago, 1952, p. 293.

52. P.C. Hoffman, op. cit., p. 33.

53. D.W. Davies, op. cit., p. 23.

54. A. Briggs, *Friends of the People,* 1956, pp. 98–9.

55. Mass Observation, *Portrait of a Shop,* H.D. Willcock (ed.), 1947, p. 207.

56. Ibid., p. 186.

57. R. Bentall, *My Store of Memories,* 1974, pp. 160–61.

58. Interview with Douglas and Rose, former employees of Bainbridge's during the 1920s and 1930s, 21 July 1994.

59. P. Joyce, *Work, Society and Politics,* Harvester, Brighton, p. 147.

60. IADS *Newsletter,* 11, November 1947, contains a scathing attack on Ford.

61. M. Corina, op. cit., p. 78.

62. A. and J. Airey, op. cit., p. 120. Many firms, however, continued with the commission system, frequently combining it with discount.

63. *Draper's Record,* 6 February 1932. A. Briggs, op. cit., p. 160.

64. T. McBride, op. cit., pp. 675–77; D. Hoffman, *Frank Lloyd Wright's Fallingwater,* New York, 1978, p. 8.

65. R. Bentall, op. cit., pp. 104–5.

66. Ibid., p. 55.

67. Ibid., pp. 107–8.

68. Ibid., p. 106.

69. R. Martin and R.H. Fryer, *Redundancy and Paternalist Capitalism*, Allen and Unwin, London, 1973.

70. P.C. Hoffman, op. cit., p. 182.

71. Ibid., p. 181.

72. Ibid., pp. 173–8.

73. Ibid., pp. 193–4.

74. Ibid., pp. 194–7.

75. Ibid., p. 186.

76. Ibid., p. 194.

77. A. Flanders, R. Pomeranz and J. Woodward, *Experiment in Industrial Democracy. A Study of the John Lewis Partnership*, Faber, London, 1968, Chapter 2, *passim*.

78. Ibid.

79. Ibid., p. 45.

80. Ibid., p. 36.

81. Ibid., p. 37.

82. Ibid., p. 40.

83. Ibid., p. 192.

84. IADS *Newsletter*, July 1948; July 1952.

85. A. Flanders *et al.*, op. cit., Appendix D.

86. Ibid., p. 102.

87. Ibid., p. 101.

88. Douglas and Rose interview, op. cit.

89. J. Woodward. *The Saleswoman: A Study of Attitudes and Behaviour in Retail Distribution*, Pitman, London, 1960.

90. Ibid., p. 22.

91. Ibid., p. 20.

92. Ibid., p. 23

93. Ibid., p. 36.

94. Ibid., pp. 66–9.

95. Ibid., p. 11.

96. Ibid., p. 29.

97. Ibid., pp. 50–51.

98. R.Q. Gray, *The Labour Aristocracy*, 1976.

99. S. Porter-Benson, op. cit., p. 263.

CHAPTER NINE

THEORIES ON CONSUMER SOCIETY:
THEMES, TRENDS AND PROBLEMS

A growing literature on the theory of consumption has emerged during the last decade. Historians and social scientists have engaged in a lively debate in their attempts to construct models and typologies of consumer behaviour. Few of these writers deal explicitly with department stores but, given the centrality of the *grand magasin* in the retail revolution and its subsequent impact on trends of consumption, these theories do require consideration. The debate on consumer culture has accelerated during the last decade with the growth in popularity of cultural studies, and the perspectives employed range from Veblen's classic study on *fin de siècle* conspicuous consumption, Marxist notions of commodification, Freudian concepts of the unconscious and male sexual domination, adaptations of Gramsci's thesis on hegemony, Debord's 'Society of the Spectacle', through to post-modernism. Given such a spectrum, the debate is often highly confusing and at best can only provide the historian with useful insights rather than a structured approach. Nevertheless, these insights can be illuminating and a brief survey of the literature is not without reward.

Veblen is an obvious starting-point. His sharp, penetrating, mocking analysis of America's new economic elite in the late nineteenth century is a key founding text in American sociology.[1] Generations of writers ranging from J.K. Galbraith to Veblen's near neighbour from backwoods Minnesota, Garrison Keillor, have continued the tradition of mocking over-consumption and share Veblen's commitment to homespun, republican ideals that stretch back to Jefferson and resonate with Weber's 'Protestant Ethic'. On the positive side, Veblen was the first major writer to highlight the point that consumption has cultural as well as economic aspects. Yet his model of conspicuous consumption and display is simplistic. 'The orgies of display at Rhode Island and the parading of ornamental wines on Fifth Avenue established both patterns of consumption to be emulated by the rest of society and became the benchmark for modern status divisions.' Jackson Lears, in a fine, perceptive essay, has drawn attention to the fundamental weaknesses in the Veblen model. Lears has noted that:

> Veblen's top-down model of cultural domination melded with his desire to stress the irrationality of consumption. As a result, his psychology remained narrow. His thinking was, to be sure, a step beyond the simple-minded utilitarianism of orthodox economics, but he still reduced social rituals to one-dimensional examples of 'pecuniary emulation': ... Veblen's furious assault on display amounted to an 'attack on culture itself' ... 'a sweeping dismissal of art, religion and nearly all sensuous or material cultural forms'.[2]

Veblen's perspective, however, has proved extremely durable within American scholarship. William Leach, in a major new book, argues that between 1880 and 1930 the culture of the USA shifted from being centred upon rural, producer, self-reliant, republican values to one that was 'preoccupied with consumption, with comfort and bodily well-being, with luxury, spending and acquisition, with more goods this year than last, more next year than this.'[3] This transformation, according to Leach, was created by an alliance of banks, manufacturers, large retailers, particularly Field, the Straus Brothers and Wanamaker, alongside a new 'brokering class', including 'urban museum curators and art school instructors ... university professors ... economists ... advertising agents ... specialists who created the "light and colour" for places like Time Square, and professional model agencies that brokered female bodies'. Writing in the tradition of Warren Susman, Leach depicts the pre-1880 period as a golden age of honest toil and simple pleasures which has been swept away by the culture of consumption:

> For some Americans the continued power of consumerism has led to further degradation of what it means to be an American or what America is all about. For others this evolution has only enhanced the country's appeal, making it appear more like an Emerald City, a feast, a department store to which everyone is invited and entitled.[4]

Leach is clearly perturbed by the morality of consumer society and argues for 'a larger vision of what it means to be human, a fuller sense of being, and a refusal to accept having and taking as the key to being or the equivalent of being'.[5]

Leach's evangelical thesis is supported by a wealth of detail and he applies a highly novel approach which links a broad range of new cultural practices in order to demonstrate the emergence of a new consumer mentality. The Leach–Susman perspective has not gone without challenge. Jackson Lears, himself a former advocate of the Susman 'Nineteenth Century Protestant Producer Culture' – 'Twentieth Century Secular Consumer Culture' model, has noted that,

> We are just beginning to glimpse the ways that this expanding world of goods was represented in popular culture, but preliminary evidence suggests that it may be a mistake to argue a shift from the plodding nineteenth century to the carnivalesque twentieth: the carnival may have been in town all the time.[6]

Leach spends much time exploring the work of L. Frank Baum, a key member of the 'brokering class'.[7] Jackson Lears, on the other hand, makes similar cultural claims for P.T. Barnum and his followers whose antics transfixed Americans in the 1840s, half a century before the 'Land of Oz'. Lears further argues that the notion of an unrestrained culture of hedonism enunciated in the last decades of the nineteenth century is misguided. Veblen may have observed the excessive display of the *nouveau riche*, but this activity was restrained by a new emphasis amongst WASP elite groups upon 'a certain kind of cleanliness, purged of decadent hedonistic associations'.[8]

This tension between hedonism and self-restraint is usually expressed in condemnatory remarks by elite observers on the consuming patterns of lower or new social groups. Veblen's critique needs to be located within this enduring tension rather than as the first attack against the new consumerism. The following passage is instructive:

> On arrival at North Villas, I was shown into what I presumed was the drawing-room. Everything was oppressively new. The brilliantly-varnished door cracked with a report like a pistol when it was opened; the paper on the walls, with its gaudy pattern of birds, trellis-work, and flowers, in gold, red, and green on a white ground, looked hardly dry yet; the showy window-curtains of white and sky-blue, and the still showier carpet of red and yellow, seemed as if they had come out of the shop yesterday; the round rosewood table was in a painfully high state of polish; the morocco-bound picture books that lay on it, looked as if they had never been moved or opened since they had been bought; not one leaf even of the music on the piano was dog-eared or worn. Never was a richly furnished room more thoroughly comfortless than this – the eye ached at looking round it. There was no repose anywhere. The print of the Queen, hanging lonely on the wall, in its heavy gilt frame, with a large crown at the top, glared at you: the books, the wax-

flowers in glass-cases, the chairs in flaring chintz-covers, the china plates on
the door, the blue and pink glass vases and cups ranged on the chimney-
piece, the over-ornamented chiffoniers with Tonbridge toys and long-necked
smelling bottles on their upper shelves – all glared on you. There was no look
of shadow, shelter, secrecy, or retirement in any one nook or corner of those
four gaudy walls. All surrounding objects seemed startlingly near to the eye;
much nearer than they really were. The room would have given a nervous
man the headache, before he had been in it a quarter of an hour. I was not
kept waiting long. Another violent crack from the new door, announced the
entrance of Mr Sherwin himself.[9]

Mr Sherwin was a successful large draper and the narrator, Basil, was
'the second son of an English gentleman ... Our family is one of the
most ancient in this country'. This extract, from the Wilkie Collins
novel *Basil*, was written in 1852. The carnival was clearly 'in town' by
the mid-nineteenth century in Britain and critics were as harsh as Veblen
in their lampooning.[10]

   Veblen's ideas have had an important impact on the growing debate
between historians on the origins and nature of modern consumerism.
McKendrick, in a seminal essay on late eighteenth-century Britain, has
argued that a new consumerism emerged during this period amongst
the upper classes. He draws attention to the selling and display techniques of Wedgwood, the pottery entrepreneur, how Wedgwood imbued
his products with class and status meanings and how the purchase of
these goods was a form of upper-class emulation by middle-class
buyers.[11] McKendrick's chronology has been challenged by a number of
writers who point to similar processes in earlier periods.[12] More
importantly, other scholars have challenged McKendrick's emulation
model. Lorna Weatherill, for example, has clearly shown from her work
on wills that different social groups gave different meanings to objects
and that there was a distinct tendency amongst those lower down the
social hierarchy to favour different products from the upper classes.[13] A
good example of this is furnished by the pottery industry itself. In
north-east England manufacturers were conversant with and utilised new
production techniques similar to Wedgwood's but their wares, from the
'canary yellow' of late eighteenth-century Tyneside, through the pink
lustre of nineteenth-century Sunderland pottery with its prints of local
industrial scenes, sailors' ditties and Friendly Society emblems, to the
gaudy colours of twentieth-century Maling, were bought by a prosperous local market that was impervious to the niceties of Wedgwood's

'Jasper'.[14] Fashion clothing students have also raised serious doubts about the emulation thesis. The work of Lois Banner has demonstrated 'that the pacesetters in the beauty sweepstakes were courtesans and chorus girls who were often aped by their social betters'.[15] In our own period, the 'Afro' hairstyle and punk have travelled up the social ladder, and in the summer of 1993 Parisian scouts for leading fashion houses were chasing the 'Convoy' through English country lanes in search of 'grunge' inspiration. Yet we should caution against outright dismissal of emulation. Furniture, for example, has over the years been very slow in style changes and a unity of form can be easily detected between social classes. Frank Pick's Council for Art and Industry reported in 1937 that 'What was fashionable in furniture with the well-to-do becomes, in time, fashionable with poorer folk. This is due to the fact that second-hand furniture is the main supply for homes where expenditure upon furniture must be severely curtailed.'[16]

Veblen was, however, the first theorist to engage with and go beyond Marx's distinction between 'use value' and 'exchange value'. This distinction, which has dominated Marxist scholarship on consumption, often allies itself with Veblen's scorn. Generations of Marxists have looked upon the 'world of goods' in modern society as a device to increase profit and exploitation and impose control via the 'false consciousness' of consumerism. Marx himself was silent on what things would be like in a socialist society where production was organised under the concept of 'use value'. We can, of course, facetiously speculate upon this theme: would we all wear the same plain clothes à la Maoist China?, would 'things' come wrapped in plain brown paper without adornment or would they be printed in the style of Morris and co.? Would we all eat the same fare in communal canteens before retiring to group discussions on literature and art? This last point highlights the problem of Marx's Utopia: how do we make a culture if we are bereft of the language of goods? This is not to deny that goods would not exist in such a society but who would decide which goods were made, what they should look like and what purpose they would serve? Baudrillard has, in a telling essay, noted that none of us would come into the market-place of such a Utopian society happy to receive our share of 'use value' products. None of us would be the consumer equivalent of the 'noble savage'. Our needs and desires are as complex as society itself.[17]

The Marxist tradition of equating consumerism with the production of 'exchange value' and profit still has some important adherents. One school of thought in this area has focused upon twentieth-century mass production, scientific management, the deskilling of work and the emergence of compliant consumers necessary for such industrial re-structuring. Stewart Ewen has been particularly prominent in relating these developments to the rise of the modern advertising industry. Ewen's 'Captains of Consciousness' are the market-place equivalent of the 'Captains of Industry' whose function is to shape the needs and desires of consumers to fit what leaves the factory gate. More import-antly, the commodity, on passing through the sacrament of advertising, becomes a major element in social control. Ewen concludes with the claim that since the 1920s, 'commercial culture has increasingly provided an idiom within which desires for social change and fantasies of libera-tion might be articulated and contained' and that people need to redefine their social needs, but to what he is silent.[18]

This Marxist notion of false consciousness and social control being articulated by the world of goods is given a further refinement in the work of Rachel Bowlby. Her perspective is a heady mixture of Marxist commodification theory, Freudian psychoanalysis and the spectacle theory of Debord. Bowlby utilises these themes to create a world where women are dominated economically and sexually by the ethos of the department store:

> It was above all to women that the new commerce made its appeal, urging and inviting them to procure its luxurious benefits and purchase sexually attractive images for themselves. They were to become in a sense like prostitutes in their active, commodified self-display, and also to take on the one role almost never theirs in actual prostitution: that of consumer.[19]

For Bowlby, the passivity of women shoppers is guaranteed by the entrapment of what Debord has termed the 'spectacle de la marchan-dise'. For Debord, society has become a 'spectacle' where 'the real world changes into simple images, simple images become real beings and effective motivations of a hypnotic behaviour'. Debord adds 'the prin-ciple of commodity fetishism, the domination of society by intangible as well as tangible things, which reaches its absolute fulfilment in the spectacle, where the tangible world is replaced by a selection of images which exist above it'.[20]

This perspective may have appeal to literary theorists seeking yet another bolt-hole in *Rive Gauche* nonsense but such arrogant, con-spiratorial interpretations of consumer behaviour are of little use to historians trained to seek out complexity and agency in social action. A more fruitful Marxist approach is presented by the followers of the Italian Marxist, Gramsci. The concept of 'hegemony', central to Gramsci's revision of Marx, analyses the role of ideas and value systems in modern society and how these constantly shift through a process of negotiation between the dominant and subordinate classes. This emphasis on 'negotiation' leads Marxist thought out of the blind alley of 'false consciousness' and allows for a more meaningful analysis of everyday life. A number of consumer theorists have utilised Gramscian theory to make telling analyses of the world of goods. Elizabeth Wilson's *Adorned in Dreams* is a seminal text on fashion which explores the creative resistance of women against the fashion industry.[21] In a similar vein, Dick Hebdidge, in an analysis of the motor scooter and 'mod' culture, has shown how young people appropriated an apparently mundane product, designed to allow adults to make short journeys cheaply and cleanly, and reinvested it with a whole new universe of meaning.[22] This idea of consumer delinquency has provided rich pickings for cultural theorists. For example, the work of Fiske celebrates the tearing of jeans, shoplifting and the misuse of shopping malls by teenagers.[23] In this perspective, consumer culture becomes a somewhat romanticised arena for a 'permanent revolution' by the subordinate classes. M.J. Lee, in a more sober Gramscian analysis, warns against such romantic excesses. Society in general, and consumerism in particular, is, for Lee, far more complex than a straightforward dominant, subordinate model: 'In the field of consumption, consumer goods should not be seen as the mere objects of a semiotic democracy, but rather as the objects through which social struggles are conducted and social relationships between groups articulated in everyday life.'[24] Lee further argues that Fiske's tendency to 'overstress this aspect of cultural consumption is to reduce the realm of everyday social experience merely to the social experience of sub-ordination...'[25] This insistence on a more complex Gramscian approach concludes by drawing attention to the unevenness of social groups and the widely varying distribution of power within and between classes: 'Consequently, any theory of popular culture which attempts to shoe-horn all cultural practice into a simple distinction between the "dominant and the subordinate" will be forced inevitably to neglect the uneven distribution of cultural competences, power and capital as these are dispersed amongst "the subordinate" classes themselves.'[26] At first sight, this appears to be a sensible, if somewhat obvious, approach. 'Power' and 'capital' can be measured and analysed but what is meant by 'competences'? The failure to explore this term undermines this otherwise useful analysis. Does he mean some of us are better shoppers than others? more skilful at budgeting? more subtle in our patterns of resistance? Despite Lee's support for Baudrillard's rejection of the 'use value–exchange value' couplet, his notion of 'competences' resonates strongly with the judgemental Marxism that he is anxious to reject.

Another positive perspective on consumerism is provided by a very different theoretical tradition to that of Marxism. Several followers of the French sociologist, Emile Durkheim, have provided novel interpretations on consumer society. The social anthropologist, Mary Douglas, in her path-breaking book, *The World of Goods*, co-authored with Barron Isherwood, admonishes critics of consumerism and forcefully argues for a more enlightened approach. Coming from anthropology, a subject which has always perceived the circulation of goods as highly important, Douglas is extremely well equipped to embark on an analysis of modern Western consumerism. For Douglas, goods form a symbolic system, a type of social discourse that is as essential to society as oral or written modes of communication. In this perspective, goods are used to give meaning to the rhythms of everyday life. A good example is the use of best china to underline the importance of a particular meal, such as a birthday tea or Christmas lunch. Goods also serve to articulate social rules: 'It is all right to send flowers to your aunt in hospital, but never right to send the cash they are worth with a message to "get yourself some flowers".'[27] Objects are also used to signify one's position in a particular social formation, and Douglas perceptively analyses the use of 'information goods', such as the telephone, as essential items in the maintenance of middle-class life-styles.

The French sociologist, Bourdieu, has pushed this line of thought even further. Bourdieu's concept of 'cultural capital' explores the growing importance of taste, style and education in modern society.[28] The social background of individuals, and the quality of their education, serves to determine their access to cultural capital. With much insight, Bourdieu explores how people on similar income levels can have widely varying tastes and life-styles. A small shopkeeper, for example, may have the same income as that of a schoolteacher. But the teacher's superior education and access to the intellectual media often results in an aesthetic sensibility that would be alien to the less educated shopkeeper. The appreciation of abstract art, the love of modern jazz, regular visits to

museums and galleries, a sensitivity to architectural styles, are all in-
dicators of an individual with access to large amounts of 'cultural capital'.
Bourdieu links refined taste and a well-developed aesthetic sensibility to
the exercise of power in society which, in the late twentieth century, is
increasingly dependent upon access to cultural as well as economic
capital.

By contrast, the working class, denied access to education and
possessing only minimum 'cultural capital', consume goods that are
readily accessible in terms of meaning. Rhythmic popular music, senti-
mental, undemanding wall pictures, low-brow television shows, the
tabloid press and heavy meals high in protein, are judged to be part of
a working-class culture of instant gratification. Patterns of consumption
are, therefore, largely determined by the individual's social and educa-
tional background, and serve to impose the 'distinctions' that are increasingly important to the complex social structure of advanced societies.

Both Douglas and Bourdieu have much to offer to the scholarship
of consumerism. Their related perspectives, with an innovative blend of
anthropological, sociological and, in Bourdieu's case, Marxist insights,
have done much to further our understanding of consumer behaviour.
Yet there remains a problem to both in that individuals are largely
perceived as being driven by the demands of 'social facts' and 'solidarities'. A diametrically opposite view is presented by the Weberian
sociological tradition to which we must now turn.

Weberian ideas and concepts have been utilised in the work of Colin
Campbell in his attempt to create a model of consumer subjectivity.
This analysis begins with a trenchant rejection of most consumption
theories from Veblen to Bourdieu, on the grounds that the majority of
writers impute meaning into the behaviour of individuals without
recourse to the subjective intention of the actor.[29] For Campbell, most
writers on consumption are primarily concerned with consumers
conforming to a pre-ordained schema of behaviour, often devised by
the theorists themselves. Rather than 'conform', Campbell is more
interested in people 'confirming' their own sense of 'character'.[30] By
focusing upon the individual, Campbell creates a typology of consumer
action that can escape the shackles of social structural determination.
By following Weber's method of 'ideal type' analysis, Campbell explores
the evolution of various 'character types', from the aristocrat to the
romantic bohemian. What distinguishes modern consumerism in this
analysis is 'a distinctive form of hedonism, one in which the enjoyment

of emotions as summoned through imaginary or illusory images is central'.[31] In other words, the enjoyment of imagining ownership is more important than the act of consumption itself. Campbell continues, 'the romantic ideal of character might have functioned to stimulate and legitimate that distinctive form of autonomous, self-illusory hedonism which underlies modern consumer behaviour. It does this by providing the highest possible motives with which to justify day-dreaming, longing and the rejection of reality, together with the pursuit of originality in life and art; by so doing, it enables pleasure to be ranked above comfort and counteracts both traditionalist and utilitarian restraints on the expression of desire.' This romanticism is expressed by the tendency of the 'middling classes', the engine of the consumer revolution, increasingly to purchase 'expressive goods' such as pictures, china, mirrors, musical instruments and clothes. This, according to Campbell, when taken with 'parallel developments [such] as the rise of the modern western fashion pattern and the modern novel … does strongly support the claimed connection with romanticism'.[32]

Much of what Campbell describes will no doubt resonate with many (middle-class!) readers of this book, but similar personal connections were probably made in the discussion of Bourdieu. Perhaps the truth, as usual, lies somewhere between, or is a mixture of, the two approaches. What is not in doubt is that Campbell's collection of consumer action under the umbrella of 'romanticism' results in the production of yet another uni-causal theory of consumerism. In reality no single theory can account for the complexity of consumer behaviour. The Weberian approach needs to develop more 'ideal types' of consumer character that take us beyond romanticism. Indeed, it needs to consider rational shoppers who budget meticulously, pride themselves in spotting bargains and who abhor waste. Given the prominence of 'rationality' to Weberian thought, this is a curious omission. Nevertheless, Campbell's attempt to explain consumer subjectivity needs to be both applauded and developed by social scientists. At the other extreme, Marxists and Durkheimians need to be more open to the complexity of human beings and go beyond slotting consumers into various models of structural determination. Judgemental accounts of consumerism still proliferate, but must be resisted. One recent text concludes with an appeal for an international religious crusade against the putative excesses of consumerism.[33] Many writers fail to make the distinction between 'consumerism' and 'shopping', consumerism being usually presented as the passive acceptance of what is on offer in the marketplace. Yet over a century, from the 'tabbies' of the late nineteenth century to the foragers in the present-day bargain basement, customers and managers have pitted their wits against each other. The conclusion that each has a good idea of what the other is up to is inescapable. Above all, we need to keep in mind the wide variety of shopping experiences. To take the department store as an example, on any day we confront the bargain-hunter in the basement, the parents buying their children's school clothing, a couple buying white appliances or a television after lengthy research through copies of *Which?*, the browser gazing at the expensive designer label clothes, women meeting socially in the coffee shop, children being bought toys ... the list is almost endless and warns against simplistic generalisation, and also defies the embraces of even the most complex social scientific models. This is particularly the case in the labyrinth of meaning and action that accompanies the relationship between women and the department store – which is the subject of the next chapter.

Notes

1. T. Veblen, *The Theory of the Leisure Class: An Economic Study in the Evolution of Institutions*, Macmillan, New York, 1899.

2. Jackson Lears, 'Beyond Veblen. Rethinking consumer culture in America', in S.J. Bronner (ed.), *Consuming Visions, Accumulation and the Display of Goods in America, 1880–1920*, Norton, New York, 1989.

3. W. Leach, *Land of Desire. Merchants, Power and the Rise of a New American Culture*, Pantheon, New York, 1993, p. xiii.

4. Ibid., p. 388.

5. Ibid., p. 390.

6. J. Lears, op. cit., pp. 76–7. Susman's influential thesis is forcefully set out in W.I. Susman, *Culture as History: The Transformation of American Society in the Twentieth Century*, Pantheon New York, 1984, especially the Introduction.

7. W. Leach, *Land of Desire*, Chapter 2, *passim*.

8. J. Lears, op. cit., pp. 77; 90–1.

9. Wilkie Collins, *Basil*, Oxford University Press, Oxford, 1990 edition, p. 61.

10. Ibid., p. 2.

11. N. McKendrick, J. Brewer and J.H. Plumb, *The Birth of Consumer Society: The Commercialisation of Eighteenth Century England*, Hutchinson, London, 1982, Part I.

12. G. McCracken, *Culture and Consumption: New Approaches to the Symbolic Character of Consumer Goods and Activities*, Indiana University Press, Bloomington, 1990; Introduction.

13. L.M. Weatherill, 'The meaning of consumer behaviour in late seventeenth

century and early eighteenth century England', in J. Brewer and N. Porter (eds), *Consumption and the World of Goods*, Routledge, London, 1993.

14. R.C. Bell, *Tyneside Pottery*, Frank Graham, Newcastle upon Tyne, 1971. See also J.C. Baker, *Sunderland Pottery*, Thomas Reed, Sunderland, 1984.

15. Cited in J. Lears, op. cit., p. 74.

16. Council for Art and Industry, *The Working Class Home, Its Furnishings and Equipment,* London, 1937, p 43.

17. J. Baudrillard, *Selected Writings*, Polity, Cambridge, 1988, p 64.

18. S. Ewen, *Captains of Consciousness. Advertising and the Social Roots of Consumer Culture.* McGraw-Hill, New York, 1976, pp. 219–20.

19. R. Bowlby, *Just Looking. Consumer Culture in Dreisser, Gissing and Zola*, Methuen, London, 1985, p 11.

20. G. Debord, *Society of the Spectacle*, Black and Red, Detroit, 1970; no pagination! Readers interested in other applications of Debord's theory may wish to look at 'What Miss Kilman's petticoat means: Virginia Woolf, shopping and spectacle', *Modern Fiction Studies*, Vol. 38, No. 1, Spring 1992.

21. E. Wilson, *Adorned in Dreams*, Virago, London, 1985.

22. D. Hebdidge, *Subculture: The Meaning of Style*, Methuen, London, 1985.

23. J. Fiske, *Understanding Popular Culture*, Unwin Hyman, Boston, MA, London, 1989.

24. M.J. Lee, *Consumer Culture Reborn*, Routledge, London, 1993, p. 54.

25. Ibid.

26. Ibid., p. 55.

27. M. Douglas and B. Isherwood, *The World of Goods*, Allen Lane, London, 1978, p. 58.

28. P. Bourdieu, *Distinction*, Routledge, London, 1984.

29. C. Campbell, 'Understanding traditional and modern patterns of consumption in eighteenth-century England: a character-action approach', in J. Brewer and R. Porter (eds), *Consumption and the World of Goods*, London, 1993..

30. Ibid., p. 47.

31. Ibid., p. 48.

32. Ibid., p. 54.

33. R. Bocock, *Consumption*, Routledge, London, 1993, p. 118.

CHAPTER TEN

WOMEN AND DEPARTMENT STORES: SOME ECONOMIC, SEXUAL AND POLITICAL AMBIGUITIES

Women play a central role in any study of department stores. For over a century and a half they have been the majority amongst the crowds of customers that have thronged through the large establishments and for most of the period women have dominated the workforce. Susan Porter-Benson has captured this female world with a telling quotation from a 1910 trade journal:

> Buying and selling, serving and being served – women. On every floor, in every aisle, at every counter, women ... Behind most of the counters on all the floors, ... women. At every cashier's desk, at the wrapper's desks, running back and forth with parcels and change, short-skirted women. Filling the aisles, passing and repassing, a constantly arriving and departing throng of shoppers, women. Simply a moving, seeking, hurrying, mass of femininity, in the midst of which the occasional man shopper, man clerk, and man supervisor, looks lost and out of place.[1]

Edward Filene went so far as to describe his Boston Store as an 'Adamless Eden'.[2] Yet apart from Benson's seminal study on American women shop workers, McBride's work on Parisian shop girls and Leach's subtle exploration of the store's political dimension, historians and social scientists alike have paid scant attention to these great female in-stitutions.[3] At a more general level, however, many of the theoretical perspectives on consumption surveyed in the previous chapter do have important things to say on the relationship between women and the world of goods. But there is no consistent model that satisfactorily accounts for this relationship, rather we have a large assortment of concepts and insights, some of which are useful while many are contra-dictory. To bring order to what is often a confusing picture, this chapter will examine the connections between women and consumption around the organisational categories of the economic, sexual and political, and hopefully the reader will excuse the frequent excursions outside the store into the wider world of retailing which are necessary to capture the richness of this most complex area.

Writers in the Marxist tradition have explored the economic connections between modern industry, retailing and women. Stuart Ewen's influential study *Captains of Consciousness* describes how the modern advertising industry has worked throughout the present century to create strong desires amongst women to consume the increasing flow of mass-produced goods. Following the insights of Henry Braverman, Ewen argues that women were systematically 'deskilled' of many of their traditional domestic functions, ranging from home cooking, washing, through to the domestic manufacture of clothing. Thus processed food, washing machines and a vast armoury of kitchen appliances and ready-made clothing reduced the housewife from being a skilled artisan to a mere factory operative. Stripped of her former talents the housewife became highly susceptible to the products of the beauty industry which were often accompanied by advertisements that played on her personal and sexual fears.[4] Rachel Bowlby has also analysed the creation of the desire to consume amongst women and she has used the Marxist concept of commodification to explain this process (see Figure 20):

> 'What does a woman want?' is a question to which the makers of marketable products from the earliest years of consumer society have sought to suggest an infinite variety of answers, appealing to her wish or need to adorn herself as an object of beauty. The dominant ideology of feminine subjectivity in the late nineteenth century perfectly fitted women to receive the advances of the seductive commodity offering to enhance her womanly attractions.[5]

Other writers have focused upon women workers in retailing, citing long hours, the living-in system, poor wages and the tenacious resistance to trade unionism by employers as another aspect of women's economic exploitation. Moreover, women workers were subjected to the most sophisticated paternalistic regimes ever devised by modern capitalism. These themes have been analysed more fully in a previous chapter which deals with the workforce but it must be noted at this stage that the issues presently being dealt with operated on both sides of the counter. The Marxist tradition and its various subspecies may have an initial attractiveness but are they not somewhat conspiratorial? They certainly present women as passive economic actors in the process of retailing. Let us take a walk around the stores and high streets to find out if this is really the case.

First showing outside London!

THE GLASS HAT

Here to-day at FENWICK'S

Sensational introduction from PARIS!

A glass hat . . . transparent . . . glinting . . . with a picture brim to see your eyes and curls! But wearably 'pliable, and stitched with a band of soft blue velvet. A romantically lovely hat, rushed from Paris to London . . . from London to Fenwick's . . . to you. See it to-day in the French Hat Salon **78/6**

FENWICK Ltd., Newcastle-on-Tyne.

Figure 20 'The Glass Hat' (*source*: courtesy of Fenwick Ltd).

During the 1880s the *Draper's Record* was in no doubt that a major threat was posed to the economic well-being of the department store by the behaviour of 'tabbies'. Referred to in America as 'Jays', 'tabbies' distinguished themselves by spending long periods in stores inspecting and trying on many items, availing themselves of subsidised refreshments and other facilities and leaving without making a single purchase. Special training schemes were advocated for floor-walkers to deal with this menace and there was growing concern that 'tabbies' were increasingly resorting to a store's free delivery system where goods, after further inspection at home, would be returned without payment! Even women making purchases could be awkward customers:

> Grandma was no believer in 'shoddy', and when the girls had a new frock she saw to it that the stuff was good; she would make a special trip to Manchester for it, and in her black bonnet and heavy sequinned black velvet cape, was a formidable figure at the dress-material counter of Lewis's in Market Street. The young man serving would take great pains showing her many rolls of cloth, and she would finger them for a long time, and ask innumerable questions as to their serviceability before deciding. If it was for a winter frock she would, in order to satisfy herself that it was 'nowt but wool', request the assistant to snip a bit off and apply a match: if it wouldn't burn then it was wool all right and not 'shoddy', and Grandma would give her order. If the material was for summer frocks she demanded an assurance that it would wash and not ruck up under the iron, and in spite of her country speech and downright ways she was always given good service.[6]

The effectiveness of the advertising industry is, of course, a highly contentious subject of debate which has produced no clear conclusions, but it is worth noting that one of Britain's most successful retailers, Marks and Spencer, rarely advertise. The allure of sumptuous display is another questionable area. Take the case of these two old women whose conversation about the Gateshead Metro Centre, Europe's largest and most luxurious shopping mall, was recently overheard in Wallsend High Street:

> Wor Betty's man run us ower. Hev ye not been? Like a palace ... foontins, plants, ... aal spotless! Band playin' while ye get yor coffee. Loads o' stuff. Gans for miles. Just aboot ivvorythin' ye cud think on! Naw! A didn't buy nowt. Couldn't see owt A needed![7]

Window shopping has always been a popular pastime for women which may well be a form of escape into a phantasmagorical dream world, but almost certainly encompasses the highly rational activity of comparing prices and quality. As early as 1857 a middle-class housewife wrote of her love of window shopping, 'in the crowded West End street'.[8] But this was Mrs Karl Marx and one suspects that she knew a thing or two more about the power of commodities than the average Victorian housewife. It could, of course, be argued that the windows which attracted Mrs Marx were simplistic and technically tame in comparison to the magical vistas that emerged in late nineteenth-century Chicago, but we need to keep in mind the fact, clearly presented by William Leach, that the major innovator of the new display forms, L. Frank Baum, was a committed feminist who saw his work as an enhancement of women's lives, not as a form of systematic deception.[9] These examples from nineteenth-century 'tabbies' to working-class women in modern shopping malls illustrate continuity in women's ability to peel off the veneer of unreality that often surrounds the shopping experience.

Similar positive points can be laid against the charge that the advertising industry in harness with mass production capitalist industry foisted new products on women. This is an important theme to this study, as for much of the period under review the department store was in the forefront of marketing new items. Were many of these products useless, as Ewen's study implies, and was their main purpose to deskill women? Take laundry as an example: labour historians in recent years have become sensitive to the role of women in working-class life away from the workplace and some have vividly described the tyranny of washing clothes in the pre-machine era, particularly in families where the men were occupied in dirty jobs such as mining.[10] Vacuum cleaners, electrical irons, modern cookers, do make life easier and they do create more time to pursue non-domestic activities. Voicing similar sentiments, design historians have pointed out that useless, or poorly-designed, products rarely create a sustainable market.

It must be conceded that the vast majority of women shop in a highly rational manner, and most base their purchases upon a carefully controlled budget. Seen from this perspective, women emerge as rational actors who have made the majority of economic decisions in what is undoubtedly Britain's most successful industrial sector. If we shift our focus to what is on the counter we cannot ignore the growing importance of women buyers, who have been increasingly employed by department stores since the late nineteenth century. These women often execute highly important decisions upon which the success and indeed

Figure 21 Fenwick's senior staff, 1932. Twenty-eight of this company's forty-seven top managers were women. Note how confident and comfortable they appear (*source*: courtesy of Fenwick Ltd).

the survival of their store depends. Moreover, the choice exercised by women buyers can often make or break many small and middle-sized firms of suppliers. The sensitivity of women buyers to their customers and market, real or potential, has long been prized by department store entrepreneurs. The illustration (see Figure 21) of the senior management team of Fenwick's in 1932 clearly demonstrates the importance of women to department store management. Indeed it would be un-imaginable to find so many women exercising so much power in any other sector of business and industry.

Marguerite Boucicaut took over the helm of the Bon Marché upon the death of her husband and she was responsible for the often remarked upon staff harmony in the store.[11] Louise Jay was co-founder with her husband of the Samaritaine and they subsequently ran the business jointly.[12] Macy's in New York owed much of its early success to Margaret Getchell, a relative of Roland Macy, who was the store's first super-intendent and chief executive.[13] Yet these are the exceptions that prove the rule that in business generally women rarely reach the very top: a situation that reflects the broader theme of the unequal distribution of

Figure 22 'Queens of the Proletariat': saleswomen in Baltimore, 1909. Their highly polished boots were often commented upon in Paris. Their American sisters were just as fastidious (*source:* courtesy of Mr Bob Jones, Northern Herald Books).

power between the sexes. But, nevertheless, department stores were the first institutions that opened the door of middle and high management to women, thereby creating perhaps the first career structure with genuine prospects of promotion for women in the modern period.

Most women, however, had to endure long hours, tight discipline and often the iniquities of the living-in system. Low pay and the lack of effective trade union organisation was a major problem for British workers. In contrast, McBride has described the world of late nineteenth-century Parisian women store workers in a much more favourable light. These women, known in Paris as the 'Queens of the Proletariat', enjoyed wage levels that were four times higher than those of local industrial working women, had access to paid holidays, maternity leave and, in the years prior to 1914, could increasingly afford to rent their own apartments and create a life-style not unlike the 'ambitious young bourgeois women'; see Figure 22).[14]

The experience of Parisian women employed in the *grands magasins* reflects the larger size of these stores and the accompanying need for managers to develop newer, more modern forms of paternalistic industrial relations. Certainly by the 1930s the larger British stores were offering similar, if less lavish, perks to their workers. Similarly, the large American stores, such as Marshall Field, in the 1890s had long ended the living-in system, practised discipline and promotion through meticulous records of staff performance, employed education officers for staff training and operated a sophisticated personnel management system. We also need to keep in mind McBride's reminder that in Paris men formed the majority of store workers prior to 1914.[15] This was the reverse of the American experience, where competition from commerce for male clerical staff gave women the ascendancy in department store employment by the 1890s.[16] We unfortunately lack precise data for Britain on this subject but a reasonable guestimate would be that Britain was somewhere between the two, with women dominating the sales floor by the Edwardian period.[17]

The theme of the department store and sexuality is as complex as the economic, and equally riddled with contradictions and ambiguities. Rachel Bowlby, in her study of women and department stores based on the novels of Gissing, Dreisser and Zola, is in no doubt that the *grand magasin* was a major venue for the economic and sexual subjection of women. Her curious mixture of Freud and vulgar Marxism may have appeal to literary critics but its utility to historians is negligible. A much more fruitful approach has been applied by Walkowitz in her study of women and Victorian city centres and by Valverdé who has investigated the late nineteenth-century unease over the relationship between finery and the morality of women.[18] These two authors, in their separate studies, explore a world of dangerous space for women, the fear of white slavers lurking in the powder rooms of large establishments and the moraliser's nostrum that a love of fashion is the slippery slope to the brothel. These late nineteenth-century urban myths may have little grounding in reality but Valverdé and Walkowitz clearly demonstrate the potency of such fears in late Victorian middle-class discourse.

The 'liminal' nature of the department store was central to this theme. The *grand magasin* was perceived as 'marginal space', a place where the rules of everyday polite society were stretched and occasionally broken. Indeed it could occupy that same section of the late Victorian mental map as Brighton beach.[19] If the popular image of Brighton involved undressing on the shore and the 'dirty weekend', the department store could offer fare that was equally *risqué*. The reading rooms of the *grands magasins* were used, it was claimed, by women to write letters to their lovers; while in France, Miller has noted the popular literature on men known as 'frotteurs'. These characters were reputed to circulate the department stores in order to 'follow the crowds in order to rub up against them'.[20]

The department store certainly provided an abundance of fuel for this bonfire of sexual innuendo. The women workers in the large stores were frequently the subject of Pygmalion fantasies, particularly in the realist novels on *grands magasins* ranging from Zola's work on Parisian stores through to Boehme's novel set in a large Berlin establishment.[21] The women workers' background added to this perception. Most were recruited for their attractiveness and many stores preferred provincial young women who readily deferred to their metropolitan customers. Thus many were not only attractive but also cut off from their families, living either above the shop or in their own apartments. Their knowledge of fashion and keen dress sense marked them out from other young women and it was not uncommon for crowds of young men to be found waiting outside the staff entrance of department stores at closing time.[22] In reality these women were establishing a life-style that today is shared by many young women from a variety of occupations; but because they were the first, comment and discussion were inevitable.[23]

A large number of social critics from a variety of backgrounds were quick to condemn this new urban life-style. Foremost amongst these was the great Victorian journalist, W.T. Stead. Fresh from his famous 'virgins for sale' exposure, Stead turned his attention to the alleged connection between women department store workers and prostitution. Stead chose Chicago as the venue for this work, which resulted in his famous study, *If Christ came to Chicago*, written during 1893, the year of the Colombian Exposition. Stead could find little fault with Marshall Field's store but he was convinced that Field's success had torn the social fabric of Chicago society by ruining small traders and by stimulating his rivals to employ young girls and pay poor wages. 'Young children are employed as cash girls in Chicago at a much earlier age than would be permitted in Europe, and in more than one of the great stores ugly stories are current of wages being fixed at a rate which assumed that they would be supplemented by the allowance of a friend' (see Figure 23). But Stead was in no doubt that 'Not food but clothes, not plain clothes but finery, that is ... the want that drives many to a life of shame.'[24]

Figure 23 A cash girl, Baltimore, 1909 (*source*: courtesy of Mr Bob Jones, Northern Herald Books).

Despite his many excursions and interviews with key figures in Chicago's low life, Stead's thesis rests largely on hearsay. Talking to Selfridge on the subject he did manage to extract the fact that, 'three girls in the last five years had gone bad' at Marshall Field's.[25] Stead, probably aware of Field's famous employee records system, did not challenge this figure which, given the 3,000 sales staff employed in the State Street store, is remarkably low. He found a similar picture at Field's main rivals, The Fair, and Siegal, Cooper and Co. Elizabeth Beardsley Butler's 1907 investigation of women's work in a variety of Pittsburgh trades is a classic text on women's labour history, but her discussion of department store workers resonates more with Stead's moralising than a scientific social survey. This study did find some evidence of prostitution amongst store workers. One of the cases cited by Butler concerned Rose, who:

> was employed at the ribbon counter. She had a mother and two sisters dependent upon her, and her mother was always urging her for more money.

She began while still in the store to 'make money on the side'. The management discovered this and dismissed her. She left for a city in Ohio; went into
a house of prostitution there from which she sends her mother money.[26]

Two points stand out from this example: first, did Rose's mother's
'urgings' include the suggestion of prostitution?; and secondly, we need
to note the management's unwillingness to tolerate such activities. This
last issue tallies with the general policy of Pittsburgh stores to employ
girls with family ties who needed to 'only work for pin money'.[27]
Butler also conceded that, 'Some stores have a waiting list of applicants
… Competition for positions in the stores is indeed often so keen as to
create a shortage of workers in the factory districts, much more in
domestic help.'[28] Such demand, coupled with Butler's insistence upon
the moral danger of department store employment, could suggest a
stampede into prostitution in early twentieth-century Pittsburgh. Yet
despite her wide research, including police sources, Butler only cites
four instances of shopworker prostitution and offers no quantitative
evidence on its prevalence amongst the city's 7,500 female store employees. This is clearly insufficient to justify her claim that, 'in the moral
jeopardy of shop girls lies one of the most widespread and serious
social problems of the women-employing trades'. Moreover, given the
prohibitive expense of appropriate working clothes incurred by new
employees, only women from the better-off working and lower-middle
classes could hope to find employment in local stores.[29]
    Britain also had 'muck-rakers' who were convinced that the depart-
ment store was a major source of vice. The Fabians and Christian
Socialists shared views similar to Stead's. The Revd R.J. Campbell in
January 1909 caused a controversy with his claim that shopgirls were
paid so badly they were forced to sell their bodies.[30] Campbell received
support from the Bishop of London who broadened the attack to
include the 'living-in system'. By the end of February, Lloyd George,
whose major backers were Welsh department store owners, was giving
legal advice to store proprietors on how to counter the Campbell
allegations.[31] The issue in Britain was always enmeshed with the living-
in system and the 'latch-key' scandal; the latter was probably another
popular rumour that some store proprietors supplied keys to the
women's living quarters rather than wage rises and thus turned the
upper floor of some stores into brothels. As in Chicago there is little
evidence to support these allegations against the morality of shop-

workers. The present writer has only found one instance of men on shop premises after closing. This was in 1887 when 'two gentlemen' entered the sleeping quarters of Howell and Co., Cardiff, claiming they, 'thought it was a brothel'. Given Howell's reputation for employing devout Methodists and the store's well-known evening hymn sessions in the dormitory the conclusion that the 'gentlemen's' advisers were playing a practical joke is inescapable.[32]

The sexual innuendo that was aimed at department stores, despite the lack of hard evidence, did stick in the popular imagination. In 1906 a new West End play, *The Heroic Stubbs* by Henry Arthur Jones, included a salesgirl character who uttered the line, 'What's the use of being virtuous in a store?' The ensuing publicity over these words caused an outcry in the trade press. Ironically the trade press itself was partly responsible for perpetuating this innuendo.[33] As early as 1887, largely reflecting the conservative nature of British stores, the *Draper's Record* carried a story on the evils of the American practice of employing women buyers. The article claimed that women could be tempted by 'fancy dresses' which would have no appeal to male buyers; the conclusion was that 'In business as in the more tender pursuits of l'amour the wiles of wicked men prove too much for the average woman.'[34] The following year the same journal carried a lengthy piece on Parisian women store workers which questioned the women's morals, claiming they flirted with male customers whom they often met later on assignations. Despite these male incursions on to the sales floor, there is evidence which indicates how women contrived to exclude men from the feminine terrain of the department store. The women workers in Marshall Field's were noted for their scornful giggling at men who accompanied their wives in the store. These 'Molly Husbands' suffered both the ridicule of breaking late nineteenth-century gender stereotypes and the subtle tactics of both women customers and workers defending their 'space'.[35] Many stores appeared to have colluded in this process of male exclusion by providing 'Men's Shops' with separate access (see Figure 24). One Blackpool store even went so far as to provide a men's room replete with newspapers, free cigars and coffee.[36] By the 1890s the feminine domination of department store interiors was heavily underscored by the advent of new window display techniques. Apart from Christmas, Arthur Fraser and his colleagues concentrated their artistic endeavours upon women's fashion. These new electric vistas proclaimed the femininity of the *grand magasin* to all who passed by.

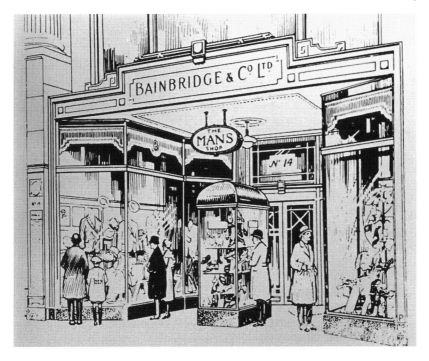

Figure 24 Bainbridge's, Newcastle 'Man's Shop', 1932. A separate entrance for the nervous male! (*source*: courtesy of Newcastle upon Tyne City Library).

The reputation of store proprietors could also often serve to perpetuate the immoral reputation of the department stores. Whiteley's extramarital activities and the apartments which he kept for his young saleswomen mistresses were the subject of much metropolitan gossip. When Mrs Whiteley discovered the 'Universal Provider's' activities as a 'ladies' man' she left the marital home and petitioned for a divorce. Separation, on terms heavy to Whiteley, rather than divorce was the result of this action, but the press made much of the 'Great Whiteley Divorce' which confirmed his 'ménage' at Kilburn with Louisa Turner, a pretty young assistant from the 'Universal Provider's' toy department.[37] There were suggestions that Whiteley also had a relationship with Louisa's sister, Emma, and it was the latter's illegitimate son, Horace, who murdered Whiteley with two shots to the head in the midst of the store's January sale in 1907. Lambert, Whiteley's early biographer, concluded that the 'Universal Provider' 'reap[ed] late in life a bitter harvest from the wild oats he had sown so gaily in the heyday of his man-hood!'[38]

No other proprietor equalled Whiteley in public sexual scandal, but his activities did throw into question the conduct of his colleagues. W.T. Stead, during his Chicago sojourn, concluded almost in surprise that Marshall Field's possessed, 'none of the scandal, such as rumour has persistently associated with other dry goods houses in Chicago and elsewhere'.[39] Field's partner, and the genius behind the State Street store, Selfridge, was certainly out of the Whiteley mould; Selfridge's woman-ising, high living and heavy gambling ensured that the sexually promis-cuous department store proprietor theme established by Whiteley in the 1880s continued in the popular press well into the 1930s.[40] Even that somewhat staid Methodist establishment, Bainbridge's of Newcastle, took on a certain *frisson* during the 1930s thanks to the activities of one of the founder's grandsons. Jack Bainbridge was Newcastle's premier inter-war playboy. He toured the streets in his pale blue Rolls Royce, had a reputation for 'entertaining' actresses and showgirls at his home, known locally as 'Virtue Villa', and young women on Tyneside were banned from attending parties if his name was on the invitation list. Jack's activities appear to have dented the family's reputation and the Fenwicks of Newcastle, the major business rival to Bainbridge's, expressed their unease when young Pamela Fenwick announced her engagement to G.M.V. Bainbridge. The Fenwicks, who shared a strong commitment to local Methodism in the late nineteenth and early twentieth centuries with the Bainbridges, now looked upon their former religious allies as 'wild and flamboyant'.[41]

The sexual dimension of department store life was closely associated with another social phenomenon, shoplifting, an activity that taxed the minds of many Victorian commentators. Pilfering from shops is as old as retailing, but what captured the popular imagination in the second half of the nineteenth century was that much of this crime, especially in larger stores, was committed by middle-class women.[42] The song, 'Ladies, Don't go Thieving', sold on London Streets in 1867 and widely sung in music halls, expresses both the scale of shoplifting and popular astonishment at finding it practised by the well-to-do:

> Oh, don't we live in curious times,
> You scarce could be believing,
> When Frenchmen fight and emperors die

And ladies go a-thieving.
A beauty of the West End went,
Around a shop she lingers,
And there upon some handkerchiefs
She clapped her pretty fingers.
Into the shop she gently popped;
The world is quite deceiving
When ladies have a notion got
To ramble out a-thieving...

Whiteley estimated that for every male he caught, 300 female shoplifters were detected and these were drawn almost exclusively from the middle and upper classes.[43] Abelson, in her important study of shoplifting, has noted that 'the carnival atmosphere found in some of the new department stores must certainly have contributed to the sense of rules being suspended and normal inhibitions being cast off in the anonymity of the crowd. Shoplifting thrived in the "buzz and excitement of a busy store"'.[44]

Apologists for this middle-class female misbehaviour stressed the 'innate weakness' of women which could be activated into criminality by the atmosphere of the store.[45] Abelson demonstrates that middle-class shoplifters generally got off lightly when caught. Early store detectives usually came from a working-class background which could lead to great tension when arresting middle-class customers.[46] Many stores, fearful of such tensions resulting in bad publicity, sent miscreants on their way after a gentle ticking-off. If a court case did ensue the defence usually cited biological factors, particularly those associated with menstruation, which usually guaranteed a dismissal, a binding-over or at worse a light fine. Biological factors were amalgamated with psychoanalytical theories in the interwar period and the defence often claimed that shoplifting was a form of sexual gratification reflecting frustration at home.[47] The class dimension to shoplifting is inescapable as the following two cases reported in the *Draper's Record* in 1932 demonstrate. The first involved a well-off woman from Harrogate who was caught stealing goods worth £4. 4s. from a large store. Her defence called Dr B. Foster, a specialist in shoplifting, who told the court that the defendant was suffering from 'Psychical Asphenia' which was caused by 'biological changes'. The court appeared to have been convinced by Dr Foster's theory, the defendant being bound over for two years with no

Figure 25 'A Lady gone a-thieving' (*source*: British Library).

fine imposed.[48] Two weeks earlier two working-class women were arrested in Bainbridge's Newcastle store in the act of stealing 'various items'. These two women put up little defence and called no experts to speak on their behalf in court which sentenced them both to 15 months' hard labour.[49]

Sexual innuendo, lecherous men and shoplifting all suggest that department stores were extremely *risqué* establishments. Yet there is much evidence which presents a more sober picture. The background and behaviour of store staff, particularly women, as we have seen, was a major area of discussion. The evidence at hand, however, suggests a different interpretation from that presented in popular late Victorian discourse. The prostitution scandal fuelled by W.T. Stead, the Reverend R.J. Campbell and the Bishop of London was never based on any firm evidence. Even in Chicago, Stead failed lamentably to demonstrate his thesis. The recruitment policy of many stores reflects the care that many proprietors took over their choice of staff. It is surely counter-intuitive to assume that proprietors would be lax in their hiring procedures given the front-line position that sales staff performed in terms of service, politeness and financial responsibility? Bainbridge's women workers of marriageable age were desired by the respectable young labour aristocrats. Josiah Wedgwood, the future cabinet minister, served a premium apprenticeship at Armstrong's Elswick works. Living the life of a labour aristocrat, he described with pride his morning routine:

> I fancied myself as a skilled workman in that closest and richest of Trade Unions – The Boilermakers and Shipwrights. Six feet high with a cloth cap, scarf tied round the neck, white moleskin trousers, with a hammer poking out of one pocket and a steel rule out of another, I swaggered to work with a sense of mastery that no office job can ever supply. There was a girl who worked at Bainbridge's, whom I passed every day, a very nice girl if I had been a working man.[50]

Wedgwood courted the girl for a while but conceded that she was suitable for a labour aristocrat but not for the son of one of the nation's major industrial families.

What is often overlooked is that sexual attraction is two-way traffic. It also needs to be borne in mind that in Britain and France for most of the period prior to 1914 men formed the majority of sales staff. In America, before the exodus of male workers into commerce, the relationship between women customers and male assistants was frequently the source of comment. For example, at Marshall Field's one incident involved Mrs Robert T. Lincoln, the deceased president's daughter-in-law, who 'pleased at the gracious treatment she received, impulsively removed a rose from her gown and fastened it on an embarrassed salesman's lapel. "I raised it in my garden", she told him, "and I want you to have it".'[51] A.T. Steward of New York, it was noted, preferred to employ males: 'He hired the most handsome men he could obtain because he noted that ladies who shopped in his store liked to gossip and even flirt with them.'[52] Perhaps similar incidents took place in Britain; the trade press, for example, reported in 1888 that West End stores were insisting that male assistants shave off their moustaches.[53]

The evidence bears out the argument that late Victorian and early twentieth-century unease over the sexual aspects of department store life was based largely on rumour and innuendo. Nevertheless the fact that department stores were talked about in such a manner does need explaining. The obvious solution to this problem, the newness and scale of the *grands magasins*, has generally been overlooked. Department stores were novel institutions and their scale often dominated the burgeoning city centre. The demise of the old 'walking city' with its patterns of sociability based upon face-to-face relationships was replaced by the anonymity of the modern metropolis. The department store often formed the hub of the growing central area with its teeming crowds. The women customers and workers in the stores were highly visible yet, in contrast to older patterns of urban life, also highly anonymous. This is not to argue that women shopping was something new; as Vickery has shown women had long been central to the control of consumption.[54] Rather it was freedom afforded to such large numbers of women by the new type of shopping that caused unease in a society dominated by patriarchal values. With hindsight we can see, as McBride has argued, that these women, particularly the workers, were pioneers of the new urban sociability. McBride has shown that Parisian women workers in the *grands magasins* pursued a life-style which shocked contemporaries. Many could afford their own apartment, visited cafés and bars and shaped and enjoyed new forms of leisure, which have become the norm in modern society.[55]

Politics, women and department stores may seem a curious trio, but it is nevertheless highly important and central to the theme of this chapter. Some commentators have emphasised the passive nature of shopping as a female experience. Simon Frith and Howard Horne, for example, see women shoppers pursuing an 'idle experience, an opportunity for nostalgia, daydream and desire'.[56] Such a perspective appears far removed from political action, yet the historical record is peppered with many instances of the politicisation of women consumers.

E.P. Thompson's seminal essay on the moral economy and bread

Figure 26 Women's Territory! Fenwick's Newcastle Sale, 1912. It was obviously hot inside – note the confidence of the women customers, opening windows for access to the balcony for fresh air and the chance to give progress reports to friends at street level (*source*: I am indebted to Professor Norman McCord for supplying this illustration).

riots is an early example of women acting in a political and sometimes violent manner in the market-place. Clare Midgley's study on women's protest movements against slavery, which focused upon the boycott of such goods as cotton and sugar, continues this tradition into the nineteenth century.[57] Nigel Todd's recent work on popular politics in north-east England has uncovered the formidable 'butchers' strike' of 1871, where women in the Northern Coalfield established an efficient, broad geographical organisation which involved the boycott of meat in protest against high prices. The fact that their mining menfolk endured a diet of herrings for several months is testimony to the strength of this particular women's movement.[58]

Nearer to our subject, women store customers were the major recruits to the Early Closing Movement established in 1856. The Early Closing Movement was similar to the Shoppers' Leagues, largely female organisations which emerged in France and America. The tactics of these organisations involved the picketing and boycotting of stores with a reputation for long hours and poor working conditions and the gradual reduction of working hours ahead of legislation is testimony to their effectiveness. The League in Baltimore even went so far as to employ a social scientist to investigate both the working conditions and home circumstances of store workers.[59] Women's customer organisations extended beyond concern for the well-being of workers. In 1887 a 'group of Bond Street women ... issued a decree against wearing garments which included feathers from small birds'.[60] This campaign, which has a strong late twentieth-century resonance, has been analysed by Alan Haynes.[61]

A more direct political link between women and department stores has been analysed by William Leach with his usual subtlety. Leach concedes that American department store selling techniques, particularly after 1890, with their emphasis on colour, light and marketing, worked to reinforce gender stereotypes – men were often provided with separate doors and the colours in the 'manshop' were usually rugged and 'masculine'. But Leach argues that the new consumerism also challenged sexual differences by providing a raft of professional employment for women both inside the store and in the important related areas of fashion journalism, advertising agencies, dress design and the management of cosmetic firms.[62] This empowerment of some women, together with the growing emphasis on service, gave rise to a new form of feminine individualism: 'the customer is always right' and the customer

TAKING THE LAW IN ONE'S OWN HANDS.

Fair but Considerate Customer. "Pray sit down. You look so tired. I've been riding all the afternoon in a Carriage, and don't require a Chair."

Figure 27 Sisterly Solidarity. This *Punch* illustration shows the concern, often organised, felt by women customers for store assistants (*source: Punch*, 14 July 1880).

is usually a woman. Leach demonstrates clearly the speed with which department store proprietors picked up this changing mentality. Numerous department stores in America gave their much-prized windows over to suffragists for suffrage advertisements and displays. The women themselves adopted department store display techniques in their visual material and invited department stores to advertise in their journals. John Wanamaker went so far as to give his staff time off work to attend suffrage meetings and demonstrations. Leach concludes:

> Their [women's] participation in consumer experience challenged and subverted the complex of qualities traditionally known as feminine – dependence, passivity, religious piety, domestic inwardness, sexual purity and maternal

nurture. Mass consumer culture presented to women a new definition of gender that carved out space for individual expression similar to men's and that stood in tension with the older definition passed on to them by their mothers and grandmothers.[63]

Leach's imaginative interpretation of the new consumer culture generated by the department store is in stark contrast to the zombie-like women portrayed by Bowlby. He is certainly correct in emphasising the political importance of the new female consumer mentality. Leach does, however, neglect the historical continuities of women using their power as customers for political purposes as outlined above. Nevertheless, by shifting the focus away from women as passive consumers and towards a perspective that views women as rational actors who often articulated their concerns through the 'world of goods', we move nearer to reality.

The British experience in many respects parallels the American one analysed by Leach. Department stores were the main advertisers in the suffrage press and, more importantly, the store provided territory that could be used as a venue for political purposes. The important women's movement in Newcastle which undertook campaigns of bombing, civil disobedience and window-smashing, used Fenwick's tea-room as their headquarters.[64] The department store since its birth had always presented a political dimension, its association with Liberalism was well known and it had frequently served as a venue for a range of campaigns from a concern for staff conditions to animal welfare. Yet in a sense this should come as no surprise. Labour historians, for example, have long known that to find the authentic voice of working-class women's politics during the late Victorian and Edwardian period they look not to socialist or even trades union archives but to the records of the Women's Co-operative Guild.[65] Consumption witnesses the exercise of power by both the seller and the buyer. Women have long been aware of this and have been highly innovative in expressing their power for the common good as well as for themselves and their families.

Notes

1. S. Porter-Benson, *Counter Cultures*, 1988, p. 76.
2. Ibid.
3. Ibid.; T. McBride, '"A Woman's World": department stores and the evolution of women's employment', *French Historical Studies*, Vol. X, Fall 1978; W. Leach,

'Transformations in a culture of consumption: women and department stores 1890–1925', *Journal of American History*, 71, September 1984.

4. Ewen, *Captains of Consciousness*, 1976, part 3, *passim*.

5. Bowlby, *Just Looking*, 1985, pp. 31–2.

6. M. Penn, *Manchester Fourteen Miles*, Caliban, Horsham, 1979, p. 41.

7. T. Hadaway, 'Comic dialect', in R. Colls and B. Lancaster (eds), *Geordies. Roots of Regionalism*, Edinburgh, 1992, p. 88.

8. M. Marx, 'A short sketch of an eventful life', p. 130, in R. Payne (ed), *The Unknown Karl Marx*, New York Public Library, New York, 1971.

9. W. Leach, *Land of Desire*, 1993, p. 57.

10. R. Colls, *Pitmen of the Northern Coalfield. Work, Culture and Protest*, Manchester, 1987. Rob Colls succinctly summarised this situation: 'The colliery produces coal as much by the pounding of the "pit wife's poss" as by the nicking of the pitman's pick.', p, 135.

11. M, Miller, *The Bon Marché*, pp. 224–5.

12. Ibid., p. 44.

13. R.M. Hower, *History of Macy's*, p.65.

14. T. McBride, op. cit., p. 681.

15. Ibid., p. 666.

16. R.M. Hower, op. cit., p. 195.

17. The difficulty of accurately enumerating British retail workers by gender is discussed in L. Holcombe, *Victorian Ladies at Work*, 1973, especially Appendix 3.

18. J. Walkowitz, *City of Dreadful Delight. Narratives of Sexual Danger in Late-Victorian London*, Virago, London, 1992. M. Valverdé, 'The love of finery: fashion and the fallen woman in nineteenth-century social discourse', *Victorian Studies*, Vol. 32, No. 2, Winter, 1989.

19. R. Shields, *Places on the Margin. Alternative Geographies of Modernity*, Routledge, London, 1991. discusses 'liminality' in the context of modern society. See especially Chapter 2.

20. M. Miller, op. cit., pp. 192–3.

21. Zola's *Au Bonheur des Dames* has received much attention. See, for example, Bowlby, op. cit., Chapter 5 and Dreisser's work which has been discussed above. Boehme's *The Department Store. A Novel of Today*, New York, 1912, is less well known. It does, however, present a fascinating Zolaesque account of life in a Berlin store.

22. R. Pound, *The Fenwick Story*, 1972, p. 38.

23. T. McBride, op. cit., p. 679.

24. W.T. Stead, *If Christ Came to Chicago!*, 1894, pp. 234; 244.

25. Ibid., p. 244.

26. E. Beardsley Butler, *Women and The Trades, Pittsburgh, 1907-8*, University of Pittsburgh Press, Pittsburgh, PA, 1984, pp. 305–6.

27. Ibid., p. 306.

28. Ibid., p. 307.

29. Ibid., p. 305.

30. *Draper's Record*, 2 January 1909.

31. Ibid., 6 February 1909.

32. Ibid., 10 December 1887.

33. Ibid., 10 February 1906.
34. Ibid., 24 December 1887.
35. L. Wendt and H. Kogan, *Give the Lady What She Wants*, 1952, p. 277.
36. *Draper's Record*, 28 April 1906.
37. R.S. Lambert, *The Universal Provider*, 1938, pp. 158–62.
38. Ibid., p. 162.
39. W.T. Stead, op. cit., p. 62.
40. G. Honeycombe, *Selfridges*, pp 51; 58.
41. A. and J. Airey, *The Bainbridges of Newcastle*, 1979, p. 160–7.
42. E.S. Abelson, *When Ladies Go A-Thieving. Middle Class Shoplifters in the Victorian Department Stores*, New York, 1989, is a recent scholarly survey of the phenomenon.
43. R.S. Lambert, op. cit., p. 126.
44. Abelson, op. cit., p. 143.
45. Ibid., p. 188.
46. Ibid., p. 139.
47. Ibid., p. 197.
48. *Draper's Record*, 30 July 1932.
49. Ibid., 16 July 1932.
50. J. Wedgwood, *Memoirs of a Fighting Life,* Hutchinson, London, 1941, p. 35.
51. Twyman, *History of Marshall Field*, 1954, p. 29.
52. Hower, op. cit., p. 193.
53. *Warehouseman and Draper's Trade Journal*, 18 February 1888.
54. A. Vickery, 'Women and the world of goods: a Lancashire woman and her possessions, 1751–81', in J. Brewer and R. Porter (eds), *Consumption and the World of Goods*, London, 1993.
55. T. McBride, op. cit., p. 679.
56. Quoted in C. Gardner and J. Sheppard, *Consuming Passions: The Rise of Retail Culture*, Unwin Hyman, London, 1989, p. 57.
57. E.P. Thompson, 'The moral economy of the crowd', *Past and Present*, 1971. C. Midgley, *Women Against Slavery. The British Campaign, 1780–1870*, Routledge, London, 1992.
58. N. Todd, 'The Red Herring War of 1872: women's rights, butchers and Co-ops in the Northern Coalfield', in B. Lancaster and P. Maguire (eds), *Towards the Co-operative Commonwealth,* forthcoming, 1995.
59. E. Beardsley Butler, *Saleswomen in Mercantile Stores. Baltimore, 1909,* New York Charities Publications Committee, New York, 1912.
60. *Draper's Record*, 15 October 1887.
61. A. Haynes, 'Murderous millinery: the struggle for the Plumage Act, 1921'. *History Today*, Vol. 33, July 1983.
62. W. Leach, 'Transformations in a culture of consumption: women and department stores, 1890–1925', *Journal of American History*, 71, September 1984, p. 331.
63. Ibid., p. 342.
64. D. Neville, 'The Tyneside Suffrage Movement', unpublished MPhil thesis, Newcastle upon Tyne Polytechnic, 1992.
65. J. Gaffin and D. Thoms, *Caring and Sharing. The Centenary History of the Women's Co-operative Guild*, Co-operative Union, Manchester, 1983.

CHAPTER ELEVEN

THE DEPARTMENT STORE
AND SOCIETY:
THEMES AND TRENDS

This study has largely concentrated upon the department store up until the Second World War. The subsequent period will be covered in a further volume which will analyse post-war retailing trends. It is, however, worthwhile to flag some of the major developments that have taken place in recent decades to gain a sense of continuity and change with the relevant issues covered in this present work. Rapid changes have become a hallmark of modern retailing and department stores have not shirked from this often difficult process. By adopting a long perspective, the importance of the themes in this study will become more apparent.

Despite reports of their impending demise, department stores have proved remarkably enduring. Jefferys, in his classic study, estimated the department store sector having between one and two per cent of the total retail trade in Britain in 1900, rising to between three and four per cent by 1920. Using the difficult and awkward data contained in the 1950 Census of Distribution, Jefferys arrived at a figure of *c.* 5.6 per cent for the department store share of retailing.[1] There were, however, many fluctuations within this upward trend. For example, in the unusual market conditions of the post-war period, department stores took 10.9 per cent of all sales in 1947 against a backcloth of rationing and utility schemes.[2] But this short-term success was checked by fundamental shifts in the structure of the market.

The rise in working-class income during and immediately after the war was partly achieved at the expense of middle-class salaries. By 1953 the International Association of Department Stores (IADS) was reporting serious problems amongst British up-market stores and in 1955 it was urging its British members to target the 'prosperous council house tenant'.[3] Harrods responded to the new circumstances in the market by taking over stores in Birmingham, Manchester and Sheffield in the hope of tapping the large number of skilled workers in those cities.[4] Brown's of Chester was one of the first luxury stores to give serious attention to the new pattern of income distribution. As early as 1943 Harris, the Chairman of Brown's, who also wrote on economics and psychology, employed a team of Mass Observation investigators to advise him on how to make the store more appealing to working-class customers.[5] The Mass Observation archive, which contains the documents on the Brown's survey, offers rich insights into the social attitudes of the period as well as the problems faced by the store in its attempt to reposition itself in the market.

Working-class customers of Brown's expressed unease inside the store about how 'the assistants, unless you are well-dressed, treat you like dirt ...' Others complained of the restaurant, where 'the service is pretty rotten ... the sweet had no sugar on at all'.[6] These attitudes appear to have been reciprocated by the staff, a workforce highly trained at serving a high-class clientele. The highly-paid manager of the restaurant, with a background in classy London restaurants, had difficulty in coping with the tastes of working-class customers. Fish and chips, served up as 'Breaded fillet of plaice with French fried potatoes, garden peas and tartare sauce' was one compromise, but the manager, nevertheless, was aghast at the size of the portions demanded and the working-class tendency to 'eat with their knives'.[7] A shopwalker wanted 'the best of the artisan type', but hoped that 'we'll never go down to the lowest'. Nevertheless, Brown's did have some success; one investigator reported that women from socio-economic class 'C' 'now wander about as if they own the place'. When one of these customers was addressed as 'madam', she retorted, 'I'm not madam, simply missis'.[8]

A range of other strategies were employed to make the stores more comfortable for working-class customers. The commonest was to remove the counters and introduce self-service. This was the path favoured by Whiteley's, but the Bayswater store was forced to abandon the system in the face of customer hostility.[9] This was a serious blow for Whiteley's and confirmed their geographic fate. The ageing, fixed-income clientele of Whiteley's won back their cherished counters. An industry report noted, however, that 'traditional counter customers' had no potential for growth and that the majority of stores were changing rapidly to self-service.[10]

Illustrious *grands magasins* from Beales of Bournemouth, to Debenham's of Oxford Street, moved over to self-service and 'island shelving systems' with greater ease than that experienced by Whiteley's. Beatties of Wolverhampton went a stage further in attracting working-class customers when it became the first department store to use television to advertise its January sale in 1957.[11] These tactics proved highly successful, store profits were growing rapidly during the late 1950s and the number of department stores rose from 360 in 1950 to 533 in 1957.[12] We must note, however, that much of this growth in numbers was the result of stores, destroyed by bombing, being rebuilt. It is also worth keeping in mind that the move to attract working-class customers had been well under way during the 1930s, particularly amongst the Debenham provincial stores based in the prosperous Midlands and southern manufacturing towns. Bentall's of Kingston is a good example of this type, seeing sales increase by 70 per cent during the 1950s.[13] By 1960 the majority of stores had successfully adapted to the trading conditions of post-war Britain and were reaping the benefits of the consumer boom. Visually, the stores had dramatically changed, counters disappeared and self-service was the norm. Behind the scenes, stores were being equally innovative – by 1961 it was reported that many of the larger stores were utilising computers for stock and account control.[14]

Many commentators have drawn attention to the role played by the ending of Resale Price Maintenance (RPM), and the introduction of Selective Employment Tax (SET) in 1965, in revolutionising British retailing. These two events certainly placed pressure on staff levels and marketing policy, but this process was already well under way during the 1950s as stores adapted to the phenomenon of rising working-class prosperity. Working-class customers did not share the store loyalty of the middle class and were more prone to shop around for a bargain. Department stores were restricted by RPM in their pricing policy, but nevertheless continued their search for market advantage. Keddies, the large Southend department store, opened Britain's first discount shop in 1960.[15] But the most dramatic development took place in Market Street, Newcastle – arguably the birthplace of the department store.

Market Street had been suffering during the 1950s from the drift of customers northwards to Fenwick's and Northumberland Street. A branch of Binns, the Sunderland-based group that was part of the Fraser empire, had, for many years, traded in adjoining premises to Bainbridge's. Sharing a similar, but diminishing customer base, competition between the two was intense. Binns tried to gain an advantage by giving account customers a two and a half per cent discount on bills paid within a month.[16] Bainbridge's, now part of the John Lewis Partnership, decided that this tactic undermined their policy of 'Never Knowingly Undersold' and responded by reducing all prices by two and a half per cent. This clear breach of RPM was the opening salvo in the campaign to end fixed prices.[17]

The ending of RPM and the introduction of SET in 1965 put pressure on department store labour costs. The number of tills was reduced and shop-floor staff management became highly streamlined. By 1967 the John Lewis Partnership had organised its sales staff in the 'manning the bridge' system in their quest for greater efficiency.[18] Apart from pressures brought by the mid-1960s' legislation, department stores were also feeling the impact of the new fashion boutiques which quickly dominated the young-fashion market. In 1959 the teenage market was estimated to account for 8.5 per cent of national personal income and this figure accelerated during the 1960s.[19] Some department stores such as Harrods reacted to this trend by opening their own in-house boutiques. The Knightsbridge store's famous 'Way In' was opened with much publicity in June 1967 by Sir Hugh Fraser, himself attired in a lilac shirt, corduroy suit and floral tie.[20] The most dramatic entry into the youth market came from the Lewis's group, with the opening of 'Miss Selfridge' in September 1966. The 'Miss Selfridge' concept was the brainchild of Winifred Sainer, sister of the company Chairman, and involved the setting up of a new team of buyers and designers. The success of this boutique within a store on Oxford Street encouraged the company to introduce similar operations in other stores throughout the country.[21]

The youth market presented wider problems to department stores than trends in clothing fashion. The teenager had been a social phenomenon since the mid-1950s and by 1970 a growing section of the population identified with a cultural style that was rapidly transcending the apparel market. One of the first entrepreneurs to spot this trend was Terence Conran. His mid-1960s' Habitat Store in Chelsea provided the perfect domestic background for a generation which, through its musical and fashion allegiances, was consciously rejecting the style of its parents.[22] Perhaps the most dramatic manifestation of this cultural shift was the opening of Biba in the Derry and Toms building, recently sold by the House of Fraser, in Kensington High Street. Biba's brief existence involved the take-over and refurbishment of a large department store by a small, but successful fashion boutique, backed by money from the Dorothy Perkins' chain.[23] Despite Biba's short existence it did have a major impact upon British retailing. For example, the refurbishment involved a stripping back to the building's 1930s' art deco style, the Palm Court restaurant was reopened, and the beauty of the store was celebrated in its own right. An innovative merchandising policy, which interestingly pre-dated some of the large Next stores by over a decade, involved the theming of a wide variety of items from belts to baked beans. The Biba concept was probably ahead of its time and the Kensington High Street experiment was soon abandoned.[24]

Biba's audacious use of the Derry and Tom's building was more than just a straw in the wind. Two decades of chasing the working-class pound and efficiency drives had reduced many department stores to a bland conformity. The individuality of stores, nurtured for decades, was disappearing under a welter of keenly priced branded goods and a boring interior of uniform fixtures and fittings. Moreover, the working-class income advantage that many of these developments had been designed to attract was diminishing. Wage freezes and growing un-employment were providing major obstacles to growth of the lower income market. Not surprisingly the *Draper's Record*, surveying the industry in 1974, counselled that department stores 'must trade up' to survive.[25]

The following decade saw the closure of many smaller department stores. Old familiar local names, ranging from Brixton's Bon Marché to Brown's of Workington, ceased trading. This was largely a response to geographical factors; many of these stores had found that their upper working and middle-class customers had moved on and the residents that remained preferred the new discount stores. Other closures, par-ticularly the John Lewis Partnership store in Finchley, reflected the important emergence of the Brent Cross Shopping Centre. Often wrongly described as an out-of-town shopping centre, Brent Cross, in reality, is north London's missing major retail area and has to be viewed as one of London's four major suburban centres, along with Croydon, Kingston and Romford. Taking advantage of its position alongside the North Circular Road and an enormous residential catchment area, Brent Cross has proved highly successful. This success, however, owes no small measure to the centre's two key anchor tenants, Fenwick's and the John Lewis Partnership stores.

The need to have major department stores as anchors has proved crucial to post-war shopping developments. Coventry Precinct, Britain's first new shopping centre, has never been a success and the local

authority for many years blamed the precinct's disappointing performance on the fact that it possessed only one department store. Similarly,
the high number of vacant units that has plagued Manchester's Arndale
Centre could be blamed on the absence of a department store tenant.
By contrast, Eldon Square, Newcastle's 1970s' inner-city mall, is one of
Britain's most successful shopping developments, thanks to the presence
of the John Lewis Partnership's flagship, Bainbridge's store, and Fenwick's
mammoth headquarters building. Fenwick's for most of its history
restricted its operation to Newcastle and Bond Street. The company
cautiously moved into Leicester in 1962, but it was not until the 1970s
that Fenwick's undertook their major expansion.[26] Fenwick's was one
of the first companies to realise the subtle changes that were taking
place in the geography of retailing. This quiet revolution consisted of
the rise of the 'shire town' as a regional shopping centre. Bath and
Chester had, of course, pioneered this trend at the end of the nineteenth
century, but the process rapidly accelerated after the mid-1960s. By
opening stores in Canterbury, Tunbridge Wells, York and Windsor,
Fenwick's has reaped the benefits of car-owning customers combining
shopping with a visit to a pleasant historic environment. It is easy to
speculate about the effect of, say, the Leeds middle-class family driving
to York, having tea at Betties and shopping at Fenwick's, upon the
businesses of central Leeds.

Fenwick's expansion strategy resulted in the company becoming the
second most profitable department store group by 1989.[27] This success
demonstrates that department stores with an imaginative management
can still play a central role in retail development. The major anchor
sites occupied by department stores at the new out-of-town malls,
including the Metrocentre at Gateshead, Meadowhall at Sheffield and
Lakeside at Thurrock, are testimony to companies such as Bentall's and
House of Fraser's desire to be at the leading edge of retail trends. The
mixed reports on the success of these new malls, however, makes even
provisional assessments extremely difficult.

Ironically, while some stores have been moving into new mall-based
premises, others have placed a new emphasis upon their original sites.
In 1987 Harrods removed the drab 1950s' and 1960s' fittings from the
Knightsbridge store in a return to Edwardian splendour. Many other
major London stores have followed suit in what also has to be viewed
as an international phenomenon, with *grands magasins* from the Bon
Marché in Paris to Marshall Field's, State Street, Chicago, undergoing

hugely expensive refurbishments to return the buildings to their original historic splendour. These refurbishments have emphasised the cathedral-esque nature of the buildings. Stained glass domes, marble pillars and intricate plasterwork have been repaired and restored as department store bosses seek to gain an advantage over rivals on the High Street and in the new malls. Store owners have been quick to notice that for many customers it is not just what you buy but where you buy it that is also important. Shoppers carrying often mundane branded goods in the plastic bags of the *grands magasins* have been a common sight for over a decade. Some may mock such behaviour as snobbish, but why should we condemn people for choosing to shop in a beautiful building? Moreover, they shop in a building that costs the owners dearly and the prices of many items are as keen as those found in the chain stores. Biba's in the early 1970s enunciated a new era for large stores. The style-conscious generation of the 1960s was perhaps not wealthy enough to support the Kensington store in the early 1970s, but as they prospered in the 1980s, many stores set out to attract them by emulating the example of the Derry and Tom's refurbishment.

In 1988 the president of Walker Group/CMI, the leading American store designers, listed ten rules for department store design. These included, 'Stores should be fun'; 'Marble is the linoleum of the 1980s'; 'Design is a silent salesman'; 'Everything that a customer sees from advertising to architecture to sales promotion and merchandising should speak with one voice'.[28] Selfridge, of course, had preached similar commandments on State Street almost a century earlier and he himself had been following a route already established by Boucicaut. Economics also shows strong continuity. Boucicaut's sales and Selfridge's bargain basement were vital to their stores' success. January and Summer Sales are of extreme importance to the industry's well-being and Marshall Field's monthly 'Deep Discount Sunday' is a major attraction in Chicago. The importance of sales and discounts clearly shows that the majority of customers retain their rationality when they enter these regenerated 'secular cathedrals'.

Department stores have existed for so long that they have become embedded into our psyche and they form an integral part of the pattern of everyday life. A Mintel survey in the late 1970s claimed that forty-seven per cent of British women visited a department store at least once a month and twenty per cent of all adults at least once a week.[29] When Bet Lynch of *Coronation Street* goes on a shopping spree it is announced to the nation that she is off to Kendal's. Similarly, the fictitious 'Underwood's' of Borchester is a venerated institution of the Archers, along with the 'Bull' and Nelson's wine bar. That keen observer of middle-class England, the novelist Barbara Pym, frequently refers to department stores in order to throw light on complex characters and situations. *No Fond Return of Love*, set in the London of 1960, contains many humorous accounts of suburban life in the metropolis. The main characters live in an area which 'took the overflow from Kensington and Harrods **do** deliver'. But Pym underlines the borderland nature of the area by noting that Pontings' white sale catalogue was stuffed in the letterbox! Elsewhere in her novels, vicars' wives are invariably wearing clothes from Schoolbreds.

Pym's world is one of women shoppers but the gender of shopping has changed dramatically in the post-war period. The days of the 'Man's Shop', with its discreet separate entrance, have long passed. In the immediate post-war period, shop assistants at Brown's told the Mass Observation investigators that they had witnessed an increase in the number of men accompanying their wives on shopping expeditions. The Mintel survey of 1978, which claimed that ten per cent of all adult men visited a department store at least once a month, indicates that male prejudice about shopping was beginning to break down. A visit to any high street or mall on a Saturday visibly demonstrates the growth of male participation in the experience of shopping. Men still insist that the purchase of 'technical' products, such as home electrical goods, requires their 'expertise'. Men are also reported to be more prone than women to impulse buying. These two points may explain why many department stores position items such as televisions and hi-fi on the far wall of the top floor or some other difficult-to-get-to space. Despite this growth in male participation in shopping, a strong continuity in the economic 'basket power' of women is still evident. A research report published in June 1982 claimed that over eighty per cent of all domestic purchases were made by, or influenced by women.[30]

The feminisation of the workforce, which has been progressing since the 1890s, accelerated after 1945. A survey published in 1957 reported that 798,000 people worked in Britain's non-food retail sector, and of these, seventy-one per cent were women, compared with sixty-four per cent in 1931. Moreover, forty per cent of women workers in this sector were married, and of these, sixty-eight per cent worked full time. Part-time work for women in retailing has increased dramatically during the post-war period.[31] By 1961 it was reported that thirty-nine per cent of women workers in the high street chains were part-timers, an increase of eight per cent in four years.[32] Department stores which require a more skilled workforce than variety stores employed nineteen per cent of their women workers on a part-time basis in 1961, slightly less than half the proportion of the chains. A subsequent survey published in 1969 unfortunately grouped department and variety stores together. This report showed that seventy-five per cent of staff in these stores were women, and of these, 28.9 per cent worked part time. These figures are on the high side for department stores but nevertheless confirm the trend of the growing domination of the workforce by women in department stores.[33]

Department stores, with their high proportion of administrative staff, buyers and managers, and the necessity in many departments for skilled sales staff with specialised product knowledge, do not lend themselves as readily as other retail outlets to a casualised labour force. This is clearly reflected in wage levels. The *Business Ratio Report* on wages in retailing in 1989 shows that the highest level of remuneration was paid in the major department stores followed by variety stores. Marks and Spencer, for example, were ranked eighteenth in this survey, behind the major department stores.[34] The working week has also been steadily reduced. The Industrial Society survey of 1969 reported that department store workers in London were employed for 39¾ hours per week; those in the provinces worked a forty-hour week. This comparatively skilled workforce was also highly profitable. The *Business Ratio Report* of 1989 placed Selfridge's and Fenwick's at the top of the retailing league table of profits per employee.[35]

In 1993 the popular British press reported surprise at the announcement by Harrods that it was considering employing only graduates as sales staff. These reports clearly indicate that retailing is still held in relatively low esteem. The articles in the press also suggest that the public is largely ignorant of the complex, sophisticated organisation that constitutes a department store. Most stores contain a greater range of items than that found in a modern aircraft. Moreover, the velocity at which these items move is constantly changing and requires highly skilled control and monitoring. This problem has been germane to department stores since the late nineteenth century. Little wonder that late Victorian proprietors favoured well-educated grammar school girls, the equivalent of today's graduates, to work in these complex institutions.

Managing department stores has been a challenging task in the post-war period. The era of the entrepreneur pacing the store and managing on the hoof has long passed. Bosses have adopted a much lower profile, employing expert managing teams and often recruiting high-flyers from other industries. Hugh Fraser, who flamboyantly gambled away his stores on the roulette wheels of Monte Carlo, was perhaps the last of the entrepreneurs whose buckaneering behaviour attracted widespread attention.[36] The demise of Fraser certainly had strong parallels with that of Selfridge. Even firms which remain family-owned have increasingly sought management board members from outside the dynasty. Fenwick's in 1954 appointed two non-family board members for the first time, although in the same period young Christopher and John Fenwick were placed at Harrods and Dickens and Jones for a year, a traditional method of training the young members of department store families.[37] The growth of business studies and marketing at university level since the 1960s now provides stores with a steady supply of managerial trainees.

Despite this influx of expertise, life for the department store remains tough and highly competitive. Between 1971 and 1989 the number of department stores fell from 818 to 580.[38] Many of these were small stores with a working-class customer base. Joyes of Grays, Essex, which ceased trading in the early 1970s, was trapped in a hinterland of working-class residential areas. The more mobile locals were increasingly attracted to nearby Romford, the less mobile to discount stores. Yet Roomes of Upminster, also in south-east Essex, has continued to prosper in this middle-class commuter town, riding the tide of rising middle-class incomes.

Many of the other casualties include stores which had long specialised in credit trading with the local working class. Shepherd's of Gateshead, and Parish's of Byker, Newcastle, both closed – victims of alternative forms of credit such as credit cards, and the rise of 'discounters' for big ticket items such as electrical appliances and furniture, located in edge-of-town 'sheds'. The relative decline in the price of major consumer durable items over recent decades also served to loosen the link between these credit-based stores. The recent crash of the Lewis Group of Stores, following the management buy-out from Sears, its former parent company, is indicative of the problems faced by those stores which traditionally traded at the lower end of the market.

Geography, however, remains the traditional enemy. The nervous eyes of city-centre store bosses keep a careful watch on the out-of-town malls and pray that Britain does not follow the American trend. The recent announcement by House of Fraser that it is closing its Binns store, Market Street, Newcastle, highlights this problem. Binns occupies the old Bainbridge premises and is the oldest department store building in the world that is still trading. House of Fraser, having endured poor results from Binns, Market Street, for a number of years, caused mainly by the northward shift of retailing in Newcastle , have decided to concentrate operations in Tyneside upon their new store at the Metrocentre. More important competition comes from the rapid growth of shire towns, and it is easy to speculate about the consequences of this trend upon the urban neighbours of Bath, Chester, Harrogate, Leamington Spa and York. Yet geography can also be kind, particularly upon those stores located in the large regional shopping centres. The Management Horizons 1984 survey on the size of shopping centres outside London places Glasgow, Newcastle, Edinburgh and Manchester in the first five positions. In Glasgow, the largest, retailing continues to be centred in the Buchanan Street district, the location of Fraser's. Newcastle, which to the surprise of many is England's largest centre outside London, is dominated by the Northumberland Street–Eldon Square complex. Fenwick's, with entrances to both, is an institution that is as well known to northerners as the city's football team. Recently described as a 'satellite town off Northumberland Street', this historic store, already massive in size, is about to undergo a £19 million pound enlargement. Princes Street, Edinburgh, has been the home of several large stores for more than a century. Both locals and tourists continue to flock to Jenner's, a store whose timbered galleries provide the city's most beautiful retail environment. In Manchester, Kendal Milne's continues to present itself as the 'Harrods of the North'. What is also noteworthy is that these cities were pioneers of the department store in Britain. Moreover, Glasgow, Manchester and Newcastle have lost much of their industrial, manufacturing base. All three would be far poorer economically, culturally and socially without their vibrant city centres and historic stores. The modern world owes a great debt to those Victorian entrepreneurs, workers and customers who created such jewels in so many of our great cities.

Notes

1. Jefferys, *Retail Trading in Britain*, 1954, pp. 21; 61.
2. IADS *Newsletter*, January 1949.
3. Ibid., July 1955.
4. Ibid., March, 1955.
5. *Brown's of Chester. Portrait of a Shop*, Mass Observation Survey, 1947, p. 205.
6. Mass Observation Archive, Brown's of Chester, Box 3, File D.
7. Ibid., Box 3, File B.
8. Ibid.
9. IADS *Newsletter*, June 1956.
10. Ibid., February 1959.
11. Ibid., July 1957.
12. Ibid., January 1959.
13. Ibid., May 1960.
14. Ibid., November 1961.
15. Ibid., November 1960.
16. Ibid., February 1960.
17. Ibid.
18. Ibid., September 1967.
19. Ibid., January 1959.
20. Moss and Turton, *A Legend of Retailing*, 1989, p. 207.
21. Honeycombe, *Selfridges*, 1984, p. 177.
22. B. Phillips, *Conran and the Habitat Story*, Weidenfeld and Nicolson, London, 1984.
23. IADS *Newsletter*, January 1972.
24. Ibid., April 1975.
25. *Draper's Record*, 31 August 1974.
26. R. Pound, *The Fenwick Story*, 1972, p. 118.
27. *Business Ratio Report*, 1989.
28. IADS *Newsletter*, November 1988.
29. Ibid., April 1978.
30. Ibid., June 1982.
31. Ibid., March 1957.
32. Ibid., October 1963.
33. Ibid., March 1969.
34. *Business Ratio Report*, 1989.
35. Ibid., November 1967.
36. Moss and Turton, op. cit., p. 238.
37. R. Pound, op. cit., p 113.
38. *Business Ratio Report*, 1989.

INDEX